Cuttyhunk: Life on the Rock

15 Years on a Very Small Island

A Memoir with Recipes

by Margo Solod

One Wet Shoe Publishing 2011

Third Edition
Published by   Schmidt Publishing
                (formerly One Wet Shoe Media)

                2066 E. Pickard Rd.
                Mt. Pleasant, MI 48858
                www.onewetshoe.com

ISBN 978-0-615-48539-3

ACKNOWLEDGMENTS

My heartfelt thanks go out to my readers: my wonderful wife and partner Deborah Miranda, Carolyn Ogburn, Sara Ellis Lehner, Jan Scallisi, Higgins Stewart, Donna Solod, Nina S. Brodeur, Lisa Solod, Jay Solod. Thanks to all who answered my requests by letter, email and facebook for Allen House memories. And thanks to everyone on island any time in those fifteen years, whether you made it into this book or not, just for being there. As I tell you at least 17 times in the book, I have fact-checked as much as possible. So much of this book is memory. I guess that's why they call it memoir. Any mistakes are mine alone. If more than two people correct me on something, I promise to change it in the next edition.

And many thanks to Virginia Center for the Creative Arts, where most of this book was written.

Cover photo and photos of the Allen House courtesy of Margo Solod. Cover designed by Judith Kerman. Book designed and typeset by Amee Schmidt with titles in Calibri and text in Adobe Caslon Pro. Author photo courtesy of Margo Solod.

Contents

For Starters

I watch my 15-year-old nephew, Matthew, load the last of the file boxes onto his golf cart and haul them off to the burn barrel. My father's attic is now empty, at least of Allen House papers. Thirteen boxes in all, documenting my life at the Allen House: from those first days building the public bathrooms with Hunter to the final days of the sale of the property. Thirteen boxes my sister Nina and I have spent two weeks combing through: every scrap of paper, every packet of restaurant checks, and every guest accommodation sheet to make sure no bit of memorabilia or important documentation is accidentally tossed. What to keep to commemorate fifteen years on this island, the beginning of a new chapter in the life of this one-hundred-year old inn, and its ultimate and unexpected end?

Old menus, the original handwritten guest book, pictures: all these are carefully set aside. But how to choose among the letters from guests and employees, work schedules, employee newsletters, and lists of most-often-asked guest questions, the series of ever-changing staff handbooks? In the end, everything of possible value is bundled into one box that I take away with me. I designate myself the official documentarian of the rise of the Allen House from a boarding house to an inn and restaurant written up in newspapers, magazines, and *National Geographic,* to its surprising and underhanded demise.

What goes into this book is mine alone to decide—the amusing, the poignant, the sad. There are thousands of stories and hundreds of recipes from our time running the Allen House; I have tried to pick and choose among the best. But I have little to go on besides my memory, and that of my sister, Nina, who worked beside me for twelve of those years. These are *my* recollections, and I apologize in advance if they do not match yours.

For Dad, who made it possible. I wish you had made it to publication.
And for Nina. Without you, I'd never have made it at all.

Section I. Island Bound

View from my father's porch.

Chapter 1
In Which We Begin

There was a time when the closest I came to cooking was a square of American cheese on a piece of white bread, a slice of salami on top, the whole grilled in a toaster oven. I don't think I turned on a real oven the entire time I was in college, nor for years after I graduated. During my childhood, my mother did the cooking. I'd never asked her to teach me and was confident I hadn't inherited any of her skill.

How I came to live on Cuttyhunk Island, learn to cook and eventually run a restaurant, is a story in itself.

I was working as a theatrical lighting technician for Boston Shakespeare Company when my father called to say he and his friends, Leon and George, had recently bought a boarding house on a tiny island off the coast of Massachusetts. Was I interested in doing a bit of carpentry work there?

Cuttyhunk Island lies southwest of Woods Hole, Massachusetts. It is the tip end of a chain of islands owned mostly by members of the Forbes family. It is roughly three-quarters of a mile by two-and-one half miles of sand, wind-twisted shrubs, and stones, the only place I've ever been where I could see the sunrise and sunset on the same day without doing more than looking out my window in the morning or walking to the top of the island's only real hill in the evening.

Of the other islands in the chain large enough to inhabit, Pasque has a caretaker, Naushon has summer homes and a few people who maintain them, Nashaweena has Highland cattle, Penikese has delinquent boys and their counselors, and Cuttyhunk, well, Cuttyhunk has Cuttyhunkers. Twenty-five or thirty of them in the winter, and a summer population that swells to four hundred. The town is crowded into less than a third of the available land, with the rest of the island being privately owned, some of it designated as a nature preserve. "Take nothing but pictures," read the sign leading out to this West End of the island when I first arrived, "and leave nothing but footprints."

The way my father described it, Cuttyhunk sounded extremely isolated. But I had just spent the past nine months in Boston with its crowds and constant clamor. What the hell. I told him yes, not realizing that one word would alter the course of the next fifteen years of my life.

I arrived at the dock in New Bedford to catch the ferry Alert to Cuttyhunk, duffle bag and toolbox in hand, with a head full of unanswered questions.

I dropped my stuff in a pile next to total strangers and looked at the odd mix of people and boxes of freight surrounding me. What had I signed on for?

Twenty minutes later, looking at heavy fog, choppy water and the small, antiquated wooden ferry I had just boarded, my more immediate question was just how seasick was I going to be before I got there?

Very. Very seasick. It was not an auspicious beginning.

There were less than a dozen of us trying to keep our balance on the wooden planks that passed for seats as the ferry pitched and rolled, but I felt by far the greenest, in every respect. I was so happy to walk down the gangway when we finally hit land that I didn't care *where* that land was. By the time I located the old tan-and-white Volkswagen van with the Allen House logo parked at the end of the splintered wooden dock, Steve, head chef and general manager of the inn, had figured out who I was. Identification couldn't have been difficult as it turned out I was the only stranger on the boat.

As we drove up the road from the dock the fog began to burn off, and Steve pointed out the general store and across from it, the post office. Just before we turned left into the rutted lane that passed for a driveway, he waved at a road lined by stone walls heading up the island's only real hill. Just up there, he explained, was the town hall, the school, the library, and the church. Almost every public building on the island seemed to be contained in the equivalent of a small square block.

We slowed to pull into the potholed driveway, and there it was: The Allen House. Two stories of classic New England saltbox architecture, cedar shingles a faded marine gray I would come to know intimately, scraping, sanding and painting one side of the building each year with the strongest of lead-based marine paints that would barely last against the fierce salt laden winds until I got back to that side four years later. A red roof I would patch and re-patch with asphalt shingles that never quite matched in color, climbing out of an upstairs window and hauling myself and my tools up to sit on the peak, which gave me one of the best views in town. The Allen House.

The Allen House property consisted of two main buildings, three cottages, and a tiny splintered, sagging outbuilding for housing staff

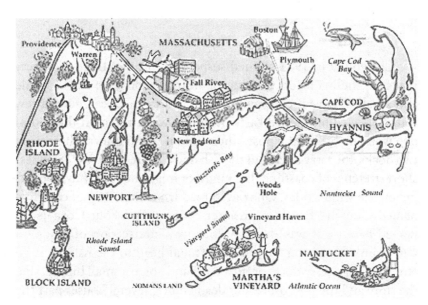

New England Map—Cuttyhunk is in the center.

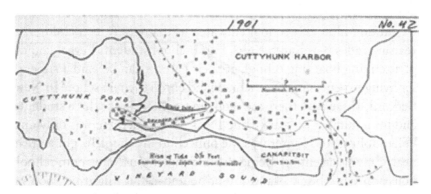

Map of Cuttyhunk Harbor—circa 1901.

Chapter 2
Where We Are

Cuttyhunk in 1981 seemed suspended in time. There were very few cars, the main forms of transportation along the island's mile and a half of paved roadway being golf carts, mail jeeps, and a few three-wheeled motorized carts. The store was a room off the end of one woman's house, the post office a room off another's. There were two docks, the ferry dock and the fish dock. There were two "beaches", short stretches of coastline that might or might not be sandy, depending on the winter tides. One paved road led from a strip of coastline named Church's Beach to an intersection called Four Corners, so named because it was the only four-way intersection of roads on Cuttyhunk. There you could turn left and head to the fish dock, go straight to the ferry dock, or turn right and go up a small hill, passing the store and the post office and dead ending several houses past the Allen House. Across from the Allen House, another paved road ran up the island's only real hill, (always referred to by us as "the" hill) and dead-ended at its apex. Beautiful stone walls lined this road, with breaks for entrances to the Town Hall, the library, the one church that served all denominations, and one of the few one-room schoolhouses left in America.

At one time, this school educated as many as fifteen children a year in grades K through eight. High school students have a choice of attending boarding school, or their parents can be paid a stipend for living expenses to take them off and enroll them in school in New Bedford. These days there are rarely more than two or three students, and for a number of years while I was on island, there was only one. When John Paul Hunter was the only child in school, he got a great deal of media attention. Being the one student in a one-room schoolhouse on Cuttyhunk Island might be unusual, it might be good or bad for learning development. But I watched John Paul grow up, and I can attest to the one thing that student was guaranteed to be: lonely.

The library was even smaller than the schoolhouse. Yet it was wonderful in a number of ways, offering a wide variety of choices, from the mysteries and biographies most of the islanders preferred to the large section of nautical and sailing books that the Allen House guests enjoyed perusing. As you walked in the front door, you saw an oversized map on the wall of every shipwreck that had occurred off the Cuttyhunk coast or in Vineyard Sound since the 1600s.

Cuttyhunk has its own church: a small, simple building with a punched tin ceiling, decorated primarily by religious mosaics made entirely of different shades of natural clam shell. The mosaics were made by Manny Sarmento, a longtime islander who had learned the art of clamshell mosaic as a sailor. When I first arrived, the church had both a pastor who lived on island for the summer, and a priest who flew in every Sunday on the seaplane. The priest has long since passed away and a priest at the Catholic Mass is an irregular sight these days. But the church continues to host Methodist and Episcopal services, as well a Sunday school and a Methodist hymn sing. There's no excuse for missing church on Sunday on Cuttyhunk Island. The pastor calls you to worship with a large bell housed in a small steeple with a striped bass weathervane on top; you can hear it all over the island.

Chapter 3
Solitude

Hunter and I finished the men's room and I left for my summer theater job in Rhode Island. I had grown tired of repertory work and couldn't stop thinking about the island, so in September, after what I'd decided was my final job as a lighting technician, I returned to the Allen House to help finish out its season. With no job, no prospects, and no idea what to do next, Cuttyhunk seemed the obvious solution to fill the next couple of months, and to postpone any decision I would have to make about my life.

By September, the busy summer season was over at the Allen House. The only remaining staff were Steve, his wife, Jan, a tall slim woman with an almost unflappable smile, Jimmy, Steve's teenaged nephew, and me. Jimmy ran the van to and from the dock with customers and gear, and washed dishes. Steve cooked and managed the kitchen. Jan and I ran the front desk, took reservations, sold t-shirts, made beds and cleaned rooms. Jan waited tables with some help from Enna, Leon's wife, who also did the books and acted as hostess. Leon played gentleman innkeeper and worked with Steve on ideas for increasing business, making repairs, and fine-tuning the general day-to-day running of the inn.

Leon and his wife, Enna, along with my father and their mutual friend, George, bought the Allen House in 1979 from Ken and Mildred Fullerton, who had purchased it seventeen years earlier from Clarence and Lucille Allen. George and my father were more interested in the property itself, as land rarely came up for sale to outsiders, but Leon and Enna had dreams of being gracious host-innkeepers in their retirement years. The Allen House had once been a lovely inn, serving up lobster and clam feasts to boatloads of tourists who ferried over from New Bedford for Sunday outings, but for the past seventeen years, Mildred and Ken had run it as a boarding house for fishermen. The public bathrooms, gift shop, and laundry that I had been brought in to help construct were only the first in a series of improvements designed to restore the Allen House to its Clarence and Lucille glory days and, hopefully, even a step beyond.

Leon discovered Steve running a country club in Worcester, Massachusetts, and convinced him to come run the Allen House. Together they were going to build something beautiful. But Leon and Enna had quickly discovered running a twelve-room, three cottage inn with a full seventy-five-seat restaurant was not exactly a retirement job.

The season ended on Columbus Day. Steve, Jan, Jimmy and I spent a few days cleaning a summer's worth of grime and grease from the kitchen, nailing plywood over the porch windows in case a nor'easter hit, stripping the rooms and bagging the bedspreads and curtains in garbage bags with mothballs to keep the mice away, and generally battening down for an island winter. Then we went back to our off-season lives, which in my case meant an unhappy winter in Providence, Rhode Island trying to figure out what to do with the rest of my life.

As spring approached and I found myself no closer to an answer, I decided to take Steve up on his offer of a full season of employment as general dogsbody, hoping that sometime in those next six months, I could come up with some direction for my life.

Steve wanted me to come to the island early and do some painting and refinishing work, and I was happy for the chance to escape Providence. I didn't realize I would be in that creaky old building alone, and the first nights on my own were a bit uncomfortable. But after I decided anything haunting the 100-year-old house would have shown itself to me the first or second night, I relaxed into my main project, stripping the linoleum tile off the kitchen floor and sanding and refinishing the wooden boards underneath. I began to enjoy my solitude, rarely seeing any one of the twenty-five or so permanent residents on the island except when the Alert arrived twice a week from New Bedford bringing supplies, mail, and the occasional visitor. I'd meet Hunter at the boat and we'd load up whatever supplies and building materials Steve had ordered into Hunter's ancient, faded-blue Chevy pickup and haul them up the hill to the Allen House.

After we'd unloaded the truck by the back kitchen door, I would walk across the lawn to the Post Office to say hello to Ellen, the postmaster, and check for my personal mail and Allen House reservation requests. Then I'd head across the street to the store for a candy bar and enough cigarettes to last me until the next boat day.

When I arrived on Cuttyhunk, the store was a medium-sized room added onto the back of Ginger's house. I don't name the store because it didn't have a name. It was literally *the* store on the island, Ginger's legacy from her father, Muggsy, who had run the store for years. Ginger was almost exactly my age, and for a few of those early years we were friends, but as we had really nothing in common besides the island, gradually we drifted apart.

I rarely heard a human voice between Tuesdays and Fridays. The wind had blown down the TV antenna during the winter, so the three fuzzy television channels we ordinarily got during the season were unavailable. And it was several weeks before I thought to ask Steve to bring a radio down with him on his twice-monthly weekend trip, when he would come to help me with the bigger projects and in general, check up on me to make sure things were going okay, and I hadn't freaked out and left the island without notice. It wasn't easy to stay in touch. In order for him to call me, he had to hit the timing exactly right and catch me when I was within hearing distance of the pay phone in the lobby. Any call I wished to make either required standing at the pay phone with rolls of quarters or making a collect call. Telephone calling cards were unheard of back then unless you had a phone of your own, and that would have required having a permanent residence. I didn't make many calls.

Just as I was beginning to enjoy my island solitude, Dave arrived. He was a big, messy bear of a man whose hair and clothes always looked like he'd just gotten up from a nap. Dave had done some remodeling for Steve in Worcester, and Steve thought he was the perfect man to take on projects at the inn. Leon and Enna wanted to modernize the place a bit by turning an upstairs linen closet in the main house into a second bathroom so the six rentable bedrooms would share two baths instead of one. Plans were also drawn up (so to speak, . . . I never saw an actual building plan the whole time Dave worked with us) to remodel the existing bathroom, adding a tub/shower combination and some crazy modern improvements such as a vanity, a mirror larger than a pocket handkerchief, and even an exhaust fan, bringing us, if not into the twentieth century, at least closer to the nineteenth. Dave also ripped out ancient, leaking sinks in rooms six and seven at the end of the hall and put a closet in each room. These improvements were welcomed by most of the guests, although I did hear one old gentleman later say he didn't think much of our "fancifying" efforts.

Dave did it all: rewiring, plumbing, tiling, remodeling, repair, even new construction. His work wasn't always perfect, and he didn't always arrive on the day he said he would, but when he came, he stayed, and when he was there, he worked. Jan liked him because he worked for a reasonable fee. Steve liked him because he ate whatever was put in front of him and rarely asked Steve for help. I liked Dave because he taught me things in the few minutes every day I was allowed to stop scraping and painting. After a while even Hunter gave Dave grudging respect.

When Jan and Steve were on-island I rarely saw them; as soon as supper was over, they would disappear to their apartment in the house below the inn. But with Dave arrived a nightly poker game, and Steve soon became a constant fixture. Not only Steve, but islanders I'd heard about but never met started showing up at the Allen House each night around 7:30, congregating at one of the big tables in the inside dining rooms. Cases of beer became a staple on the weekly grocery list. I was invited to join the game, and I learned most of my poker skills from Dave as well. He was a killer player: quiet, unflappable, with a great poker face.

The makeup of the game changed depending on who was on-island. When the tides ran so they weren't out fishing in the evening, one or more of the three striped bass fishing guides who worked out of the Allen House would show up, and the games got rowdier. Roland and George, two of the guides, were heavy partiers when they weren't working. They drank apricot brandy, as a rule. Joe, the third guide, kept himself pretty tightly under control. He showed up at the games far less frequently, and would rarely have more than a beer or two a night. A.P., a tiny man who even with his white hair and thick glasses seemed ageless, and who'd had a hand in building at least half of the island's houses, was another regular fixture at the table. Charlie, who ran fishing charters out of his own house, could usually be relied on to show up with his bottle of bourbon. Steve, Dave, and I drank beer, but Steve drank a lot more of it than Dave and I did, and noticing who drank what and how much became my first lesson in spotting a poker "tell." The secret between winning or losing at an Allen House poker game was quite simply not to get drunk.

Steve lasted three years. When he and Jan left, I took over management of the Allen House with my sister, Nina. That story comes along in a few chapters, but Nina was an even better poker player than Dave. Eventually, she won so much that she was no longer allowed in the game.

Poker game in the original tv lounge. From left—Dave, Betty, Jimmy, me, (I can't recall his name, I think it was Michael) and Steve.

Kitchen Cuisine

Chapter 4
So Much For the Theater

During my first complete season at the Allen House, the opening staff consisted of Steve, Jan, Jimmy, a day cook whose name I have mercifully forgotten, and me. Steve and the day cook were to run the kitchen and dining room, Jan the front desk, gift shop, and inn. Until the season picked up and we could hire more help, Jimmy and I would fill in everywhere else—van driving, dishwashing, housekeeping, cleaning, and maintenance. The new day cook was in his late fifties or early sixties, and large enough so I wondered if he would be able to move in the cramped space between stove and counter. I also wondered how he would fare in the heat of summer. Although I questioned Steve's decision to hire a man who seemed so physically unsuited for the job, I learned over succeeding seasons just how hard breakfast/lunch cooks were to come by. And as difficult to keep. The fat man was gone by Memorial Day, but not before consuming our entire stock of cooking rum and brandy. Steve finally became suspicious of him when the crème de menthe we used for parfaits started disappearing. I suppose we were lucky we got rid of him before he'd had a chance to go through the vanilla and almond extracts as well.

The day cook traditionally occupied tiny room number four upstairs, a room too small to be considered rentable. I had been temporarily housed in my old room in the annex, a single room with no view, considered the least desirable of the useable rooms, often rented to one of the fishing guides, except during the height of the season.

It was taken for granted that I would move to the girl's side of the staff housing shack once high season began, a move I dreaded as the shack was noisy and crowded as well as being damp, moldy and slowly self-destructing. That move never happened. By the time the season officially started July 1, I was firmly ensconced in room four upstairs, where I would remain for the next three years.

I am an early riser, preferring sunrises to sunsets, and getting up with the dawn gave me a few precious moments to myself before the day started. I noticed Steve, too, was up by five, setting up the kitchen and trying to get a jump on his day before the fishermen showed up at six demanding an early breakfast so they could go ready their boats for the day's charters. Without the fat man to help, Steve was cooking breakfast, lunch, and dinner in addition to ordering food, planning menus, running the kitchen and dining room and taking responsibility for cleanup and repairs on the main house, annex, and cottages. I felt sorry for him, working until ten or eleven at night and then having to rise again at dawn, seven days a week, and a few days of watching him convinced me there wasn't much to setting up the kitchen for breakfast. Given a list, I could do the job easily and allow Steve an extra hour's sleep, something he could really use. My day was only twelve hours or so long and seemed easy in comparison. I offered my help and Steve accepted.

Breakfast setup was a breeze, and within a week I was handling the simple pre-season lunch set up as well, albeit with very detailed lists. Barely a week after that, I found myself in the kitchen all morning learning to flip eggs and make pancakes. Penny, Steve and Jan's dog, probably gained five pounds from all the broken eggs I fed her.

As soon as I mastered breakfast, at least at the slow spring pace, Steve taught me how to cook lunch. Except for grilling burgers to the correct temperature, which required a long learning curve and a lot of sliced-into burgers, lunch was easier than breakfast. The menu consisted mainly of sandwiches, and as long as I was well-prepped, lunch was a piece of cake compared to flipping eggs, stirring a cast-iron pan of home fries, keeping bacon from burning, and remembering to get the French toast out of the batter before it disintegrated.

The third week in June, Steve threw me a fastball. He was going to leave me alone in the kitchen for breakfast and lunch. He'd contracted to cater a wedding on the other side of the island well before the day cook debacle, and there was no one else. He told me to take it slow and I'd be fine. On his way out the door, he shouted over his shoulder, "If you're still here and alive when I get back, I'll teach you to work dinner."

Chapter 5
Off to School

After my first season in the kitchen, I decided a little professional training might be a good idea if I was serious about cooking. I thought I just might be. Restaurant work seemed like theater work, fast-paced, long hours, and no one minded if you moved from job to job. And the pay was certainly better.

With this in mind, I enrolled in Johnson and Wales Culinary Institute. I lasted two semesters. Only one thing saved Johnson and Wales from being a total waste, but that one thing made up for everything else. Personally and professionally, I had one of the luckiest breaks of my life: I met Higgins.

She sat in back of me in nutrition class, and made sarcastic, wildly funny remarks under her breath about the absurdity of the class, the dress code, the school experience in general. On our first break, I sought her out. She sported a punkish haircut with a dyed blue streak that did not exactly endear her to our teachers. But as it was the only form of protest the school officials hadn't thought to write into their ridiculous dress code, I loved her for it, and within two days had talked her into coming out to the island one day that spring and taking a look at the Allen House. I had no authority to hire people, but I knew I had to convince Steve to take Higgins on. She would be terribly out of place on this conservative little island, but so was I. I needed her.

Steve was not impressed, to say the least. Higgins wasn't exactly wowed by him, either, yet something about this tiny, isolated island appealed to her, and by the time we left to return to school on the mainland, she had agreed to work the coming season. Steve said she didn't have enough experience to be hired full time in the kitchen so she'd be doing dishes and some prep. But if she could prove herself he'd move her up. By July we had hired another dishwasher and Higgins was prepping full time.

Chapter 6
If I Had a Hammer

After my first and Steve's third year in the original kitchen, it was more than obvious the kitchen and dish room *had* to be remodeled before next season.

The dish room was a tiny, dark closet of a space, with one small window cut into the side wall so waitstaff could place bus bins of dirty dishes on a shelf. Similar battered wooden shelves covered the rest of the room's walls, and a narrow door led to the kitchen and allowed the dishwasher to enter his cave and emerge with a load of clean dishes. Under one counter was an antique dish machine which held two racks of dishes or silver and took eight minutes to complete a cycle. Fast compared to your own dishwasher, but the average restaurant dish machine has a cycle of forty-five to ninety seconds. We were perpetually behind, and whoever washed up often worked well past midnight on Friday and Saturday nights in that close, airless room. The Allen House dish room in the early days was the closest the island came to corporal punishment.

The kitchen wasn't much better. In the height of summer it was a furnace, with a single box fan turned backward to pull hot air outside. The only other source of ventilation besides a small fan in the broiler itself was the kitchen door, opened to a small concrete patio between kitchen and shack.

The broiler, an ancient six burner Garland stove with a flattop grill, and two beat-up deep-fat fryers all radiating heat comprised "the line." The rest of our equipment consisted of a small, two-door commercial reach-in refrigerator and two other old household refrigerators, a lovely sixties avocado number facing our side of the kitchen, and a plain white one next to it, turned the other way for the waitstaff. The waitstaff had a sink next to their refrigerator and a small Formica countertop upon which to work. It was impossible to imagine cooking seventy-five meals a night in that space. But we did.

The kitchen remodeling was our grand enterprise. The plans Dave and Steve sketched out on a napkin over lunch one day looked extremely professional. That was the way we had always done things in the theater. Sketch it out, build it, and then draw the fancy, scale blueprints from the finished product. Dave and Steve simply skipped that last little part.

They gutted the dish room and boarded up the window to the dining room, hung fluorescent lights, and added four feet by breaking through into an old pantry. A real Hobart dish machine was installed, all the plumbing upgraded, and a window cut through to the kitchen so we could actually communicate with the dishwashers. Only the original doorway was left. The dish room was bright and clean and now looked totally out of place.

Then Dave started on the kitchen. First he boarded up the window next to the broiler, and installed two actual, if well-used, commercial exhaust fans. I spent days cleaning caked-on grease and grime off them. We were on a tight budget, and my time was worth a helluva lot less than a brand new exhaust fan.

Dave moved the outside kitchen wall out four feet as well, utilizing some of the dead space between the kitchen and shack, and the extra space gave us room to put the refrigerators side-by-side and still have space for an old, top-opening, four-tub ice cream freezer. This was placed lengthwise and helped to define even further our new concept of "the line."

In front of the line was where waitresses worked. Behind the line was where cooks worked. Waitresses did *not* go behind the line in Steve's kitchen. He claimed it was for safety reasons, and it made sense. But you didn't want to be around him when someone broke his rule.

With our amazing, freshly painted, newly tiled, florescent-lighted, semi-ventilated kitchen came a whole new range of possibilities. We still had to wear bandannas tied around our foreheads as sweat rags, but it became possible to work beyond nine o'clock in the morning in summer without perspiration pouring into our prep. And we still periodically dunked those bandannas in a container of water we kept in the refrigerator during meal service, grateful for the momentary coolness. I remember one hot July night when Steve ripped his faded blue bandanna off, dunked it in the cold water, slapped it against his face, and promptly passed out. Luckily he was nowhere near the grill at the time.

That kitchen was where I learned to play with food. We had several weddings off premises during the inaugural summer of the new kitchen, and they required much larger quantities of things than we usually made. Steve came in to the kitchen one day to find me trying to stir a huge vat of pasta salad with a long kitchen spoon.

"You'll be at that all night," he said, and, going over to the sink, scrubbed up his arms like a surgeon. He took the pasta salad from me and plunged both hands in.

"This is the only way to stir a big amount of anything," he said.

It's true. You can't really make meatloaf for forty unless you get in it up to your elbows. If you use your cupped hand and thumb like the parts of an ice cream scoop, you can fill muffin tins, measure out cupcake batter, and even mold cookies twice as fast as you can any other way. Think about it. Your hands and arms are the perfect kitchen utensils. Easy to clean, extremely versatile, and impossible to lose or have someone borrow and not return. Try it at home sometime. Plunge your hands right into that salad or meatloaf. Frost a cake with your fingers dipped in warm water. It feels great. It is exactly what your parents always told you not to do. Play with your food. Hell, become a cook and play with everybody's food.

From Steve, I learned our basic baked stuffed lobster recipe, bread-crumb stuffing, chowder, our apple crisp. All of our most requested recipes. Of course, he might have stolen them from someone else. It's what cooks do.

Steve taught me how to flip an egg over easy and back again without breaking the yolk (the trick is to flip a piece of toast or stale bread in a small sauté pan thirty to one hundred times, or until you get the wrist flick down pat.) But, if your eggs come over on the ferry and spend six hours in the sun between the two docks before they go back into the refrigerator, you get an egg with a delicate yellow center and a soft, runny white. It is unbelievably hard to keep an egg like that from breaking. Your best bet is to crack each egg into a cup and pour it carefully into your heated pan, which gives you a fifty/fifty chance of making it. The eggs that broke as they slid into the cup became scrambled eggs or French toast batter; the eggs that broke in the pan become staff breakfast.

The first time we ran out of eggs *and* Ginger at the general store ran out of eggs (oh, the trips to the store in the middle of breakfast: "Ginger, how many eggs can I have? How much bread? Can I buy all your maple syrup?") was a Monday in spring when we'd had an extra heavy Sunday breakfast. The boat didn't run till Tuesday.

An island woman saved the day by bringing down several dozen eggs from hens she kept by her house at the top of the hill. Those eggs! High orange yolks and perfectly round whites that hardly spread at all; you could flip an egg like that over and back five times and not break it. Hell, you could play catch with an egg like that. I remembered those eggs fondly the rest of the summer, as egg after egg slid into the ruined pile, to be fed to staff, Penny the dog, several stray cats, and any fishing guide who wandered by.

Steve taught me many of his old Navy cook tricks. One, great for making masses of perfect egg salad, consisted of boiling and peeling several dozen eggs, then smashing the eggs through the bottom of a fryer basket with your hands. Out came perfectly diced eggs, the exact size and consistency for egg salad. I've never been tempted to try this trick with any home sieve as I hate egg salad, but I have to admit this was the best looking stuff I ever saw.

And the ultimate way to perfectly grease a grill for pancakes and French toast: a piece of salt pork cut about 4"x6" and soaked in water until all the salt is removed. You cut a handle into the rind large enough to get a couple of fingers through. A paring knife is the best tool for this job. Hook your first and middle fingers through the handle in the rind and slide the block across the grill every few batches of pancakes or French toast. The salt pork leaves a grease slick the exact thickness desired. When the bottom of the pad becomes hard from the heat, just slice it off and start fresh. We averaged one two-inch thick piece every couple of weeks, but then, we cooked a lot of breakfast.

Here I must apologize to all those vegetarians who ate pancakes at the Allen House those fifteen years. My only excuse is that I wasn't particularly well informed in those days, and to be honest, it just never occurred to me to mention it. After all, I did tell you about the bacon grease in the home fries, and the salt pork in the chowder. Didn't I?

When I taught Higgins how to flip eggs using the "Steve" method, she successfully began flipping eggs over easy after only thirty toast flips. At least she was successful until Steve came into the kitchen. He had a way of simply appearing behind you, not sneaking exactly, but you'd never hear him. And he never showed up, or so it seemed to us, until Higgins or I had just made a major mess or mistake. The first egg Higgins flipped in front of anyone besides me she flipped directly onto the toe of Steve's boot.

The most people Higgins and I ever served for breakfast was two hundred thirty-four, between 7:30 and 10:30 on a Sunday in July, back when nobody else on the island did anything for breakfast fancier than a muffin-to-go from the Bakery. The most people I ever served for breakfast alone was a hundred and two. Higgins holds the record at one hundred twenty-three.

My sister Lisa invented the famous Allen House blueberry walnut pancakes because she refused, in her own words, to eat "mushies" (blueberries) without "crunchies" (walnuts). We never charged any extra *not* to put the blueberries or the walnuts in, even though Higgins wanted to, because it was so hard to remember.

Higgins insisted the Allen House buy some decent egg pans. She seasoned those pans for days, and babied them lovingly. God help the dishwasher that tried to scrub one of them with water. Higgins tried to make sure they never even went near the dishroom. When, years later, Jimmy (Higgins's future husband, though we didn't know that at the time) accidentally threw a pan wrapped in an old towel away, he spent an entire Sunday searching for that particular bag of trash at the dump. This should have tipped us off their relationship was more serious than any of us had thought.

Recipe for Apple Crisp

Steve passed on to me many recipes that became Allen House favorites and this one became a staple on our menu. We couldn't imagine a meal where we didn't offer apple crisp. Some people even ordered it for breakfast. And it was Steve's recipe, unchanged, that we used for twelve years. What most people didn't realize was that this recipe came straight out of the Navy cookbook. Steve had merely adapted the quantities so he only needed to make one pan at a time instead of the usual 20 he had made in the Navy.

Filling:
One number 10 can sliced apples
1 cup sugar
2 tablespoons cinnamon
3 tablespoons cornstarch

Topping:
¾ pound margarine
1 pound brown sugar
1 cup flour
Approximately 5 cups whole oats

In a hotel pan, mix together first four ingredients. For topping, cream margarine and brown sugar, then add flour, then add oats until mixture crawls out of the mixing bowl. Crumble mixture lightly over apples. Bake at 350° for 45 minutes–hour until apple mixture bubbles and browns.

The first time my dad's older sister Fran visited the inn she had the apple crisp for dessert. As soon as she returned home, she sent me a combination apple peeler/corer, with a note saying she felt awful about how many apples I had to peel by hand. I never had the heart to correct her, and the peeler stayed in its box until we closed the inn.

Island Delights

Chapter 7
It's Only a Quahog in Rhode Island

The wedding that was to alter the course of my life was for Wyatt Garfield Jr., so I suppose in a way Wyatt is responsible for my subsequent career move into the restaurant business.

The Garfields were a generations-old island summer family, but only one of their offspring, Seth, actually worked on the island. Seth Garfield ran a shellfish farm, growing oysters in the West End Pond and dredging little neck (hard-shell) clams from the waters around the islands. Seth hadn't been in business much longer than we had when we started running the Allen House. He sold to some mainland restaurants, but a good portion of his summer business came from the shellfish bar he ran from his shack on the Fish Dock. He took orders for shellfish platters, sold whole shellfish for steaming, shucked clams and oysters to order in the shack. He also had a skiff that went around the harbor every night at cocktail time and shucked shellfish right at boat-side.

This looked impressive, especially as Seth tended to employ young island kids. We bought our shellfish from Seth, but although we also shucked to order, we did so in the kitchen, which wasn't as impressive. We *had* to shuck in the kitchen. Even if we'd had the personnel to have someone stand at an oyster bar and shuck shellfish, that wouldn't have been possible with the product Seth sold us.

We called the clams Seth sent up the hill to us lipless wonders. Lips are the tiny ridges where the two shells meet. In order to open a hard-shell clam you have to insert a clam knife or other sharp instrument between those edges and slide it in far enough to slice the muscle and pry the clam open. When the clams were as fresh as Seth's, they closed up tight at the slightest movement. After the jostling they took coming up the hill in his truck, opening them was no easy task. When Seth's staff broke the lips off, it made a difficult task damn near impossible.

Every night, Seth's young employees would take a load of fresh oysters and clams out in their flat-bottomed skiff. They wanted to work as fast as possible, and look as good as possible in order to get big tips, so if their knife slipped and "ripped" the lips off a clam, they just threw it back in the bucket and grabbed another. I'd have done the same thing, if I had been out there. What I *didn't* appreciate was when we placed a Friday night order for five dozen little neck or cherrystone clams and four and a half dozen came with no lips.

Now, I'm not saying Seth did this deliberately. Not at all. I am sure it was an employee. And of course our pride *(Seth's shuckers can't open this but I can)* kept Higgins and me from sending them back, unless they were truly impossible to open. Seth always exchanged those with good grace, and for a few days at least half the clams we'd receive hadn't been touched by a shucker's knife.

For a few days.

Chapter 8
Claws!

We bought our lobster locally as well. Cuttyhunk lobster is famous for its freshness, and rightly so.

There were two working lobstermen when I arrived on island, but Dickie was slowly phasing out his business, so we dealt with Bruce. Bruce closely resembled a combination of fisherman and pirate with his Hollywood good looks, dark skin, and gold earring. He was a kind and easy-going man. Carolyn, his wife, ran the lobster shack on the dock and took care of business. She was as tough as Bruce was soft, but she was fair. An added attraction at their shack that we weren't so crazy about was Carolyn's side business. If you were coming off a boat for lobsters you could buy them, pay an extra dollar a pound, come back at six that evening, and Carolyn would have them cooked and ready for you. This cut into our lobster dinner business. Of course, boiling lobsters at her house was illegal from a health inspector's point of view, but there wasn't a food-related business, including ours, that could pass a strict health inspection. Fortunately, Cuttyhunk didn't have a health inspector.

Bruce went out every day the weather was decent and pulled his traps. He kept the collected lobsters in several large cages under the dock by his shack, and that's where we picked them up nightly for the restaurant. If we had a big party, Bruce would deliver two dozen lobsters or more, and in July and August he would generally drop off two dozen each Friday afternoon. The rest of the time we'd send our van driver down on a "lobster run" around four in the afternoon. It was always a challenge to try and get just the number of lobsters needed that night so they would be as fresh as possible. Too many and you took the chance one would die on you; too few and you'd run out.

You can't cook a dead lobster. The moment they die they begin to decompose. The same goes with any shellfish. Crabs, oysters, clams, mussels. If you aren't sure it's alive, don't cook it. And for god's sake don't eat it raw.

We sold a fair amount of lobster, even though our prices were high. Bruce didn't give us much of a break. He didn't need to. Most of the season he could barely keep up with his demand down at the dock.

But the Allen House had a specialty that brought lobster lovers in. Baked stuffed lobster, Steve's way. I think he made it up; I've never seen the dish prepared quite the same way anywhere else. Instead of the creamy crabmeat and breadcrumb mixture you find in most restaurants, we used whole shrimp and scallops. The dish was heart-stopping good. We didn't make much profit on it, and it was a lot of work, so we buried baked stuffed lobster in the middle of the menu. Restaurant research shows people tend to order the first, second and last things on the menu, rarely from the middle.

The waitstaff loved to sell them. They were our most expensive item. Bigger check, happy customers, bigger tip. And people were always happy with that dish. In fifteen years, I never had a single baked stuffed lobster sent back to the kitchen.

We had one waitress who outsold all the others. She could sell a baked stuffed lobster every other table. I half-seriously suggested she was paying people to order them just to torment me, but Peggy was a nice young woman from a lovely summer family, and she insisted she wasn't doing anything special. One night I cracked the kitchen door and watched her wait on a large table of fishermen. Parties of six or more were seated at large tables in the inside dining room, and they were the only tables you could really see from the kitchen. Except for table thirteen, but that comes later in this story.

As I watched, Peggy began to describe the dish.

"They take the lobster," she said, "and split it down the middle."

She illustrated this by running her hand in a straight line from her neck to the bottom of her apron. The fishermen's eyes followed her hand.

"Then they pull it open," she illustrated this by holding both hands between her breasts and then pulling them apart while thrusting her chest out.

"Then," she continued, "they stuff it with shrimp and scallops," miming stuffing something from her neck to her knees.

The fishermen were mesmerized. Four out of six ordered the baked stuffed lobster. When I demonstrated for Peggy at the end of the night what I'd seen her do she was mortified. She was totally unaware of what she was doing. The other waitresses loved it, and they all threatened to copy Peggy unless I gave them free ice cream sundaes that night. It was a small price to pay to avoid even more baked stuffed lobsters, and a great joke we told for years.

We had a waitress at the Allen House one season that had a relative of the Ba Ha'I faith, and she told me that she thought the Ba Ha'I believed that when you died you could be eternally damned to be killed over and over again in the manner in which you had taken the most lives. I have never been able to decide if I will be eternally split open and placed under a broiler, or eternally shucked.

Baked Stuffed Lobster, Allen House Style

One 1 ¼ to 1 ½ lb. lobster
3 large or 5 medium shrimp
5 sea scallops
1 cup seasoned bread crumb mixture
Melted butter

Lay one large lobster on its back, and with a sharp knife, split the lobster down the middle. Try not to cut through the back shell. Split open the lobster and remove the lungs. You may either remove or leave the liver and roe, depending on your taste. Brush the inside of the lobster with melted butter. Insert a skewer at the bottom of the tail and up the back of the lobster to keep it from curling under the broiler. Broil the lobster for approximately 2 minutes and remove from heat. In a separate pan place three large shrimp peeled and deveined, and five scallops. Brush with butter and sprinkle with granulated garlic. Broil for approximately 1 minute. Spread a small amount of seasoned crumb mixture inside the lobster and drizzle with butter. Put the three shrimp in the body of the lobster and line scallops up down the tail. Drizzle with butter and cover with crumb mixture. Drizzle over crumb mixture with butter. Place lobster in 400° oven for 12 to 14 minutes, depending on size. Remove from oven, brush claws with butter for a shiny look and serve. Caution—this is not a diet dish.

Seasoned crumb mixture

1 cup bread crumbs
1 cup finely ground Ritz crackers
2 tablespoons dried parsley
2 tablespoons paprika
1 tablespoon each white pepper and granulated garlic

Mix together with enough clarified or plain melted butter to moisten thoroughly.

Inn Fare

Chapter 9
By Any Other Name

In the beginning of my tenure, the Allen House consisted of the main house, the annex, and three cottages. In Allen House history the beginning was just the main house and it wasn't even called the Allen House, but The Poplars. No one I asked could ever tell me why, only that as far as anyone knew; the building had never been anything but an inn. When Clarence and Lucille Allen bought the place they re-named it the Allen House. The building we referred to as the annex was actually built out on the West End as Coast Guard housing. After World War II, when the government deemed a first line of defense was no longer needed against German submarines attempting to capture Wood's Hole Oceanographic Center, the station was disbanded and moved to Menemsha on Martha's Vineyard. Clarence and Lucille bought the sleeping quarters and had the building moved across the island to where it now stands, approximately thirty feet from the main house. The annex was moved using mules that pulled it over a series of logs set one in front of the other. Imagine moving a two-story building over a mile long rough track, swamp on one side and cliffs leading down to crashing surf on the other.

I moved with great glee out of the cramped quarters of room four into room two of the main house when I became a manager. This had been Ken and Mildred's room, evidenced by the deep claw marks in the door from their two golden retrievers.

It was a big room, with great cross ventilation and a private sink, but it was directly over the original kitchen and all the hot water pipes ran through the horsehair plaster walls. On Friday fish-fry nights the combination of the smell and the heat was enough to kill you.

When we re-did the kitchen the first time and put in an extra hot water heater, we installed both ventilation fans and a cut-off switch for the boiler, so we could redirect hot water away from the pipes leading to the second floor. This had an added bonus of correcting the plumbing in the bathrooms so that hot water no longer ran to the toilets. This quirk might have been useful, even appreciated in the cold winter months, but it could be quite a shock to a guest sitting down for the first time on a warm summer evening.

Room one wasn't much better than two in terms of view, but there was a little less kitchen noise and heat, and more importantly, it had the amazing changeable bed. This was simply two twin beds joined by a headboard, with the beds on coasters so that they could be combined with the help of a pad into a king, or separated slightly into two twins. Room one turned out to be extremely popular with two types of houseguests; the ones who wanted something larger than a double bed, which was the largest any other rooms offered, and gay and lesbian couples, who weren't sure if they could ask for a double bed, but who clearly did not want two twins.

Because of me, we advertised in a lot of gay and lesbian travel publications, but it still took us a while to figure these particular housing requests out. When we finally caught on, we began telling prospective guests who asked for room one that we had two lovely front-facing rooms in the annex that had both a twin and a double bed. That way, if the couple felt the need for secrecy they could mess up both beds each night to "fool" the housekeeper.

Room five was the smallest of the rentable rooms in the main house, but it had a front view and there was something charming about its slanted ceiling under the eaves. Across the hall were the bathrooms, and at the end of the hall lay rooms six and seven. These were identical, with twin beds, hideous carpet, and turquoise plastic headboards. They were also in the worst shape, their sink plumbing having burst inside the walls at some point.

Because of the condition of these rooms, when Dave came to redo the bathrooms, he brought his wife Betty. They sheet rocked both six and seven and Betty wallpapered them. Of course, then those rooms looked so nice and neat compared to the bulging, cracked, and often repaired hundred-year-old horsehair plaster in the other rooms that we vowed as soon as we had a little spare cash we'd do the whole main house.

We never got past room five. Not until the ceiling in room three gave way several years later, by which time Steve and Jan (and therefore Dave) were long gone. A huge crash in the middle of the day sent us sprinting upstairs to find seventy-per-cent of what once was a plaster ceiling spread across the room, with huge chunks of it lying on the bed. Thank god the room was not rented at the time.

I do not even wish to imagine . . .

Several years of activity in the attic caused by staff housed up there must have gradually loosened the plaster from the lathe. If you have never seen an old horsehair plaster and lathe wall or ceiling, you might not realize that nothing really holds the plaster to the lathe (thin strips of wood nailed to beams) except the plaster's own sticking power. The physics of plaster, lathe and gravity had never crossed my mind until I looked up through the hole in the ceiling of room three.

We sheet-rocked every ceiling in the main house immediately. Every room except room four. We still housed a cook there, and it never hurts to keep employees on their toes. Hell, I had spent three years staring up at the bulging, cracked ceiling, wondering when it would give way. Why deny others that same thrill?

A steep flight of stairs (yes, only one, in violation of every fire code known to man) outside room three led down to the inside dining rooms. These were dining rooms for houseguests when Ken and Mildred ran the inn, the porch being too steeply slanted to hold more than a rocking chair. These rooms had great huge plate glass windows with a beautiful view of the harbor. When Leon and Enna took over, they leveled the sloping porch floor with large plywood wedges. The wedges went from flat to a good six inches at the outside wall, and the resulting space was large enough to hold a table and four chairs.

We managed to squeeze thirteen tables onto that L-shaped porch. The moment we did that the inside dining room became pariah-land. No one wanted to be seated there, and they'd wait forty-five minutes for an outside table even if it was going to be too dark to see anything outside by the time they were seated. We finally solved this problem by putting several large tables in the inside rooms and making them required seating for parties of more than five. We also made those rooms non-smoking. Yes, they still allowed smoking in restaurants in those days. Even in Massachusetts. There's a half case of Allen House ashtrays in my sister's basement to prove it.

At the short end of the L after table thirteen was the ramp. God, how our waitstaff hated the ramp. It was just long and steep enough to work up a little too much momentum coming down with a loaded tray, and to really feel it in your calves after you'd gone up two hundred times in the course of a day. The ramp led to the gift shop, and at the top was an area we used for salad and dessert preparation. The waitstaff not only had to go up to the cash register with each guest check, they also had to go up and down with every salad and dessert order. No wonder "the ramp" always seemed to come out of waitstaff's mouths in a sort of snarl.

The gift shop was the newest part of the main house, a large square room where Ken and Mildred fed anyone who wasn't a houseguest. This was also the area that brought me to the island in the summer of 1981, to help Hunter build public bathrooms. At the same time we put in an L-shaped counter that ended up serving as reception counter, front desk, information center, restaurant and gift shop register, and later, the place to purchase laundry and shower tokens. The person manning this small but vital area was also in charge of answering our illegal extension from the phone booth.

The public areas were a royal pain in the ass. Luckily, I was not responsible for seeing to their policing and cleanup. I only came into the picture for spring re-painting and replacement of rotted wood floors in the showers, or easy maintenance like unclogging a drain or repairing a worn-out toilet with a bread tie and duct tape until a new part could be ordered from the mainland.

The annex was a much simpler building than the main house, three rooms up, three down, with a bathroom on each floor. Something about the way it was configured and the placement of stairways and bathrooms allowed us to fit one more double bed upstairs than down. I've never understood how that worked, but I'm sure Hunter would have. Sometime after the annex building was moved from the West End, a large open porch with a beautiful view of Vineyard Sound was added on.

The three cottages spread out from the annex over just under an acre of gently rolling lawn. I know exactly how large and rolling that lawn was. I cut it with a hand mower for years.

Horseplay, the cabin closest to the annex, was a medium-sized room crowded with two twin beds, the largest and heaviest dresser I have ever seen, a couple of nightstands, a chair and lamp straight out of a sixties rummage sale, and a tiny cubicle of a bathroom.

There was no closet, just a series of hooks screwed into the molding on one wall. Horseplay's attraction, aside from its miniscule porch, was a small loft over the beds, reachable by a ladder that swung down from the ceiling on a series of pulleys. The loft held two low, uncomfortable camp cots. No one in their right mind over the age of ten would consider sleeping up there.

When I arrived at the Allen House, Horseplay was already slanting downhill enough to feel a distinct tilt when you stood inside. Every year until we tore it down, the cottage slanted more, and by our third year we rented it only to couples, fearing even a child's weight in the loft. Thin cracks appeared constantly in the walls, which I repaired by rubbing in joint compound, then literally pouring in thick latex paint. When my hand went through a wall as I attempted a patch, Steve solved the problem by nailing a sheet of half-inch inch plywood to the studs and having me paint that instead.

Fowlplay was next down the line, and was our most popular cabin with fishermen. Two tiny bedrooms sandwiched an equally tiny bath, but there was an actual sitting room with ancient chairs, a sprung couch, and a "working" fireplace. I say "working" because the guys often burned driftwood in it, but when I think of that hearth and filthy crumbling chimney now, I shudder to think we let them use it.

Perhaps most importantly, the cabin had a tiny round-topped fridge perfect for holding a case of beer and was shabby enough that no fisherman felt the need to take off his boots.

That place smelled like mold from the day I walked in until the day it was demolished. We re-roofed it, repainted it with mildew-fighting paint each year and cleaned it down to bare boards every spring. But, as we discovered when we demolished it, the rot went deep into its bones. I think we probably could have pushed it over with three strong guys. I have never seen a building come down so easily.

Fairplay, the last of the cabins, was the newest and in the best shape. It had a real porch, big enough for two chairs, one room and the usual tiny bath, and was most popular with couples due to its double bed. All the cabins booked up first each summer. Not only were they private, with their own baths, but we allowed pets in them. Pets almost always meant dogs. People seldom travel with cats, although we did have several pet birds over the years.

When the consortium of three (as we called Leon, George, and my father) took over the Allen House, very little beside the most basic maintenance had been done by Ken and Mildred for the previous seventeen years. Most of the improvements made the past spring when I had come on as carpenter's helper concerned things such as the public restrooms and porch floor. The floor was necessary to increase seating. The theory behind the bathrooms was a bit unusual. Although we had a bathroom for restaurant customers off the lounge, there was no public bathroom at the dock. The consortium felt if someone walked all the way up the hill to shit in our toilets, they might be tempted to look around at the gift shop merchandise, check out the restaurant menu, or at least pick up a brochure. This proved true, although I always believed people were just too embarrassed to walk in, use the restroom, and walk out without at least pretending to be interested in something else.

As the public found the Allen House, Steve came up with new ways to part them from their cash. Within a year, two small sections were added on to the back of the gift shop, one with three shower stalls, and one with two token-operated washers and dryers. Word quickly spread down at the harbor that Cuttyhunk Island now had more reasons to get off your boat than just a chance to stretch your legs and get an ice cream cone.

The island harbor was a well-known secret for years among power boaters and sailors who traveled the eastern coast from Connecticut and New York to Block Island, Martha's Vineyard and Nantucket, but most of those who stayed in the harbor had never left their boats. Suddenly, there were incentives to do so. You could shower, do your laundry, eat lunch or dinner, and buy a t-shirt all in the same place.

We were well on our way to creating a monster.

Horseplay

Fairplay

Fowlplay

Chapter 10
Palate Cleanser

For reasons I will never understand, and now will never know as both Ken and Mildred have passed away, *someone* decided the best colors for painting rooms and furniture were lemon yellow and turquoise. Every room in the inn, the annex, and the inside of all three cabins was painted in some combination of these colors. Some had bright yellow walls and turquoise furniture, some had turquoise walls and yellow furniture, and the cabins had interesting combinations of walls and furniture mixed together.

A few rooms had been allowed to keep their original furniture colors as they had fairly decent looking bedroom sets. But wherever there was a plain wooden headboard, mismatched dresser, nightstand, or, the mainstay of most of the cabins, particleboard do-it-yourself furniture, that item sported a thick coat of bright yellow or turquoise paint.

Because of the heavy wear and tear a publicly rented room receives, every room needed painting every spring, if not a full coat, at least a touch-up. A major touch up. Jan thankfully decided to have the two newly sheet-rocked rooms wallpapered, but every other wall in the main house, the annex, and the cabins was painted the same color: True-Value (the only hardware store that would deliver to the boat) latex semi-gloss Navajo White.

Enna picked the color that first year of consortium ownership. She, Leon, and Steve were the only ones to see the Allen House in its true lemon-yellow and turquoise splendor. By the time I arrived, many of the rooms and much of the furniture had at least a coat or two of Navajo White, and Jan had sewn vanilla slipcovers for the turquoise plastic headboards on the twin beds in room six and seven. Within two years, I was as sick of Navajo White as anyone could be of such an innocuous color, and actually welcomed the chance to paint outdoors where, although everything except the trim was gray, at least there were several shades of gray. In fact, by the time I finished painting outside that first year, there were many shades of gray, as I had amused myself by painting every outside door a different color gray from the leftover paint cans I found in the annex basement. Amusing, that is, until the next spring when I had to try and match each door color in order to touch up all the nicks and scrapes.

By my second spring, enough major damage control had been accomplished inside that Steve suggested I try and clean out the annex basement. It was a less daunting task than the main house basement, a task that would take us years. The annex basement was smaller, but there were ledges at my shoulder height running the length of it, and these were crammed as full as the floor space.

One oddity I unearthed I wish now I'd kept was a box of small tools, hinges, and various inexplicable pieces-parts made of zinc, still in their WWII original wrappers. These were obviously parts Clarence had ordered during the war, just in case he needed them. Hunter scarfed those up the moment he saw them. Most of what I found were things either Ken or Clarence before him had deemed possibly useful to someone, someplace on island, at some future point.

I borrowed Hunter's truck, one of only two on island at the time, to haul stuff to the dump, but after he saw me drive by with the first load, he ambled over to the annex and met me on my return. He instructed me to pull everything out of the basement and lay it on the ground. Then *he* would come by and tell me what was junk. Probably sixty percent of what I pulled out of our basement ended up in Hunter's garage. This pack-ratting was normal behavior on Cuttyhunk as you couldn't just run out and get what you needed when you needed it, but I swore when I was finished we would actually be able to use the cellar for storage.

Between Hunter and the dump, I was finally able to clear enough space to store all the extra boards, pipe, molding, paint, and painting supplies deemed necessary by Steve and still get farther than two feet into the basement.

A clear victory. I did catch holy hell when Alan, the caretaker who Leon and Enna had acquired with the Allen House, came by to inspect my work and discovered I had thrown away some *obviously* immensely valuable brush essential to cleaning the furnace. It had just looked like a greasy, bent, rusted tangle of wire brush to me. Luckily for me, Hunter had rescued it, so I was spared Alan's full wrath.

This was in the beginning, when Alan still liked me. He was not only our caretaker but our island mentor. He knew the ins and outs of the Allen House buildings and all their secrets. His knowledge was vitally important because the houses appeared to have been plumbed by a crazy sociopath with serious ADD. I can imagine this unknown being chuckling dementedly to himself as he installed cut-off switches in areas impossible to reach, routed the hot water lines so that when you turned on the heat in the fall the toilets occasionally got too hot to sit on comfortably, and ran whole sections of pipe from one cabin to the next with no cut-offs at all in between.

Until we could get the place re-plumbed and a new auxiliary water heater installed, we were completely dependent on Alan to keep the systems going. Alan also supplied and hooked up bottled gas for the kitchen and repaired appliances. For some reason it was almost always the circulator or the regulator that went out on things. To this day, I find myself muttering circulator-regulator in Alan's down-east tinged accent whenever something goes wrong in my house.

Inn Fare²

Chapter 11
Don't Pick Up That Phone

Every winter in my first few years at Allen House, I'd picked a different city to work in, in an attempt to gain more and varied restaurant experience. I was in Charleston, South Carolina, when the call came.

"Do you think you could run the Allen House with Chris?"

No preamble, no lead in. That was my dad. I asked him what the hell he was talking about. Run the Allen House with George's son?

"Steve doesn't want to run it anymore unless we give him a piece of the pie," Dad said.

"And we don't want to give him a share. So, you've had three years under Steve. Do you think you could run the kitchen?"

I told him sure, I could run the kitchen, although I had no idea if I could or not. It's best not to show weakness with my dad, at least when you are starting out.

"But I won't run it with Chris," I said. "He and I don't get along at all."

"Well," Dad said, "You can't run it alone. Steve had Jan. Who do you have?"

I remember thinking for just a few minutes before I told him I might have a few ideas.

"Let me get back to you," I said. "But if Chris is in the deal, I'm out. Tell George that."

I thought I was pretty safe in saying that, as none of George's other kids could cook.

The notion of being my own boss really appealed to me, and although it was daunting, I was fairly confident that after the last three years, I could run the kitchen. It was the front-of-house operation that terrified me. The idea of dealing with customers all day seemed a far greater hell than sweating in a hot kitchen dealing with cooks, waitstaff, and dishwashers.

My ace-in-the-hole idea was my younger sister Nina. We'd always gotten along, and recently taken a six-week, cross-country road trip together. That's an acid test of both friendship and effective communication. Nina had spent the last several years running the folk-life pavilions at the 1982 and 1984 World's Fairs. She knew how to budget, organize, and plan. Most importantly, she was good with people. Of course, the sum total of her hotel and restaurant experience was a short stint as a restaurant hostess and an even shorter one as a Hilton desk clerk. But hell, I hadn't made anything more difficult than tuna helper when I first came to the island. She was smart. She could learn. But was she willing?

The next World's Fair wasn't scheduled to happen for six years. In fact it never happened at all. The 1984 World's Fair in New Orleans was the last of its kind. Of course, we didn't know that then. All Nina knew was she needed a quick career change, and this might be it. With what I saw as a total lack of hesitation, she said yes.

Later I found out beneath her tough exterior was a weak gut, and these seemingly spontaneous decisions sent her straight to the bathroom. Then, I was just grateful for her response. I called Dad back and informed him that if he could talk George out of trying to employ his son, Nina and I would run the place for the gang of three.

Nina wasn't able to get away from other obligations until the middle of May that year. For the first time, I found myself alone, responsible for hiring staff, organizing cleaning crews, and getting the Allen House open. There were brochures to be sent out to past customers and prospective new ones, dates to book with fishing guides, reservations to take. . .

Thankfully most reservations came in by mail, as I couldn't possibly have answered the phone in addition to cleaning, painting, replacing roofing shingles, and de-molding every surface that had ever come in contact with water.

These tasks were ones I had performed for the past several years, and ones Nina and I would continue to perform as long as we ran the Allen House. The difference was this time I was in charge.

By the middle of March, I finally had some people to manage. Several returning employees agreed to come out early and help get things up and running. Without them, I know I would never have been able to get it all done in time.

Higgins had progressed in two years to the main line cook. Her friend, Christopher, had been out for part of last year and was coming back for a full season. Hopefully, that is. We never knew who would be able to last out an entire season on "the rock" as we affectionately referred to the island, and who would run screaming.

I knew I could count on Higgins, and I was pretty sure about Christopher. My third early bird, Becky, had been out for a brief period the year before, and I was fairly sure that if Christopher didn't tease her to death (a distinct possibility), she might last the season, and my girlfriend, Annie, was on board to help.

There may have been more people, and if I left anyone out here or from any of the lists in this book, I sincerely apologize. But when you are working with twenty to thirty people every year for twelve years and three-quarters of them are new each season, memory tends to falter. I remember people being on-island together who worked for us three seasons apart, and I am constantly being reminded as I write this of people and events that slipped my mind completely. So that is my apology, for what it is worth. This is merely a remembrance. Those of you whom I have mixed up or forgotten are welcome, even advised, to get out a pen and write yourselves in wherever necessary.

Chapter 12
The Young and the Exhausted

Our second year running the Allen House, I drove to Texas in March to get Nina. She'd been answering reservation requests and trying to hire employees by phone from her winter home in Dallas, and was more than ready to get closer to the action.

That spring, Nina and I painted for a month straight, at least six hours a day. Then several more hours were spent prepping areas to be painted, washing away a season's worth of mold (always a problem in old buildings on a damp island), patching gouges and cracks in walls, changing out ropes in some old sash-weight hung windows, replacing cracked panes or rotted caulking in others.

And mail. Reservation brochures, island information and ferry schedule requests, letters from prospective employees. Mail was generally reserved for after dinner as it could be handled sitting down. After one of our usual days, a sitting position, once attained, was damn near impossible to rise from.

The mail came in on the ferry, and went out the same way. Between Columbus Day and Memorial Day, the ferry arrived only twice a week. Twice a week, that is, if the weather wasn't too bad or the boat wasn't pulled for Coast Guard inspection or hadn't broken down. And when the boat did come, it docked for three hours. *If* it arrived on time. If it was blowing more than twenty knots, the ferry would tie up at the dock just long enough to offload freight and load on mail. If you wanted anything on or off that boat, you'd better be damn quick.

Nina and I raced each week to make sure brochures were ready to be postmarked and sent out—the Post Office was only open on ferry days, so you had to be ready for that, too—and deposits ready to go to the bank. The ferry captain would take our deposit bag and drop it off at the night deposit slot on his way home. The next week he'd bring our empty bag back. He performed this service during summer, too, often carrying off thousands of dollars. We never questioned whether those bags would make it to the bank.

Nina and I developed several little rituals those months we worked alone. Promptly at noon every weekday we stopped work and headed to the lounge where the single ancient TV set resided. I would make some sort of sandwiches, or heat up some soup and bring it into the lounge, where Nina would be totally engrossed in *The Young and the Restless*, a soap opera she had become addicted to over the winters. I would set the food down and try to watch, but usually ended up peppering her with questions—*Now who is she sleeping with again? I thought he died last summer? Isn't that the same guy who played her father? Wasn't she pregnant?*

Nina tried to keep me up to date but at some point almost every day, she'd tell me to shut up. Then during a commercial she would attempt, once more, to run down the cast of characters and who had done what to or with whom. I never did get it, but I realized watching with her was a good thing, as it forced me to take a whole hour off in the middle of the day. Had it been up to me I would have gulped lunch down in five minutes and gone back to work, completely wearing myself out in the process. Nina was not, as we used to say to each other all the time, as dumb as she looked.

Another ritual dear to our hearts those long spring days was cocktail hour. Every day after washing out paintbrushes, putting away joint compound, patching materials, caulk, and putty knives, but before we had cleaned ourselves up, we had cocktail hour. I went down into basement freezers and storerooms and pulled out items left over from the season before: puff pastry sheets, sun dried tomatoes, olives, capers. I would slice chorizo ordered from Giamalvo's Portuguese grocery and make bite-sized concoctions of almost any combination available rolled into puff pastry and baked. These would be taken into the lounge where we would sit in the recliners with a beer and a plate full of spicy somethings in front of us, watch the news, and discuss the day. The news was our only real exposure to the outside world those couple of months, and the outside world seemed distant indeed.

Spring Painting Canapé Recipe

Roll out one sheet of thawed commercial puff pastry to double its size. Spread a thin layer of chopped chorizo (or any hot sausage you like) and top with a layer of frozen chopped spinach, some chopped olives, and a layer of parmesan cheese. Roll up the puff pastry into a cylinder, and put in freezer until it is easier to slice (usually about 20 minutes). Cut through the roll, top to bottom, in ¼-inch slices. Place slices flat on a cookie sheet or baking pan and bake in pre-heated, 400-degree oven for about 5-7 minutes or until brown and bubbling.

Serve hot with a flourish to your admiring sister.

Innsider Magazine *photo of Nina and Margo looking impossibly young.*

We ordered from Giamalvo's Grocery because by late winter/early spring, the Cuttyhunk store was a dark and dismal place. It was the only place on Cuttyhunk open year round, and in summer it was a bustling operation. Ginger, a slim woman with long fair hair who looked like a kid herself, housed three or four kids in her upstairs rooms and worked them ten hours a day. They made sandwiches, scooped ice cream, hauled supplies up from the dock, and ran the cash register while Ginger cut and packaged meat, baked pies and muffins with fruit that was slightly too ripe to sell, and generally ran the show. At least one of everything had a place on her shelves. Need a mousetrap, a galvanized bucket, a fishing pole, masking tape, aspirin, a toothbrush? How about a postcard, a squid jig, tape measure, sunglasses, flip-flops? No problem: Ginger had it all.

As the summer season drew to a close, Ginger would slowly let her stock run down and the store hours would grow shorter. Gone would be the fancy items people on boats bought for hors d'oeuvres and the fresh fruit and vegetables with short shelf lives. Sunglasses and flip-flops, t-shirts and hats were packed away until the next season.

After October, Ginger stopped buying fresh fruits and vegetables except for small amounts of onions and potatoes. The same went for meat, chicken, anything that might go bad before someone bought it. You couldn't blame her; the amounts she bought in winter were just too small for her to receive discounts on. Grocery stores off-island delivered to the boat cheaper than she could price the things she bought and still make a profit.

You could special order certain things for boat days, and Ginger usually got some lettuce and bananas for Mary, a tiny, bird-like woman in her seventies who relied entirely on the store for the miniscule amount of food she required. The rest of us depended in the winter on one of the several off-island stores that delivered to the ferry.

If Ginger was on-island in the off-season, she would open for an hour or two in the morning and an hour in the afternoon, but if you'd lost track of time and needed a pack of cigarettes, you knocked on her window and she'd usually let you in. When she went off-island, Hunter, who almost never went off, would open for an hour each morning and evening. When I first got on-island, Stop and Shop would let you set up an account and deliver to the ferry, but within a year they decided it wasn't worth their time. That left Giamalvo's, a small grocery in the Portuguese section of New Bedford. They were very good about going out and getting what you wanted if they didn't have it, but the quality of the produce depended on who they sent to the store, and there were often interesting mix-ups, like the time I ordered a half gallon of skim milk and got a quart of mayonnaise. And there were many winter and spring days we expected groceries, and the boat didn't run due to weather or mechanical malfunctions.

Come summer, a couple of tiny gift shops and a small bakery would open, and shellfish, lobsters, and ice cream would be available down at the dock. But only Memorial Day through Labor Day. Any other time, Ginger's store was it.

Sometimes no matter how carefully you planned, you ran out of something. And sometimes you just needed a change, wanted something, anything, different. That's when it was time for a trip to the store.

It was cold and damp in the store, the one light she turned on dim. Ginger shut down almost everything in winter to conserve energy. Energy was money. She kept one refrigerator case and one small chest freezer on, and whatever she ordered lay within. Frozen bread or milk was better than none at all, and she usually had eggs and some sort of cheese, orange juice, and butter. The freezer would occasionally surprise us with ice cream bars or cups. And there was always the candy shelf. True, around about February the Almond Joys would be more than a little on the stale side, but by then if you had a sudden craving for a candy bar you really didn't care. In fact, it was amazing what began to look tempting on a cold February afternoon when the boat hadn't run in two weeks due to ice or storms. Out-of-date Tuna Helper? *Mmmmmmm.*

Chapter 13
People Who Have People

Most Cuttyhunkers divided people into three basic groups: islanders, summer people, and tourists. Islanders were, at least to themselves, an elite group. The rest of the world might not understand what compels a person to live on a tiny island with few basic services, no entertainment or luxuries, minimal transportation to the mainland, and a bitter sea wind that blows half the year. What the rest of the world doesn't get is those are exactly the reasons people choose Cuttyhunk.

Island living takes a certain kind of person, and I quickly discovered I was that sort of person. But no matter how many winters I spent on the island (lasting out even one winter bloods you somehow, and you become something more than just a summer person, a sort of in-between species far more tolerated by natives than even someone whose family has been summering on the island for generations), I would never be an islander. Islanders were born, not transplanted, unless they married in, moved on, and stayed for twenty years. Minimum.

Summer people owned vacation homes on the island. If you rented a house each season for fifteen consecutive years, you might achieve almost the same social level as a summer person. Otherwise, renters were pretty much ignored.

There were around four hundred summer people on the island in July and August, maybe two hundred and fifty in the months of June and September. A hardy few came on-island for Thanksgiving, Easter break, sometimes even Christmas, but they were few indeed.

Of the three populations, Nina and I paid the least attention to summer people, simply because they affected us the least. We got along with most of them and were genuinely fond of a few, but as a group they held little responsibility for our survival as they provided us minimal income.

The only summer people we took real notice of were the ones who had children old enough to work. Those we wooed, trying to steal their sons and daughters away from the bakery, the lawn mowing service, or the businesses at the dock. Kids who had their own places to stay on the island were immensely valuable to every business owner due to the island's severe lack of affordable housing.

The last and most important group (unless we were dealing with island politics) was the tourists.

Islanders and summer people alike made fun of tourists, even those of us dependent on them for our livelihood. We looked eagerly for the first of them in early spring, counting boats in the harbor and at the dock each evening. We prayed for good weather Memorial Day weekend, and for June fogs to sweep in suddenly and strand boaters. Back then most sail boaters either didn't have Loran or radar or weren't comfortable depending on electronics they didn't really understand in pea soup fog. June business was always iffy, dependent on weather, and with only twelve rooms and three cottages we could barely make payroll on houseguests alone. So we watched for fog and willed those boaters to come into our harbor and be stuck, forcing them to eat at the restaurant when they ran out of food. And when the harbor was empty we used our excess employee labor on the always needed and unending painting, cleaning, and repair projects necessitated by ancient buildings poorly maintained for too long.

Summer people might complain about crowds but they knew without tourists there would be less variety in the produce at the store, no gift shops, no bakery, no fresh fish at the dock, no restaurant. Many islanders made a portion of their living caretaking summer peoples' homes in the off-season, but everyone on the island depended to some extent on tourists to raise their standard of living. In my case, they were my entire living, and I found myself wishing like hell they would start showing up about the middle of May. Of course by Labor Day, I was wishing like hell the last of them would go home.

Gus lived in his little house down by the fish dock for many years, and after Labor Day weekend he held a pond scum party—pond scum being a concoction of unknown ingredients Gus whipped up every year. It had a lethal alcoholic kick and somehow he managed to make it look exactly like its name, down to the algae floating on top. I never knew what was in it, and never had any desire to ask him. It was quite an honor to be invited to this party, for it meant that you had somehow crossed that invisible line between outsider and insider. Nina and I were invited the year we bought the Allen House.

Before that, we outsiders made do with a little party on the ferry dock. We would bring a tray of canapés and vegetables with our famous bleu cheese dip, and Ginger, who had fallen out with Gus sometime in the distant past, would bring a bottle of champagne. Then Nina, Higgins, Ginger, and I would toast off the last boat on Labor Day Monday. Everyone on the ferry always thought it was a tribute to them. In reality it was a kiss-off until next year.

Our Famous Bleu Cheese Dressing/Dip

Thin, it's a dressing, thick, it's a dip.

Makes approximately 1 ½ gallons of base.
6 pounds sour cream
¼ cup Worcestershire sauce
¼ cup garlic powder
¼ cup onion powder
1 tablespoon salt
1 tablespoon white pepper
¼ cup horseradish
6 shakes Tabasco sauce
¼ cup lemon juice
3½ cups mayonnaise
3 cups crumbled bleu cheese

Mix all ingredients except bleu cheese together, and then stir in bleu cheese gently so as to leave lumps. Thin with milk to desired consistency. This base lasts weeks in the refrigerator; just add milk as needed. Give some to your friends if you really like them.

Tourists were further divided into three main groups: houseguests, day-trippers, and "boat people." For me, in the 1980s, the term "boat people" always conjured up families of Cambodian and Hmong people walking up the hill toward town. But that's what they were called. At least, that was the *nice* name. The other term was grebes, a small, loud, annoying type of bird.

Houseguests were generally the nicest group, especially after the first two years as we learned to make our descriptions of inn and island more explicit when booking first-time guests. We described in great detail shared bathrooms, the lack of phones, radios or clocks in the rooms, doors with no locks, and the television in the lounge that got three channels on a very clear day.

We explained to our prospective guests only one of the two beaches was sandy each summer, and not always the same beach. Where the sand ended up depended on how the winds and tides ran and how many storms we'd had that winter. We'd warn there was no public transportation, nor could you rent a bike or moped, buy a drink or a six-pack, find an ATM, or use a credit card anywhere but with us. This usually weeded out the faint of heart. Those guests who decided to come anyway and those who came back year after year loved Cuttyhunk and the Allen House for what they were, not what they lacked.

This didn't mean life always ran smoothly. Many of our houseguests were, to put it quaintly, eccentric.

There was one houseguest, an older, single man, who always requested the worst room at the inn. He started out only mildly odd, stopping employees and trying to engage them in philosophical discussions about science and the nature of life, but by his third season he had started wandering around the annex clad in only a pair of stained boxer shorts, demanding cleaning supplies from the housekeeper in order to "properly sanitize" *his* bathroom because other people kept using it. Finally we had to flag his card, instructing the desk staff to tell him whenever he called we were very sorry, but *his* room was not available.

We had several flagged reservation cards, guests that for various reasons we would not allow to return. Some were simply a bit too much for our young, inexperienced staff to handle. Some were such royal pains, with constant complaints and unfillable requests that we just did not want to deal with them. Nina and I always wondered why these people would want to come back, given how miserable and unsatisfied they appeared to be. But we quickly learned that every time we thought we had people figured out, we'd be shown again how wrong we were.

One example: A woman guest tells the front desk person, "There is a mouse in my room. I know old buildings get mice and I am not complaining, I really don't mind mice, but it rustles around in my wastebasket at night and keeps me up. So please have someone take care of it."

Christopher happens to be in the gift shop and overhears. His version of the story goes like this: "There's a mouse in my room. It's the cutest little thing but it bothers me and I WANT IT DEAD!"

This of course becomes another Allen House "in" joke. Usually, by the time an employee finished an entire season, he or she has so many odd sayings, "in" jokes, and conversational puns that it could be weeks before he or she was able to be understood again by friends and family.

Day-trippers never affected business much, unless the boat was packed for some reason and suddenly 60 people showed up at once for lunch or t-shirts. In the early part of the season, when we were especially cash-strapped, we considered their business an extra gift. In the fall, when we might have one waitperson on for lunch, and suddenly someone ran in to tell us there was a horde of hungry-looking people walking up the hill, we were not quite as enthusiastic.

The last of the tourist categories, people who sailed or motored into the harbor, provided some of our best stories. Although we did have quite a few celebrities come to Cuttyhunk, usually on their way to Martha's Vineyard or Nantucket, most people who spent a night or two in the harbor or at the dock were not famous. Many of them simply acted as if they were.

Again, the majority of our customers off boats were good, fine people, and again they get short shrift in this book. They tended to pass by unnoticed, leaving only a grateful waitperson, host, or desk person in their wake. Unfortunately, it's a rare day in this business when the customers you remember are the ones who gave you a smile or a generous tip.

Chapter 14
Knock, Knock

"We have no food on the boat."

The first time I heard this I was truly puzzled. It was my very first season, and Steve and I were cleaning up from dinner service when someone knocked at the kitchen door. I looked through the glass to at a man in a yellow rain slicker peering in. Before Steve could say, "Don't answer that," I opened the door.

"I'm sorry," I said politely, "but the kitchen is closed for the night."

"Can't you fix us *something*?" the man replied.

I gestured to the cleaned-off counters, the mop bucket standing at the ready.

"I'm sorry," I said again. "Everything is shut down and put away. We stop serving at seven-thirty this time of year."

I looked pointedly at the clock. It was quarter till nine.

"But you must have something," the man replied. "We just got into the harbor, and it's raining, and we walked all the way up here."

I looked at Steve. He shook his head.

"I'm sorry," I said for the third time. "But we're closed."

"But we don't have any food on the boat," the man said.

No food. That must suck, I thought. Without looking back at Steve this time, I said,

"Well, I could heat you up some chowder, I guess. And the coffee's still on, if you want that."

"Is that the best you can do?" the man said.

At which point Steve walked around me.

"We are closed." he announced, and shut the door. Firmly.

That was the first of many, many knocks on the kitchen door over the years. People wanted to buy a pound of butter to serve with the lobsters they'd steamed on the boat, or milk, or a loaf of bread after the store closed. People had small children on the boat that would go hungry. I remember my sister Nina's reaction the first time she heard that line. By then Steve was long gone, and Higgins and I had worked out a simple system. Nina was in the kitchen sharing a beer with us as we cleaned up when her first after-hours knock at the door came.

She was just about to offer the man salad and chowder when he uttered the magic line, "We don't have any food on the boat."

Nina gave him a puzzled glance.

"You sailed across Buzzard's Bay at night with no food in the boat?" she asked, an incredulous tone in her voice. "And you have kids on board? That seems awfully irresponsible to me."

The man had the grace to look embarrassed, but stood his ground.

"Salad and chowder," Nina said firmly. "That's all I can do. Sit up in the coffee shop so the waitstaff can clean up and I will bring it to you."

The man led his family back up the ramp.

Nina turned to us. "Do you really think he doesn't have any food on the boat?" she asked.

"Nah," Higgins replied. "They have food. They just don't want to walk back down the hill and eat peanut butter or tuna fish on a cold, rocking boat."

"You're gonna see a million of them," I told her. "Here's how we've been working it. First off, they have to ask nicely. Any demanding or whining and it's over right then. We're closed. That's it."

"Then we offer them salad and chowder up in the gift shop, like you did," Higgins continued. "If they are grateful and say, 'Anything is fine, anything at all,' we might even warm up some rolls for them. *Really* grateful people get dessert."

"But the first sign of discontent and they are out the door," I said. "If they say, 'Don't you have anything else?' or 'Do we have to eat up there, why can't we eat down here at a table'. . ."

"Out the door." Higgins said firmly. "It might seem harsh, but after you've done this twenty or thirty times when all you want to do is clean the kitchen and go to bed, you develop an amazingly thick skin."

"Isn't it bad publicity, though?" Nina asked. "I mean, they're going to go down to the dock and badmouth us."

"We've kind of figured out they'll do that in any case, unless we seat them in the dining room, give them a waitperson, and let them order off the menu," I said.

And unfortunately, that proved to be the case. On the other hand, we discovered that sort of bad-mouthing never did our business much harm. As long as we did our best to accommodate people, and gave them the best service and best food we could for reasonable prices at reasonable hours, amazingly enough, our business prospered.

Recipe for Clam Chowder

Makes 8 gallons

6 large white onions
6 bunches of celery
14 large potatoes
6 cans of chopped clams
6 cans of clam juice
1 cup diced salt pork
1 pound butter
about 1¼ cups flour
6 bay leaves
¼ cup white pepper

Dice onions and celery. Peel and dice potatoes. Soak one 6" x 5" square of salt pork in water until all surface salt is removed. Score the salt pork down to the rind and slice it thinly. Render the salt pork in a large pot until crispy. Add 1 pound butter and melt. Add diced celery and onion and sweat. Whisk in flour to vegetable and fat mixture until all the fat is absorbed. Pour in 6 quarts of clam juice and 6 quarts of canned clams. Whisk mixture until flour has been absorbed. Add potatoes, 6 bay leaves and cook over low heat, stirring frequently, until potatoes are cooked through. Add one-quarter cup white pepper and cool mixture down. This is clam chowder base. Add light cream to taste just before reheating and serving.

Bits and Pieces

Chapter 15
Spring and Fall

Our first spring running the place, Higgins's old friend Christopher decided poor Becky, our new waitress, was his new plaything. He'd been tormenting her all month, calling her Bitsy, putting tape in her hair, the sort of behavior one expects from a five-year-old with a crush, not a twenty-three year-old, 6'2" queen. But this is how Christopher behaved when bored, and painting ninety percent of the walls in the main building was *boring*. I went down to the basement one day to put a load of towels in and found Becky lifting the lids on all the washing machines. She saw me watching, and pointed silently halfway down the washing machine instructions printed on the lid. **To Avoid Agitation, Lift Lid** was printed in bold white letters.

"I figured it couldn't hurt," Becky said.

Fall, that same year. It is after Labor Day, weekday business is very slow. Dinner service is over by seven-thirty, clean-up by eight. It's been a terrible year for mice; they've been getting into the boxes of individual bags of chips stored on kitchen shelves. We bait traps with peanut butter and place them in the boxes. We each pick a box. Then we sit behind the kitchen counter, beers in hand, and wait, placing bets on whose box will be the first to catch a mouse. Traps that are simply snapped do not count.

Much later: Kim, one of our waitstaff, is in the kitchen when Higgins shouts out, "Are you ever going to take this lobster out?"

Kim responds, "Lobster? I hardly know her?"

And there begins another Allen house wordplay. Any word with an "er" on the end is fair game.

"Butter? I just met her!" "Dinner? *You* dinner. You brought her." The game reached its peak when Nina and Mark were driving up to Maine one winter, with then three-year-old Matt strapped in a car seat in the back, supposedly playing with his toys. Nina said to Mark, "We get off the interstate just before Bangor." A tiny voice pipes up from the backseat, "Banger? I hardly know her!"

The infamous corner phone booth.

Got A Dime?

When you are trying to run an inn and restaurant during a busy tourist season, the island's quaint eccentricities stop being quaint and start to drive you crazy.

Take the island phone system. There were six phones on the island, all of them pay phones, and only four easily accessible to the public. Our phone lay in the antiquated booth at the end of our L-shaped dining room. We considered it our phone because we had run an illegal extension up to the desk in order to be able to answer calls and take reservations. This extension didn't allow us to call out without using a credit card. New Bedford, where most of our suppliers were located, was a local call, so to put our orders in for the next day we needed to use the phone booth. The same booth that was a favorite of our house and dinner guests. Mid-afternoons often found me outside placing orders at the phone on the post office wall, clad in kitchen whites, a roll of dimes clutched in my hand. (Local calls stayed a dime on Cuttyhunk well into the nineties.)

Not only did you have to get your order in before your dime ran out, which was sometimes difficult if you had a chatty supplier like our fish monger, Captain Frank, who always wanted to know how things were going, but you had to deal with members of the public who also were waiting, often in long lines, to use the phone and resented you trying to place six orders at a time. You had to be polite to them as most of them were either present or potential customers.

This was long before cell phones, and in the middle of the season the island swarmed with wealthy businessmen from New York and Connecticut who couldn't understand how our meat or bread orders could take precedence over a phone call to their offices. We finally got most of our suppliers to set up answering machines or services (not a usual thing for small businesses back then) so we could make our calls after the restaurant closed at 9:00 p.m. This cut down considerably on the number of people waiting in line behind us.

Our phone in the lobby was busiest when bad weather hit, as it was the only one inside an easily accessible building. Most people didn't know about the phone in A.P.'s front entryway, and his wife, Dot, liked it just fine that way. And no one was going to walk all the way up the hill to the Jenkins's to use the phone there—you'd be wetter before you got to the phone than if you'd stood in line outside. The corner phone across from Ginger's house was the most obvious. It was enclosed in a booth of sorts, but one or more panels were always blown out and there hadn't been a door on it for years. The two phones down at the dock had the same number and were always jammed with slugs or gum. The last of the six was on the wall of the post office, but if you thought the other phones weren't exactly private, try holding a conversation directly under Ellen's living room window.

The corner booth was the first number listed in the New Bedford phone book under Cuttyhunk, so it got the most nuisance calls. At least we thought they were nuisance calls, because they were never for us. People quickly learned never to answer that phone when it rang.

New staff couldn't stand it. Twelve rings in and a new kid would lunge for the phone. Sometimes it was as simple as one of Ginger's suppliers calling back with a question. That was easy, because Ginger lived across the street. But when it wasn't a caller expecting you to act like the chamber of commerce and spend an hour answering questions, it would be someone saying, "Go get Roland for me," or "Can I speak to Charlie Tilton?" and then the kid would have to play the island game of "run and find the fishing guide." Not a great game. Very time-consuming. The next time that phone rang there was one more wised-up employee who simply didn't hear it.

In 1984, when the Olympics came to L.A. and everyone had Olympic fever, our t-shirt design that year was a cartoon of a phone booth, a line of people stretching from its door into infinity. The caption read: Cuttyhunk's Official Olympic Sport.

When Nina and I first took over running the Allen House, we made a lot of "help" calls: I called Steve for answers, Nina called Jan and occasionally, Enna. Jan taught Nina a great deal about what bills to pay when, how to organize the books, and the best way to handle the register so it was harder to screw up. This last bit was important because I occasionally closed out the register on nights when I was sticking around to close the kitchen anyway. Math has never been my strong suit.

Nina did things the way Jan taught her. She kept all the books, paid all the taxes, cut all the paychecks, paid all the bills. But there was one thing Jan was unable to help us with: What to do when the register was a few cents over or under? How many times should we go over the tape before we gave up? And what did we do about it when we had to record the numbers? Jan couldn't help us because when she and Steve ran the inn, ninety percent of the time she was the one on the register. And even when she wasn't, Jan's registers somehow always balanced. Jan was a bookkeeper. Nina was an American Studies Major who'd been a park ranger, a canoe guide, and a World's Fair folk-life coordinator who also happened to be the only one in our family who could count without using her fingers. A bookkeeper she was not.

Finally, in desperation, Nina called Enna. Enna seemed surprised Nina didn't know. Hadn't she seen the coffee cup on the desk? We had noticed a chipped cup full of change on the corner of the desk but assumed it was for the phone or emergency cigarettes. No, Enna told us, it was her own personal bookkeeping system. Jan never used it, but Enna told Nina it saved her sanity. When the register was a few cents over, she said, you put the change in the cup. When it was a few cents under, you made it up out of the cup. Anything less than a dollar and you didn't have to search the tape again and again, looking for that tiny error.

Of course.

Year after year Nina turned the books over to a private accountant to be reconciled before they went to the C.P.A. who did our taxes, and year after year the books passed muster. So I guess Enna was right. A few cents here, a few cents there, even the government didn't care, as long as your taxes came out right. And our tax accountant was our uncle, possibly the most honest person I have ever met, personally and professionally. Our taxes always came out right.

Chapter 16
Wanna Buy an Inn?

Times change. Tax laws change. After three years of managing the Allen House for the consortium of three, tax laws changed so that it was no longer in their best interest to hold onto a property that lost money. And we had always lost money, because no one ever cared if we made a profit. In fact, they didn't want us to.

Now the owners wanted out. Leon had long ago decided running an inn and restaurant was not a retirement hobby. George was semi-resigned to the fact the Allen House was not going to be a job factory for his kids. If he couldn't give his kids a career there, he really had no use for the place. And my father had only wanted a piece of land on the island. This was the real reason he bought into the business in the first place, although he did occasionally enjoy playing lord of the manor. For example—

The first Memorial Day weekend Nina and I ran the Allen House we had almost no staff. Becky and Christopher were waiting tables; I was in the kitchen; Nina at the front desk. My new girlfriend Annie had agreed to come over and wash dishes later after she had closed the store for Ginger. Nobody else we'd hired could come out until later in the season.

After Memorial Day weekend, it didn't really matter. We had enough staff for the small amount of business we'd get until mid-June. But that weekend we were in a real fix. We needed a host. Nina couldn't leave the front desk; she was answering the phone, taking reservations, selling T-shirts, answering questions, and ringing up dinner checks. Truly desperate, we asked Dad to be maitre d' for the weekend.

Friday afternoon Nina ran him through the dining room, explaining table numbers, showing him where the menus were, how to read the reservation list, pour water, wipe a table off properly. She demonstrated re-setting a table in case Christopher and Becky couldn't get there fast enough. Dad accused us of acting like he was a simpleton, but Nina went over every detail with him.

Or so we thought.

Dad was a charming, sweet-talking guy, and had certainly eaten in his share of restaurants far nicer than this one. He assured us he was more than able to handle the job. With some trepidation, Nina agreed and left him to it.

I was barely aware of the dining room that night. I had my hands more than full trying to cook even a limited menu for the number of reservations we had taken and coaching Becky through her first waitress job at the same time. I had no idea anything had gone wrong until we'd managed to get through the evening, and everyone was helping clean up. I popped a beer and pulled Nina aside.

"How'd he do?" I asked.

Nina gave me one of her famous looks.

"You mean before or after I realized he'd seated half the dining room with a lit cigarette in one hand and a scotch in the other?" she asked.

Back to business. Our business. Because Nina and I decided if the Allen House was to be sold, we wanted to buy it. Desperately. There was only one slight problem. Somehow we doubted that in that particular economic climate (or any, for that matter), we would be able to find a bank willing to lend a technical theater major and an American studies major specializing in folklore several hundred thousand dollars. Especially when our biggest *combined* income year didn't top twenty-five thousand.

But we wanted the place. We thought we had earned the right to give it a try. Nina and I held massive planning sessions: how we would run the place if left to our own devices, ways we could increase business, maximize sales. All we needed was a chance.

And Dad, amazingly enough, gave it to us. He was skeptical at first, which didn't hurt our feelings. At the time it was a huge amount of money for him, and we could damage him financially if we screwed up and lost the place. He quizzed us about our plans for the future, and finally asked the key question. The Allen House hadn't made a profit since Mildred sold it to them. It hadn't had to. Now, if we bought it, it did. Did we really think we could run it profitably?

We did. And we had the numbers Nina had crunched to back us up.

Dad took the gamble. I am not exactly sure what he had to do to buy the others out, and he didn't say. I know he gave George back his house, which had been thrown into the pot as part of the original deal. And he sold the land the land Fairplay and Fowl Play sat on to Pete Lehner, George's boss, to get the money to buy out Leon. He took the property Horseplay was on for his own house.

Now the Allen House was down to the main house and the annex, and the land cut by more than half. It was actually more manageable that way. More importantly, Dad was the sole owner. And he sold the mortgage to us.

Looking back, I am still amazed he would take a chance like that on us. Amazed, and grateful. Everything I have done since has been in some way related to that sale. I gained confidence, new skills, pride of ownership. After we sold, years later, the money gave me the freedom to explore other options. I know Nina feels the same way.

Thank you, Dad.

Section II.

Surf and Turf

The original ferry Alert.

To Go

Chapter 17
Traveling Menu Column A

The first ferry I rode on made the run from New Bedford to Cuttyhunk for seventy years before being retired in 1987. The Ferry Alert was a mostly open wooden boat sixty-five feet long. It had a tiny cabin/wheelhouse that sat eight to ten in a pinch, but an over-active heater and diesel fume blow-back battled it out inside, and staying inside took someone with a stronger stomach than mine, even in the freezing winter months. Almost everyone elected to sit outside. There were benches along the sides of the boat and wooden shutters that swung down from the roof of the wheelhouse during rainy or rough weather that partially protected those seated from the elements. The key word here is partially.

But I didn't know any better. The seaplane was expensive as well as seasonal, and even more reliant on good weather than the ferry. At least the ferry ran in fog. My other, cheaper option was to try and catch a free ride with either one of the bass fishermen or Seth, the shellfish farmer, all of whom had open boats. The Alert was the lap of luxury by comparison. All the small boats docked in Padanaram, a tiny village in South Dartmouth, which was a $6 taxi ride to the parking garage in New Bedford. That was a lot of money to a kid making $275 a week in the early eighties. The ferry was $8 one way and a dollar a bag for freight, but that was a lot cheaper than the plane, more reliable in bad weather, and you docked within walking distance of the parking garage.

If I took a certain route to the Alert, I'd pass the Shumanchee, the Martha's Vineyard ferry. This was a much smaller ferry than the ones that ran from Cape Cod. It didn't even carry cars. But the size of it in comparison to the Alert always surprised me. It was like comparing a lifeboat to a cruise ship.

Yet I took that lifeboat for years, in every kind of weather. I figured a boat that old, running continuously for that long, well, somebody had to know what they were doing. Blind faith is a wonderful thing.

Chapter 18
Traveling Menu Column B

Occasionally we had to get somewhere fast, or at a certain time, so we took the seaplane. Back then, flying by seaplane to the island was always an adventure, because you flew with Stormin' Norman.

Norman had been flying to Cuttyhunk for more consecutive years than any pilot had flown continuously anywhere in the U.S., and that record had been set long before I even came to the island. He had a wall full of newspaper and magazine articles as proof. Norman worked out of a travel camper parked on a small fenced-in lot near the boat building docks in Fairhaven. You could leave your car there for $2 a day or $100 a season and his daughters, who comprised his office staff, would keep your keys and lock the gate at night to keep the cars safe. Norman always inquired when you were likely to come back, supposedly so he could move your car near the gate. But occasionally, if you had a car he liked, he'd drive it around just for fun. He often used my truck when he needed to haul something. Once, the truck was muddier than I remembered leaving it and I accused Norman, only half-jokingly, of having gone four-wheeling that weekend. He didn't deny it, just smiled.

After you'd parked where you were told, you unloaded your vehicle into one of the ancient shopping carts he kept for luggage and wheeled it out to the plane at the end of the dock, trying to keep the rusty wheels going in a straight line and the cart from going over the side. Norman never charged for freight, and split the flight cost among the passengers, so if you could arrange to go on a full plane of three and didn't have much stuff (a feat that required you have a great deal of flexibility in your schedule), it was not that much more expensive to fly with Norman than to take the ferry. And it was fifteen minutes as opposed to an hour and a half. After we took over the Allen House, that time difference came to mean more than money, and we often took the plane, even when it was just us.

Norman was an amazing pilot, winning prizes yearly in the small plane competitions he flew up in Maine. He kept his plane in a small pond next to his house. That meant as soon as the pond began to freeze, Norman was done with Cuttyhunk. He'd trade his pontoons for skis shortly after Thanksgiving and head up to Maine to compete, then put the plane away and spend the rest of the season in Florida. He didn't resume flying until April, when everything had thawed with no danger of re-freezing. When he pulled his plane, those of us left on island knew winter was coming and felt a little bit more alone. It was nice knowing he was there if you needed him.

In small aviation circles he was famous. We just knew him as Norman, the guy we felt safe flying with over water in any kind of weather. If Norman was willing to take us, we were willing to go.

This was not to say that flying with Norman always *felt* safe. He had a wicked sense of humor, and one of his favorite tricks to play on first-time passengers was to take off, fly for a few minutes, then reach around and pull a well-worn map out of the pocket behind his seat. He'd hand this map to his passenger and say something like, "I can't see so good without my glasses. See if you can locate Cuttyhunk, will you? It's somewhere near Martha's Vineyard."

Or he'd fly our new employees over tiny Penikese Island with its two lonely buildings and say, "Look, down there. There's the Allen House. Nice place, we'll just circle around and find a place to land."

Of course, that did make Cuttyhunk with its sixty or so houses look pretty good by comparison.

Norman liked to combine trips whenever possible. On Sunday runs to the island, he'd swing low over Penikese, buzz the main house and drop a Sunday *Boston Globe* tied in a plastic sack out his window. He'd deliver medicine and small, reasonably unbreakable items to them the same way. Not that he *couldn't* land there, he just saw no reason to waste the time and fuel.

A couple of years after we bought the Allen House, Norman took on a young pilot, Gid, to help him with his flights. After a year or so of "training" Gid, Norman died suddenly in Florida of a heart attack. His wife sold the business to Gid that next spring. Gid was a competent pilot, but he was no Stormin' Norman, and flying to and from the island was never quite the same.

Celebrity Dishes

Chapter 19
O., No!

Some famous people passed through our doors. My first season a man knocked on the back door, asking for the manager. Steve came out and the man introduced himself as Walter Cronkite's skipper. Mr. Cronkite was having some people for dinner. Could he possibly borrow a big lobster pot?

Steve did his best not to laugh in the man's face, explaining that we were a restaurant and we didn't loan out equipment, and if "Walter" wanted a lobster dinner he could damn well come to the Allen House.

After the man left Steve said, "That's a new one. *Walter Cronkite* wants to borrow a pot."

An hour later came another knock at the screen door. This time Steve answered it.

I saw him step outside for a minute, return, pull a large pot from under the counter and carry it outside. When Steve came back, I said, "I thought we didn't loan equipment out. Who was that for, the president?"

"No," Steve answered. "It was Walter Cronkite. I mean, it was actually Walter Cronkite. Hell, if you can't trust *him* with your lobster pot, who *can* you trust?"

Sure enough, the lobster pot came back the next morning, clean and bright, with a nice thank you note. Walter Cronkite became a regular in the harbor over the years, but he never came into the restaurant. I guess he bought his own lobster pot, too, because he never again borrowed ours.

When I told Nina this story, she didn't believe me. That was before her first season, after which she realized there were an awful lot of celebrities (and even more people who imagined they were) who visited Cuttyhunk on a regular basis.

Jimmy Dean (of country music and sausage fame) motored into the harbor almost every season on his eighty-something-foot yacht.

He would come for dinner, and if the waitress recognized him, he would be charming, sweet, and a great tipper. If nobody seemed to know who he was, he could make lives miserable. We started checking with the harbormaster as to when Mr. Dean's yacht was in and tipping off the staff, ninety percent of whom were too young to recognize his name, let alone his face. After we made sure we alerted them, our dinners with Mr. Dean went quite smoothly.

A lot of musicians dropped by on their way to the Vineyard or Nantucket. The most famous were Carly Simon, who had a nightclub on the Vineyard and stopped by occasionally, and Billy Joel, who caused quite a stir when he showed up one weekend with Christie Brinkley. John Hall of *Orleans* fame had relatives on the island and often came and played at summer events.

And there were the politicians. Lots of politicians. One afternoon Senator Dodd of Connecticut dropped his laundry at the front desk, saying he'd be back to pick it up in the morning. The desk person told him we were not a laundry service but we could sell him tokens for the washers and dryers. He demanded to see a manager. Nina politely told him the exact same thing. He bought several tokens, gathered up his wash, and headed back to the laundry room. Nina waited a few minutes to make sure there wasn't going to be trouble, then realized she hadn't heard the washer start up. She entered the laundry area to find the Senator staring at the machines. Nina asked if there was a problem and he confessed he had no idea how to do his wash. Nina graciously led him through it. I assume any mate he has now is grateful to my sister.

Then there was the man who came in after six p.m. demanding tokens for the washing machine. This wasn't a rare occurrence, but this man, when told the laundry closed at dinnertime and he would not be sold tokens, angrily and loudly demanded to see a manager. I usually sent Nina into battle in situations like these as I am a natural coward, but I was in the kitchen and by default, the closest manager. When I introduced myself and informed him no matter how important he was, the laundry still closed at six, he grabbed his bag, marched into the laundry room and stuffed two washers full of clothes. Then he liberally poured liquid detergent over his laundry.

"Now what are you going to do?" he demanded.

Me?

What *I* was going to do was go get Nina. She was great at confrontation. She was the confrontation queen. Nina came up and saw the washers and the man standing by them, his hands on his hips, smiling. Nina opened the closet door and took out a large black trash bag, which she handed to him.

"You have five minutes to get those clothes out of the washers and yourself out of this building," she announced. "And don't even think about trying to come back tomorrow and wash them. You and your attitude are not welcome here."

"I am a member of the New York Yacht Club!" he said "If you don't let me do my laundry, I will make sure you are never again patronized by a single member!"

"If they are all as rude as you, we don't want their business," Nina told him. She turned on her heel and left, telling the desk person in a loud voice to let her know if he wasn't out in five minutes and she'd call the police. I hurried out behind her. After all, I had a kitchen to run, right?

Then there were the Kennedys. Politically, I like the Kennedys. Nina does not. But none of that matters when you run an inn. Everyone is a valued customer. At least until he or she acts like an asshole. For a while, it seemed like every member of the Kennedy family made an appearance at the Allen House. Robert's kids, Ted's kids, John Jr.

One year my sister, Lisa, was visiting my dad. We were sitting on his porch one evening before dinner service, and Senator Ted Kennedy and his new wife came out onto the annex porch. We recognized him immediately. Lisa's young son, Philip, rolled his ball off Dad's porch and we told Philip to go get it and say hi to the man on the other porch, that he was a very important senator. Philip obediently went to get his ball, then went up on the annex porch and said hi. Senator Kennedy said hi back, looking up at our porch. We smiled and waved. He asked to see Philip's ball, and Philip handed it to him. Jokingly, the senator held the ball behind his back and said, "Did your mommy send you over here?"

"Yes, sir," Philip replied politely.

"Did she tell you who I am?" the senator asked.

"Yes," said Philip.

"And who am I?" the senator asked.

"You're the man who won't give me my ball back," Philip answered.

So much for our dreams of political privilege.

Our most famous, most universally liked and admired guest had to be Jackie Kennedy Onassis. She came over once every couple of weeks in the early and late seasons. She had a huge house on the Vineyard and a boat with its own captain on call. She always came during the week, always at lunch. She ate only with her captain, and never without her signature scarf and oversized sunglasses. Invariably she ordered a hamburger, rare. She always drank iced tea.

I know people by what they eat, Nina by what they wear or how they behave. The first time Mrs. Onassis came into the restaurant, Nina ran into the kitchen with the news. She might dislike the Kennedys politically, but there was something about Jackie Onassis that transcended politics. At first I thought Nina was mistaken, or joking. Higgins and I snuck several covert glances out of the kitchen doors until we agreed the woman at table six had to be Jackie Onassis. We alerted the few staff we had, informing them to respect the woman's privacy. Since none of our young staff knew who Jackie Onassis was, that wasn't too hard. Gradually, we learned to deal with her as if she were just another guest.

I was, I admit, star-struck. Nina rarely cared who anybody was. She might be somewhat impressed at first, but in the end everyone got equal treatment. She proved that once and for all with Jackie Onassis.

After she had convinced us she was right about the identity of our new guest, Nina went out to greet Mrs. Onassis and give her a menu. A moment later my sister was back in the kitchen.

"She doesn't have any shoes on," Nina said.

"What?" I answered.

"Jackie Onassis," Nina said, "She isn't wearing any shoes."

"So?"

"It's against the state health code, dummy" Nina said. "For everybody."

"And who's gonna make her put shoes on?" I asked. "Becky?"

"Oh, please god, no," Becky moaned.

"Hell," Nina said, "No shirt, no shoes, no service. I'll do it."

No amount of pleading could sway her. That might be Jackie Onassis out on the porch, but if she didn't have shoes on she wasn't getting served in Nina's restaurant.

I watched Nina go out onto the porch, lean down, and softly say something to Mrs. Onassis.

Mrs. Onassis nodded her head and spoke to the captain. He left the table, and returned twenty minutes later with her sandals, during which time she waited patiently in the gift shop, sipping iced tea. She was very gracious about the whole thing.

My relief was visceral. Jackie Onassis had shoes on.

Life as we knew it could continue.

My mother, who takes the Kennedys personally, as if they were family, was aghast when she heard the story.

"Did you know who she was?" Mom asked Nina.

"Yes," Nina answered. "And I know she can afford shoes."

Chapter 20
Lady of Spain

By the time we'd made it through the rough part of our second season, I had relaxed enough to contemplate having some fun with part of the largest salary I'd ever made. Cheryl Wheeler had been my favorite local singer/songwriter for years. Nina and I regularly ran to the pay phone and called the Vineyard radio station we listened to while we scraped and painted, requesting Cheryl's songs.

I had actually met Cheryl the winter before. I'd gotten island fever around January that winter. I hadn't realized how badly I had it until I heard the Vineyard station announce a Cheryl Wheeler concert at an up-island coffee house and youth hostel. I immediately began the first of a long series of pay-phone calls in an attempt to purchase tickets and find accommodation. I finally got through to the manager of the coffee house, who informed me the hostel was only open in summer *but* since I was from Cuttyhunk, if I brought my own sleeping bag and didn't tell anyone what he'd done, I could camp there. (I figure twenty years is long enough to keep a secret. I doubt he'll get in much trouble now.)

Donnie, the island's only boat builder and Sea Tow operator, was going to his house in Menemsha that day anyway, and he ended up taking me across the rough waters of Vineyard Sound in his open, inflatable rescue boat, both of us wearing survival suits. Proof, if any was needed, just how badly I wanted to go.

The concert was wonderful and just what I needed to get me through the rest of the winter. Afterwards the manager took me to meet Cheryl and told her what I'd done to get there. I was so star-struck I could barely mumble more than hello when she told me I must be utterly mad.

So when I wanted to reward myself, Nina, and the end-of-season employees, I naturally thought of Cheryl. Luckily, she had a midweek opening in early October, and we could book her for the not inconsiderable but not unreasonable sum (in the mid 1980s) of $350. That was *if* we paid for her to get over to the island and back, put her up for the night, and fed her.

What the hell. We requested use of the Town Hall and made a few signs. Word spread like wildfire, and by the end of the week not only was everyone left on-island telling me they planned to come, but several friends and relatives planned to come over to the island just for the concert. I just prayed most of these excited people would actually show up. Cuttyhunk had a way of closing down at night after Labor Day, and I desperately wanted enough people so that Town Hall (which seats about fifty) did not look totally empty for Cheryl.

Concert day, I called the Alert to make sure Cheryl had made the boat. Barely, I was told. The captain didn't sound too happy about that. (I later found out Cheryl had managed to wedge her van firmly inside the low-ceilinged entrance of the parking garage.)

After the excitement of just getting to the island came the shock of Cuttyhunk itself. I had warned Cheryl's manager how small the island was, but either he had neglected to pass that information on, or Cheryl hadn't quite taken it in. She was silent during the forty-five-second van ride from the dock to the inn, and didn't say much as I showed her to her room. It was the best in the house, of course, room three with its brand new ceiling, but you had to know the other rooms to properly appreciate that. Her response to my "Can I get you anything, anything at all?" was: "Yeah. A tuna sandwich, a beer and a four p.m. wake up call."

Done.

It might sound like Cheryl was a bit of a prima donna, but I thought she was holding up very well for her first Cuttyhunk experience.

We closed the restaurant to outsiders that October night, and asked our inn guests to please eat at six so every employee who wished could attend the concert.

Everyone was quite obliging and by ten till seven I was at Town Hall, setting up for Cheryl Wheeler!

I was absurdly excited, hoping enough employees would show up so she'd have a proper audience. What could be worse than *paying* to give a party and having nobody come? Then the unexpected happened. A few minutes after seven, Milt and his wife, Joan, arrived, followed shortly by Gladys and Jack, Asa and Kris, Bonnie, Ginger, even Billy, who *rarely* went anywhere socially. Soon ninety percent of townspeople left on-island were filling the rows, followed by our employees, inn guests, even a few people from boats in the harbor. I was astounded and grateful. Even Cheryl was slightly impressed.

"I thought you said I'd be playing for your employees," she told me. "This is quite some staff!"

She inclined her head toward Gladys and Jack, an island couple in their eighties, holding hands in the second row.

"Lemme guess, those are your dishwashers, right? I obviously didn't come with the right material! Next year, I'll do *Lady of Spain!*"

Next year. She said <u>next year</u>. I don't think I heard another word for the next five minutes.

"I'd like to do a song about my cats," Cheryl said after intermission. "I have to do my animal songs when I play alone, because my band refuses to play them."

The audience cheered her on. Just as she played the first notes of her song, Tom, the island cat, appeared from nowhere and strolled majestically to the center of the stage, where he sat down and, cocking his head to the left, regarded Cheryl and her guitar with interest. The crowd, all of whom knew Tom, went wild. Cheryl waited for a pause in the laughter and demanded to know who had paid the cat to do that. Tom just sat there. As soon as Cheryl finished her cat song and started on about her dogs, Tom got up and strolled off stage the way he had come.

After we closed that year, I got in touch with our specialty t-shirt maker. We'd run a very popular "original" design that year, a line drawing of Massachusetts with the Elizabeth Islands coming out in a line from what was referred to locally as the armpit of the cape. The shirt had a small x on the last island and the words "*<u>you are here</u>*" printed above. I had the designer add "*Cheryl Wheeler, Cuttyhunk World Tour 1988.*" On the back it read, "*Next Year, Lady of Spain*".

I had a couple of dozen made and as a holiday present, sent them to every staff member and fishing guide who had been at the concert. And of course, I sent several to Cheryl. Just a gentle reminder.

The Tuna Fish Dressing Cheryl Wheeler Ate

4 cups mayonnaise
1/3 cup lemon juice
¼ cup Worcestershire sauce
1/8 cup tarragon vinegar
6 shakes Tabasco
½ teaspoon white pepper
2 tablespoons dry mustard
¼ cup dried tarragon leaves

Billy's boat as he prepares to take Cheryl Wheeler off island.
She refused to fly.

More Bits and Pieces

Chapter 21
Lucky 13

Steve and Jimmy had partially cleared out the main house basement sometime before I arrived for my first full season in 1982. I knew because I could walk through it from one end to the other. Sort of, that is. Carefully. This basement was much larger and longer than the annex basement, with access through two outside bulkheads and one treacherous set of bowed wooden stairs leading down from the kitchen. It was L-shaped like the house, the short end of the L fat and wide.

Most of the long end was lined with steel shelving. Steve put a good portion of it there as a sort of pantry for cans and jars but some of it had obviously been there for many years. Behind these shelves lay darkness and innumerable vague dusty shapes. I never went behind the shelves unless I was shamed into it. *There be dragons*, as the old maps used to say.

Deep in the bowels of the basement L lay the ancient rusted beast known as the furnace, home to the dreaded circulator/regulator. Its secrets belonged to Alan and Hunter. That furnace was our only source of heat, labyrinths of pipes running hot water from it through the walls and sometimes even all the way to the ancient radiators. We needed that heat for our spring and fall guests, and in winter we kept it on low to keep the plaster from freezing and thawing, and consequently cracking even more than it already did.

The furnace pipes ran the length of the low basement, and could get **hot**. To avoid accidents and preserve heat, they were wrapped in insulation covered in disintegrating cloth. One of my first jobs every spring was to duct tape the cloth back up and cover all the loose insulation with more cloth and duct tape. Years later, when we went to sell the place, we discovered that insulating stuff was asbestos. A team in Tyvek suits and breathing apparatus removed the insulation in special bags and took it away. Oh, well. Life is dangerous. Live and learn.

My second full season at The Allen House, (and my first as a "real" cook) Dave and Steve decided to build a walk-in in the short part of the basement L, which had its own bulkhead access for easy freight storage and held only a washer, dryer, and an ice machine.

Dave and Steve got together with Alan and designed something so unbelievably against code that a health inspector from the mainland wouldn't even have looked inside before condemning it. But then, we weren't on the mainland.

As often was the case with Dave's projects, it was function over form.

A walk-in cooler is just a large insulated box with a cooling unit, or condenser, providing cold air. Dave built a plywood square, covered the walls and ceiling with pink fiberglass insulation, and nailed plywood over that. Basically, a box within a box. He lined all the walls with plywood shelves, and hung a huge, heavy insulated door that looked as if it belonged on a bank vault. Alan installed a condenser and we were good to go. All I had to do was apply thirteen coats of polyurethane every spring, sanding lightly between coats. Every spring.

It actually worked better than most of the commercial coolers I've used since. Because it was plywood, we kept it scrupulously clean. And I kept a close eye on the thermometer as the outside fan had a tendency to freeze up in the humid sea air. When it did, I sent a dishboy up a ladder with a hairdryer. They just *loved* that job. The walk-in was the only thing that worked properly in that basement. The ice machine produced enough ice for our limited needs in June, but come July, when we really needed it, it turned into little more than a repository for ice purchased at exorbitant prices from Bruce. Bruce's ice machine worked just fine. It was housed in his shack on the dock, with plenty of air circulating through gaps in the boards. Our machine, stuck in a hot, airless basement, never had a chance. No amount of care in the world could induce it to make more than a few pitiful cubes. Until September. The temperature dropped, the number of customers dropped, and the ice machine began pumping out unneeded ice at a steady rate.

Chapter 22
Stronger than Dirt

To this day, I haven't decided which was worse: cleaning the kitchen, the walk-in and the basement in the fall; or cleaning the rest of the inn come springtime. When Nina and I spent winters on-island we could do little chores like touch-up painting whenever it was warm enough. Warm enough meant we couldn't see our breath inside the rooms. But no matter how we tried, this never seemed to make a difference in the amount of work necessary when spring arrived. Spring meant washing every towel, blanket, and bedspread in the house. And spring meant carpets. Every year we rented a carpet cleaning machine and had it sent over on the ferry. That gave us three days to clean every carpet in the main house and annex and get the machine back on the boat. The carpet cleaners we used back then cost a lot more and required a great deal more physical effort than the ones currently in use, and we had to work furiously to get the job completed in time to send the machine back on the next boat. We dreaded those three days, every muscle in our bodies aching long before we were halfway through.

As bad as washing the mold off the bathroom ceilings with bleach and running the carpet machine was, for me *nothing* compared to painting the porch. Coating the walls, ceiling, and shelves of the walk-in with thirteen coats of polyurethane came close, but in the end the dining room porch floor won out.

Dave had covered the wedges he used to level the porch with one-inch thick, grade two plywood. In the process, he covered up the scuppers built into the walls to carry rainwater off the slanted deck outside onto the lawn. We cursed him for that every time there was a storm, when rain poured in through the old, warped porch windows and we had to mop up puddles an inch deep where the plywood bowed.

The porch was initially coated with dark gray polyurethane outdoor deck paint. You would think paint that tough could hold its own. But it didn't seem to matter how carefully I scraped and sanded, how many coats of paint Nina and I rolled and brushed on that damn floor, how long we let it dry between coats, by the middle of the season the floor would be gouged and flaking. Yet I never gave up. For some reason,

I was always sure that *this* spring, this spring of *all* springs, would be the one where I'd get the paint, temperature and buffing exactly right and the floor would look perfect the entire season.

It never happened.

In the fall, cleaning the kitchen after closing was a painful job. We tried to keep it clean throughout the year, but as soon as we were open three meals a day, seven days a week, meticulous cleaning was simply impossible. Fall cleaning was designed to remove every possible speck of food that could decay over the winter.

I learned that lesson the first year Steve and I closed down, when he decided we might as well leave all the cleaning for spring. The sight and smell that greeted us that next March when we opened the kitchen door is something I will never forget. The moist sea air caused every surface to grow a loathsome coat of green or blue mold. Never again.

By the time Nina and I took over, Steve had devised a workable method to fall cleanup. Any part of the stoves or broilers that could possibly come apart we took outside and leaned against a stone wall. There we blazed away at each section with a blowtorch until the metal glowed bright red and every bit of grease and food accumulated over the season burned off. This was a coveted job. But considering the danger, I usually tried to keep this job for myself. Okay, maybe it wasn't just the danger. A blowtorch is fun.

Any appliance left standing in the kitchen was scrubbed down with steel wool and heavy-duty grease cleaner that had all sorts of dire warnings as to its use and misuse printed on the back of the bottle. Even with heavy gloves on, by the end our hands were blistered and cracked. If there was such a thing as a heavy-duty green cleaner in the '80s, I had no knowledge of it.

Cleaning the kitchen usually took four days, depending on the quality and amount of help we had. That might seem a bit obsessive for such a small space, but there is no pleasure quite like walking into a kitchen that smells only slightly stale after being closed up for six months.

Chapter 23
Fire Me

Most of the time our houseguests, if occasionally strange, were at least controllable. There were exceptions. Our first year George and Roland brought over a fishing party of six young men. It was barely nine a.m. when they pulled up at the dock, but these guys were already taking the "party" part seriously.

Nina heard them coming up the hill, and as the guides checked them in, she said, "Those guys sound a little rowdy for so early in the morning."

"Don't worry," George said. "We'll take care of them. They're just a little young."

George was a cop back on the mainland, so Nina was somewhat reassured. The way the tides were running, the guides wouldn't go out until mid-afternoon. Instead of sleeping, which would be the smart thing to do as they were in for four or five hours of fairly strenuous fishing, the boys continued to party.

Shortly after noon our housekeeper ran into the kitchen.

"The guys in the annex have gone nuts," she yelled. "They just sprayed a fire extinguisher out the window of room four!"

I shot out the kitchen door as she ran up the ramp to the gift shop to tell Nina.

Our housekeeper was right about the guys going nuts. I could hear swearing and something that sounded like glass breaking. No way was I going in there alone. I ran to where George was staying and pounded on the door until he woke up.

"Your guys are going nuts in the annex," I yelled. "I mean *really* nuts. They just set off a fire extinguisher. You gotta get in there and do something!"

"Okay, okay," George said. "Let me get some pants on, I'll take care of it."

I ran back to the kitchen. We were in the middle of lunch, so I had to take George's word he would indeed take care of it.

About twenty minutes later George came into the kitchen shaking his head.

"Jesus," he said. "You weren't kiddin'." He looked at me. "They got kind of out of hand. Roland's getting the boats ready. As soon as he's done, he'll come up and we'll get these guys out of your hair."

Nina stormed into the kitchen. She saw George and demanded, "Did you go in the annex?"

"Yeah," he said. "It's pretty bad."

"Pretty bad," Nina said, "*Pretty bad?* Those guys are paying for the whole three days. All the rooms in the annex, all three days."

"Yeah," George said. "Okay. Don't worry about it. We got it covered."

"*And* all the damage," Nina continued. "I want a check for the three days before you haul their asses off-island. And I want names and addresses so I can bill them for repairs."

"Don't worry," George repeated. "Roland and I will take care of it. I promise."

"Okay," Nina said. "Just get them out of here."

I don't know what George and Roland said to those guys but it was a pretty subdued bunch I saw walking down the hill a few minutes later. George drove ahead with their luggage but made them walk to sober them up a little for the boat ride back.

I have never seen anything like those rooms, and I hope never to see anything like that again. The downstairs wasn't too bad, just a broken lamp in room three, some beer spilled on a rug and a pile of empty cans that looked like they'd been tossed down the stairs.. Upstairs was a different story. There were red wine stains all along the stair walls and it was obvious a massive pillow fight had taken place. Several pillows were split along their seams and the rest were thrown about the rooms, most soaked with beer. The walls in room four were covered with red wine stains. The bed was literally broken, the wood splintered and snapped. Broken bottles littered the floor, with several sharp gouges in our carefully restored floorboards. And of course, the fire extinguisher. Only half of the foam made it outside the window. The rest was sprayed liberally across the room and out into the hall.

I was stunned by the amount of damage. Before I could say anything, Nina told our housekeeper, "I want you to keep a careful record of exactly how much time you spend in the annex. Every minute you spend here is double-time and I'm going to charge these guys for it."

"This stuff isn't going to wash off," I said. "We're going to have to repaint at least two rooms and half the hallway."

"Double-time for that, too," Nina replied. "I don't care who ends up doing it. Just get someone on it."

Later that afternoon George returned.

"Those guys were really sorry after they sobered up a little," he said. "And they sobered up a lot over the edge of the boat on the way going back. We kind of took the rough route home." He handed Nina a hundred dollar bill and a sheet of paper with names, addresses, and credit card numbers.

"The money is extra for the housekeeper," George said. "I suggested they might want to send a tip back. And all the credit card numbers are good. If anybody makes a fuss just remember I'm a cop. I reminded them, too."

He shook his head. "I'm really sorry," he said to Nina. "I swear this will never happen again."

And it never did.

Section III. Fish Tales

Allen House Logo

Chapter 24
Swordfish a la Gertrude

That first year, when Alan still liked me and Nina, he was not only our caretaker but our island mentor.

We trusted him completely. We had no choice; there were just too many things we didn't know. Fortunately he was absolutely honest.

When he appeared at the kitchen door one June afternoon and announced, "There's a boat comin' into tha harbor with a swordfish. You'd be smart ta' to buy it for the restaurant. Do ya want me t' go down to the dock and dicker with the captain on the radio for ya?" We didn't feel we had a choice.

Alan felt we should buy the swordfish. Not to buy the swordfish would be to lose face, possibly even incur Alan's displeasure. We *might* be able to handle everything at the inn ourselves, but we really didn't want to put that theory to the test. Alan was our lifeline, our in with the islanders, our backup plan.

Obviously, we were buying a swordfish.

We knew swordfish were big. There was a stuffed marlin hanging on the dining room wall that was caught locally, and it was at least seventy-five pounds.

Nina and I talked about it until Alan returned.

"Can we handle seventy-five pounds of fish?" she asked.

"It's a lot less gutted and with the head off," I answered. "Hell, we might be able to handle a hundred."

Alan returned.

"Well, I got it," he said. "Had to go five-fifty a pound, but that's a good price. You can sell it for eight, easy. I'll go down when he comes in and gut it out and cut the head off. You don't have to pay me; I'll just take some steaks. Nothing like good fresh fish."

He started out the door when Nina, being by far the braver soul, stopped him.

"Uh, Alan," she said, "how big is this fish?"

"Won't know till he gets in ta the dock here and gets it on the scale, now will we?" Alan answered. "But not too big, I shouldn't imagine. Hasn't been a really big fish caught around here in quite some while. You're lucky I got ya this one."

He headed out the door and Nina and I looked at each other in alarm. We had just bought a fish, a big fish, sight unseen over a marine band radio.

"I sure hope we can sell it all," I said. "Or we will be running a shitload of swordfish specials."

"Yeah," Nina said. "I wish it were July instead of June. But I suppose we could freeze it."

"Let's see how much of it we can move first," I said. "We'll put the word out and sell it wholesale, too. We can be a fish market as well as a restaurant."

Dinner came and went. That early in the season we served six to seven o'clock, and rarely fed more than twenty-five people, most of them house guests. We cleaned up quickly, and waited.

And waited. It grew dark. We grew more and more apprehensive. What had we gotten ourselves into?

Finally, we heard Alan's tractor rumbling up the hill. He appeared at the kitchen door, his overalls stained and smelly.

"Got her in the trailer," he said. "I took the head and a couple of steaks. I like the cheek meat for smoking. Nothin' better than smoked swordfish, 'cept marlin. I'll unhitch the trailer and leave her here and take the check down. Man wants his money."

Nina had the checkbook ready on the kitchen counter.

"How much?" she asked.

"Well, now, let's see," Alan said. He took a pencil and a crumpled piece of paper out of his overall pocket.

"Three hundred and seventy-eight pounds at five-fifty a pound is $2,079."

To our credit, neither of us fainted. Alan misread the expressions on our faces.

"Now you know you got ta pay for the whole fish," he said. "Even though I cut off her head and gutted her down at the dock. That was the weight. Ask Marty."

We hastened to assure Alan that we trusted him and his calculations completely.

"We just didn't expect it to be so big," I said.

Nina nodded. I was talking about the fish. She was talking about the check. We were new in business, and had yet to write a check for more than $1,000, and that was for half a season's worth of t-shirts.

Now we were about to pay out more than $2,000. For a single fish. I caught the look on Nina's face. She had a weak stomach, and I knew that the moment that check was written she would be heading for the bathroom.

Alan waited in his timeless manner.

There was nothing for it. Nina tore off the check and handed it to him. Then she headed towards the bathroom, and I went outside with Alan to look at what we had just purchased.

The fish was huge, as long as I was tall and twice as big around. And bloody. Really bloody. Nina came out and we stared down at it.

"I never knew fish had red blood," said Nina.

"Oh, sure," I said. "Striped bass have red blood."

But there was a big difference between the amount of red blood a cleaned, thirty-pound striper had in it when the fishermen brought it up the hill, and this hulking carcass leaking pools of the stuff on the pavement.

Alan was back before we'd had time to fully take in what we'd gotten ourselves into. He was whistling and quite cheery, with several 25-pound blocks of ice strapped to his tractor fenders.

"Thought we could use that old bathtub Dave tore out upstairs," he said. "Haul it into the walk-in cooler and I'll get some guys ta take this fish down for you. You can put her on the ice, and if you keep her covered up and moist, she oughta be just fine 'til you sell her all."

Alan pronounced it, and it was so. Within an hour, Gertrude, as we fondly came to call her, was firmly ensconced in her walk-in final resting place. With a plastic tub under the drain hole to catch run-off, the bathtub full of ice proved to be a brilliant innovation. And swaddled in wet bloody towels, Gertrude was a frightening sight to anyone coming into the walk-in without knowing what greeted them. She looked exactly like a dead body we were trying to hide from the police.

We sold Gertrude steaks in the restaurant, Gertrude kebabs, Gertrude pasta dishes. We sold wholesale slabs of her straight from the walk-in. Gertrude sold so quickly she was gone in a week. It was an important lesson for us. Obviously, we needed to do more research into what sold on an island, and what people were willing to pay for things. Nina went down the next week to the dock and asked the captain, Marty Niemiec, if he could get us another one. Marty got quite a laugh from that. He explained he was actually a boat builder and this was a vacation break for him. He also told us he'd been extremely lucky, that the days of huge swordfish being caught off the island every couple of weeks were long over, and we would be lucky to see another fish come in that whole summer.

We kept the bathtub, just in case, but sadly, Marty was more than right on that score. Gertrude was the last line-caught swordfish I ever saw brought into the dock at Cuttyhunk Island.

Sauce for Sword
(and a little discourse on swordfish):

Mix one cup mayonnaise with 1/3 cup Dijon mustard, and add one tablespoon of chopped fresh rosemary and one teaspoon cracked black pepper. Rub each swordfish steak with about one tablespoon of the sauce for each side. Grill or broil on high about 2–3 minutes per side for a 1" thick steak.

Please don't overcook it. Swordfish, like tuna, should be served still slightly rare in the middle, or it will dry out.

If you ever get sword as fresh as Gertrude, don't even consider doing anything to it except brushing it with butter. Truly fresh swordfish will spoil you for anything else.

When buying swordfish, avoid fish that have been long-lined. This is the practice of trolling with baited hooks strung out behind the boat. Aside from being a cruel way to die (the fish essentially drowns as it is pulled behind the boat) and the fact that other fish and mammals are caught on a long line and then discarded as trash, sword caught on a long line is waterlogged and mealy compared to line-caught or harpooned fish. Line-caught and harpooned fish are individually caught and brought into the boat. You can tell a fish has been individually caught because its flesh is pink and firm. It is pink because it was caught and brought into the boat quickly, and hasn't had all the blood washed out of it. Long-lined fish tend to have gray- or white-colored flesh.

Chapter 25
True Blue

After we finished off Gertrude, we were back to buying fish from the mainland. Luckily, we had a great fish supplier in New Bedford who bought directly from the trawlers that came into port, so freshness was never an issue.

We were one of his few commercial customers, and I believe he worked with us mainly because he liked to motor out to the island for lunch on his day off. He kept us well-supplied with all our menu basics: cod, clams, haddock, scallops, sword, sole, and, when available, more exciting fish such as monkfish or tautog.

For our catch-of-the-day, we depended on the island bass guides and fishermen. For cash-in-pocket we depended on Pete. The guides sold us our signature fish, wild striped bass, and gave us bluefish when we could beg it out of them. Usually, I had to go down to the dock, retrieve it from the cooler where it might have been for a day or two waiting to be used for lobster bait, and fillet it myself. Bluefish is an extremely strong, oily fish similar to mackerel, and customers who ordered it had discerning palates. You couldn't serve them bluefish that was more than six hours old. That's how it is in an island restaurant. As a result, most of the bluefish I got off the bass guides ended up in the smoker.

You can smoke five-day-old bluefish as age just increases the flavor. Hell, you can even freeze bluefish and smoke it after it thaws with no appreciable loss of quality, as long as you freeze it while it's fresh. You couldn't pay me to eat frozen bluefish that hasn't been smoked.

Bluefish from the guides helped keep our ever-popular smoked blue on the appetizer menu and since I smoked it myself, helped offset the cost of the striped bass we *had* to serve whenever we could get it, regardless of price. But it was Pete who gave us our profit margin.

Pete built two of the three buildings that replaced our run-down cottages, and rented them back to us for a decent price so we could use them for guests. He also brought us a lot of business, since about forty percent of houseguests in those buildings spring and fall were actually customers of his, whose bills were charged to his business. All he asked in return was for a few minor perks.

We let him bring his guys in early for breakfast, made them special omelets, and they could hang around the usually off-limits kitchen. He got his own key to the back door so he could make coffee at four a.m. before heading out to fish. He thought he was doing us a favor by making coffee so we'd have it when we arrived in the morning. We never had the heart to tell him none of us cared to drink two-hour old coffee. And we made ourselves available at the drop of a hat if he needed an appetizer platter(raw oysters and clams, boiled shrimp and clams casino,) something we rarely supplied anyone else without twenty-four hour's notice.

In return, aside from being a perfect gentleman, he brought us fish. Loads and loads of fish. Even though he owned his company, he took all his customers fishing himself. Whatever they caught, we broiled large fillets of it for dinner and served him family-style on old decorated platters left over from Lucille's days. He'd always request enough fish for at least double the number of people he had, so it was a bountiful spread.

Anything else his party caught that day was ours. Free of charge. Not only did he insist we charge him for the fish he caught himself, when all we had done was prepare it, he filleted, bagged, and delivered every extra bass, blue and albacore tuna he caught that his customers didn't want to take with them. And that man knew how to catch fish. When he went after an albacore run, he was likely to bring us back thirty fish at a time, and I regularly found four or five bags of cleanly filleted and skinned bluefish in the walk-in each morning Pete was on-island.

The Clams Casino We Gave Pete for Appetizers

Stuffing for 3 dozen Littleneck clams
1 cup minced bacon
1 ½ cups onion, finely diced
¼ pound butter
1/3 cup green pepper, diced
¼ cup red pepper, diced
¼ cup seasoned bread crumbs

Sauté bacon and onion until onion is transparent. Add peppers and sauté till soft.

Add butter and melt, then stir breadcrumbs into the mixture. Remove from heat and chill. Mound stuffing over the top of each raw clam and bake at 350° until warm throughout.

Chapter 26
Stuffed Bass

When I started at the Allen House, there were three main fishing guides working out of the inn. Joe Coriea was an intense, extremely macho, old-style Portuguese from New Bedford. He was a cop most of the year. You fished with Joe when all you wanted to do was fish and fish hard. George Isobel also was a cop when he wasn't fishing, but much more laid back than Joe and for me, easier to get along with. He took out clients who liked to catch fish, but also liked to kick back and party. If you really wanted to party, you went out with Roland Coloumbe. Roland was the oldest of the three guides, a French Canadian who'd made New Bedford his home for more than 20 years. He knew how to catch fish, and he knew where the fish were, but he liked to drink as much as he liked to fish; a midnight trip out with Roland was likely to bring you home with both a good-sized striped bass and an equally large hangover.

The inn was more of a bed-and-breakfast back then, especially in the off-seasons when we catered primarily to striped bass fisherman. Fishing guides were given rooms and breakfast at a discount in return for bringing their clients to the Allen House, and as a result I saw a lot of them. George and Joe pretty much lived at the inn the months of May and October. Roland stayed with his girlfriend, Kit. She was an island girl whose parents and grandparents had lived on the island, and she had grown up on Cuttyhunk. Roland slept and ate at Kit's, but he spent his free time when he wasn't fishing at the inn, sitting around in the kitchen in the mornings hassling the cooks, playing poker in the inside dining room at night after dinner was finished, or drinking with his clients.

The guides fished the tides on the reefs off the West End of the island between Cuttyhunk and Martha's Vineyard, and the timing of their trips depended on those tides. They were never on the same time schedule as the rest of the island, and it was not uncommon to see them barbecuing steaks and drinking beer and brandy at seven in the morning.

My father caught his first and only fish with Roland. As soon as he reeled it in, he was ready to head to shore. I inherited my seasick stomach from Dad. But he'd recovered enough by the time he got to the Allen House to saunter casually into the kitchen with his fish. It was a decent-sized bluefish.

"Wanna cook this for me for dinner?" he asked.

"Yuck," I replied. "Get that thing out of here. It's the middle of lunch. Put it downstairs in the walk-in, and if you really want me to, I'll cook it for dinner." I thought by dinner he might change his mind. He wasn't particularly fond of bluefish.

I forgot all about the fish until I went into the walk-in about five p.m. and saw it sitting in a milk crate. Dad had apparently decided that was a good way to store a fish. He hadn't taken rigor mortis into account. The fish was a near-perfect U from being crammed into the crate. When I pulled it out, it stayed the same shape. There was no way I could gut the damn thing, never mind fillet it. I hoped as soon as Dad put the fish in the walk-in that he had forgotten about it. If not, Pete had delivered some fresh bluefish about an hour earlier, nicely filleted and skinned. I could broil dad a piece of that, and he'd never know the difference.

I promptly forgot about his fish again. Halfway through dinner service, I heard some sort of commotion from the dining room. Just then Nina stuck her head in the kitchen door. "You gotta see this," she said

I pointed at my broiler full of meat and fish.

"Sara, take over for a second," Nina said firmly. To me she said, "Come."

I came.

It was Dad, carrying a milk crate around the full dining room.

"See this fish?" he asked each table. "I caught this. It's my first fish. My daughter is going to cook it for me."

"You want to stop him?" I asked Nina. "Go right ahead. I think I'm just going to ignore the whole thing."

After Dad had finished dinner that night, Nina approached him.

"You are hereby forbidden to do **anything** in the dining room besides eat," she said. "Do you understand? No more fish parades!"

Dad looked up at her calmly.

"I have no intention of ever going fishing again," he said. "And anyway, Margo just cooked my fish."

I hid that U-shaped fish until one of the dishwashers could drive to the dock and leave it in Bruce's lobster bait tub. It had gone far too long without gutting to be eaten in any form. I never told my father the truth.

Sorry, Dad.

Filleting cod with Roland.

Garlic Walnut Sauce for Fish
(great for any dark, oily fish)

2 egg yolks
2 tablespoons white wine vinegar
1 tablespoon lemon juice
2 garlic cloves
¾ teaspoon salt
1 cup olive oil
½ cup ground walnuts
¼ cup fresh parsley

Place egg yolks, garlic, vinegar and lemon juice in a food processor and process until smooth. With the machine running, gradually pour in olive oil until thick. Fold in the walnuts and parsley. Spoon over cooked fish. Brown under broiler.

Chapter 27
Hot Tuna

A year after we bought the Allen House, the tuna tournament arrived. This large group of boats used Cuttyhunk as a harbor from which to go deep-water fishing for blue and yellow fin tuna. Starting from the island saved them 14 miles of traveling every morning, as well as enormous amounts of gasoline.

Nina and I felt it was absolutely wrong to have all these boats docked at the marina and not get any business from them. The tournament boats left at five a.m. and didn't return until after dinner hours. Although we could buy extra yellow-fin at a decent price and serve incredibly fresh fish at the restaurant, we felt that somehow we must be able to generate more income from these boats. They were, after all, taking up most of the slips at the dock, preventing potential customers of ours from docking there.

So, the second year of the tournament we devised a brilliant strategy to capture some of that extra cash. I would get up at three a.m. for that week and prepare breakfast pastries, egg sandwiches, and boxed lunches. Then we'd send someone down to the dock with the food and air pots of hot coffee. The employees we picked go down to the dock were not exactly happy with the early morning hours, and we had to bribe them with time off, free dessert, free meals in the restaurant, anything we could think of. We had high hopes for this endeavor.

We did sell some coffee and a few breakfast things. But the box lunches were a dismal failure. The tuna tournament guys—and they were almost all guys—were long used to bringing enough food for the entire week, and carried more than enough supplies on board to cover their every need.

After we gave up on the dock idea, we tried staying open an hour later in the evening in hopes of getting some tournament dinner business. This plan too was a failure as ninety percent of the tournament guys just wanted to grill out and party on their boats after they returned to the dock. It drove us crazy; there were boats taking up space at the dock and we couldn't get business from any of them. We were in our fast-forward phase of the business, still new enough to want to expand anywhere and everywhere we could. But this turned out to be one market we just couldn't take advantage of.

Still, for one week every year we could be sure of an unending supply of beautiful, fresh-off-the-boat yellow fin. I became an expert at filleting tuna, even slicing the cheek meat paper-thin into sashimi. We didn't sell this raw fish as we worried someone might feel sick and blame it on us. But we sent out beautiful little plates of sashimi with wasabe and pickled ginger arranged in rose shapes to special customers we knew would appreciate such a lovely (and free) hors d'oeuvre. These customers almost always ordered the tuna.

I grilled tuna fillets, I broiled tuna steaks. I used the leftover pieces in our nightly pasta special. I made bouillabaisse. If I could have figured out a way to use the tuna skin, I would have.

Once we got over our disappointment at not being able to tap into this new market, we began to look forward to the tournament every year. I made sure I had pickled ginger and wasabe brought in from the mainland, and certain houseguests booked that week a year in advance.

Tuna Marinade
(and a little discourse on fish in general):

For 4 average-sized tuna steaks.

Mix together:

¼ cup virgin olive oil (the lighter the better)

½ cup lemon juice (fresh squeezed is always best)

2 or more finely chopped cloves of garlic (depending on taste)

¼ cup fresh fine chopped oregano

Let the mixture stand for an hour or two, or up to several days, refrigerated. It just gets better with time. Just before grilling the steaks, place marinade in a shallow pan and lay the steaks in, being sure to cover each side. Grill or broil LIGHTLY. Please do not overcook a good tuna steak, you will break my heart (and the fish will dry out and taste like it came from a can).

Fresh fish. In most places that's just not true. Even if it's never been frozen, any deep-sea fish is at least a week old when you get it. Minimum. Because that's how long the boats stay out. And it is usually a lot older. Only believe the fresh fish label if it is a local fish, you live on the coast, and you watched your neighbor-the-fisherman offload it himself.

Of course, there are exceptions, but as a general rule this works. Buy your deep-sea fish frozen. It is flash frozen on the boat as soon as it is caught, and is actually fresher than "fresh" fish. Buy local fish if you live near a coast.

I know the rules of thumb. Look at the eyes of a whole fish; they should be glassy and not cloudy. Smell the fish; it should not smell of ammonia. But fish washed in baking soda and water does not smell of ammonia. It doesn't mean they are fresh. Really fresh fish does not smell at all. Of anything.

After fifteen years on the rock, I rarely eat any fish at all unless I am on the island or at the shore. Call me a snob. But after you've had fresh tuna, or sucked down a raw scallop that you dredged yourself, or filleted and skinned and grilled a slab of bass or bluefish that you watched Roland or George bring in an hour earlier, you can never look at fish the same way again.

Chapter 28
Salt Cod

One fine spring day, Mark Brodeur asked Nina and me if we wanted to go cod fishing. His two young daughters were on-island for the weekend and he wanted to give them a fishing trip. We suspected we'd been asked primarily to help with his girls, but we wanted to go fishing, so we said sure.

At least, Nina wanted to go fishing. It was one of those rare warm days you get in early spring on the island, days that make you believe winter might actually end, before the cold, damp, windy days of true spring make you wonder if somehow summer might be skipped entirely that year. I wasn't at all sure going out on a boat that was anchored and rolling in the waves was the wisest course of action for me, but it did appear to be extraordinarily calm for Cuttyhunk, and the idea of a day outside was too tempting to resist.

When we arrived, Mark was already at the dock with his daughters, Melissa and Kathryn, and Roland, who had been induced to join us. Roland confided that he didn't care much for cod unless it was fried, but he dearly loved mackerel and was planning on catching a bucketful, some to fry up for dinner and some to smoke. True to his intentions, he had a plastic mop bucket beside him on the dock.

Mark assured us this was the prime time for a large codfish run to be passing by and we were going to catch, in his words, "some serious fish." Nina and I agreed that if we caught more than enough for dinner, we would freeze the rest for the restaurant. The island practice of getting everything you could free from the sea was one we'd taken to immediately.

We boarded Mark's boat, a totally equipped, specially designed, 27-foot Boston Whaler that would have been the envy of the Coast Guard.

Designed for his daily commute from Cuttyhunk to New Bedford in any sort of weather, it had Loran, radar, sonar, and half a dozen r's that probably hadn't made it to commercial market yet. I didn't understand any of it, and quietly made my way up to the bow where his daughters sat. There was the one piece of equipment on board I understood, a fifty-gallon plastic trash can. It seemed a bit large for trash, so I asked the elder daughter what it was for.

"Oh, that's for the fish," Melissa answered. "Dad says we're gonna catch a trashcan full."

Right, I thought. Cod were usually between three and seven pounds this time of year. Quite an impressive fish for someone like me, used to lake fishing, but it would take an awful lot of fish that size to fill a fifty-gallon trash can.

We made our way out of the harbor, through Canapitsit, the cut between Cuttyhunk and Nashweena islands and headed into Vineyard Sound. Mark kept one eye on the water and one on the fish finder installed on the dash next to the radar screen. Suddenly, he cut the engines.

"Get out the rods," he called to Roland, "they're right underneath us."

Roland grabbed four rods and Mark handed them out.

"We'll take turns," Mark said, "as we get tired."

I assumed he meant as soon as his girls got bored.

Within minutes Roland got a bite, and pulled up a nice one-and-a-half pound mackerel.

"*That's* what I'm talking about," he said, and flung his hook back over the side. The mackerel he threw in the bottom of the fifty-gallon can, where it flopped in a lonely sort of way. I hoped it wasn't the only fish caught that day.

For twenty minutes no one got a bite. But the sea was dead calm, almost glassy, the sun was warm and I felt great. So what if we didn't have fish for supper?

Then it happened. Melissa got the first bite. Mark went over to help her set the hook, but she was already reeling in. Up came a good six-pound codfish. Before Mark could net it, Kathryn cried, "Dad, I got one!"

Roland went over to help Kathryn, handing me his rod as he went. Nina had already been handed Mark's, and we both felt tugs on our line at the same time. The action never stopped from that point on. The moment we threw our lines in the water, a fish bit. Within half an hour my arms felt like lead. Kathryn had long since tired of the sport and was attempting to count the squirming fish in the rapidly filling trash can, but Melissa was gamely fishing on, and I was not about to be shown up by a twelve-year-old girl. So, on we fished, four of us manning the rods, and Roland or Mark netting the fish and taking them off the lines.

Melissa finally gave up. The rest of us were totally caught up in the excitement. The school seemed endless.

Then I heard Mark say, "Damn. We got anything else?" I turned and saw the trashcan brimming with cod. Wordlessly, we pulled our lines. Roland took care of the rods while Mark fired up the engine and we headed to the dock. It was barely after noon.

When we got to the dock, Mark took the kids to the house to clean up. Nina went with him, saying she'd stay with the girls while Mark came down to start skinning, gutting and filleting our enormous catch. Roland and I dragged some coolers over to the boat and began flinging fish into them from the trashcan. It was far too heavy to even consider trying to lift off the boat.

Those few people hanging around the dock came to stare at our catch, and word soon spread across the island. Half a dozen came just to see for themselves and another half-dozen to see if Mark wanted to sell a fish or two. Twelve people was almost half the island population that early spring. Mark, being Mark, gave anyone who asked a fish for dinner, and set aside some fillets to take to the island's older population, those few who hadn't come down to see the show.

And it was a show. Even if we hadn't been on a tiny, sparsely populated island it would have been a show. Mark, Roland, and I each grabbed a fish, and the scales started flying. I was hopelessly outclassed, even as a professional chef. Mark had lived his life on the water, and Roland was a fishing guide. But every one I filleted and skinned was one less for them to deal with, so I kept on, careful to take a position at the end of the table out of their way.

Mark and Roland quickly filled the lobster bait tubs Bruce and Dickie left on the dock for fish skeletons and offal. With no other containers in sight, we began tossing the remains into the ocean. Within seconds the sky filled with raucous cries and beating wings. The shallow water teemed with seagulls and terns gulping down whole skeletons. They ate as fast as we could toss.

The coolers emptied of whole fish and filled with bags of fillets. Finally, I was left with a bloody, scaly cutting board that didn't have a fish on it. I looked up to see Roland leaning over into the can. Could we finally be done?

"Shit," Roland said quietly, straightening back up. He had a flat object about four inches wide and a foot long dangling from his fingers. "My mackerel," he said glumly.

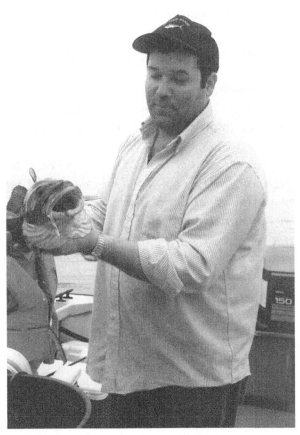

Mark and a codfish from the great cod adventure.

Ciopinno

2 tablespoons unsalted butter
3 tablespoons diced red onion
2 cloves garlic, chopped
1 pound skinless, boneless firm-fleshed fish fillet (like tilapia,
mahi-mahi or black cod), cut into 4 pieces
½ pound large sea scallops
3 medium plum tomatoes (about 15 ounces), diced
1 pound mussels (about 20), scrubbed and de-bearded
1 dozen cherrystone clams
4 snow crab claws (or split legs cut into 3 inch pieces), optional
2 tablespoons white wine
½ teaspoon kosher salt
1/8 teaspoon freshly ground black pepper
2 tablespoons thinly sliced fresh basil, plus 4 sprigs for garnish

In a large pan that is at least 2 inches deep, heat the butter over medium–high heat. Add the onion and fish and cook for 1 minute. Add the shrimp and scallops and cook, stirring occasionally and flipping the fish once, about 2 minutes more. Add the tomato, mussels, clams and crab and pour the white wine over everything. Add the salt and pepper and sprinkle with the basil. Cover and cook until the clams and mussels start to open—about 4 minutes. Discard any that don't open. Remove from heat and divide the seafood and broth among 4 soup or pasta bowels. Garnish with basil sprigs and serve.

Chapter 29
Calamari

Most years around the first week in June, squid arrived in Cuttyhunk Harbor. My first few seasons, I was barely conscious of this fact. Squidding was something little kids did, going down after dark to catch and sell them for a few cents each to fishermen for bait. I vaguely remember the guides talking about squid being in at the beginning of each season, and I'd seen the squid jigs hanging at Ginger's, vicious-looking-barrel-shaped plugs with rows of metal spikes.

The year we first bought Allen House and needed to actually turn a profit, something snapped on in my brain when I heard George Isobel say, "Well, the squid ought to be coming in any time now."

Squid. Otherwise known as calamari. Big bucks in Italian restaurants. Free for the taking sometime in the next week right from Cuttyhunk Harbor. A few questions netted me the necessary facts: You caught them off the fish dock, when the lights were turned on and shining in the water. You could use a pole, or a hand-held line as long as it had a jig on it. Hooks didn't work. You had to be patient, because some nights they didn't come at all. But when they did, there could be hundreds.

My mental calculator clicked on. Pasta dishes with calamari. Cajun fried calamari with spicy remoulade sauce. Baked stuffed calamari. And all with the main ingredient absolutely free.

I bought several from a kid at the dock and practiced cleaning them. We coated a few rings in a spicy tempura batter and dropped them in the fryer. Delicious.

Later that week, I let my prep cook, Mary Beth, off early, telling her she didn't have to clean up if she'd head down to the docks around ten that night. She was a night owl, and I knew she liked to fish. I suggested she take a dishboy with her, and gave her two poles I had outfitted with squid jigs. Then I cleaned the kitchen and went to bed.

The next morning there was a note in the kitchen when I arrived. *Look in the walk-in,* it read. I went down the basement steps to the walk-in cooler, hoping to find half a tub or so, enough for a weekend special and maybe even some to freeze for later in the season.

There were three five-gallon buckets in the walk-in. I don't know how they got them up the hill to the Allen House unless someone gave them a ride. Those buckets weighed at least forty pounds each.

Very funny, I thought. But then, I *had* told them to catch all they could. I just wished they had used a little common sense. These would all have to be cleaned and frozen immediately if they were to be any good. I dumped part of one bucket into a bus bin and hauled it up the stairs. Its contents filled one of the dish room's double sinks to overflowing. I was just about to wake Mary Beth to help me start cleaning and skinning when a furious Roland stormed into the kitchen.

"Did your kids go out squidding last night?" he roared. All the Allen House employees had, somewhere along the line, become "my kids."

I pointed to the sink. "What do you think?" I asked him.

"I think they got friggin' squid ink over every inch of my boat and they better clean it off before it stains is what I think!" he yelled, and stomped out of the kitchen.

Sighing, I went and woke them, not to help me clean squid, but to spend the morning scrubbing Roland's boat.

Squid are actually not that hard to clean. Fresh, they have almost no smell at all, just a slight briny tang. And they aren't really slippery until you strip the skin off, something you can save till last. Once you get the hang of it, it's just a few quick motions. Pull the head off the body, exposing a hollow tube. Pull out the spine (a clear, almost plastic-looking flat spike) flip the tube inside out, and remove the few guts. Grasp one end of the tube and pull the skin and fins off. That's it. I threw the heads into a bucket for striper bait.

A few quick moves. Over and over and over again, with the realization there were two-and-a-half more buckets downstairs. I was still at it when Mary Beth came back from cleaning Roland's boat.

"I'm really sorry," Mary Beth said. "It was dark, we had no idea the ink was getting on his boat."

"Never mind that," I said through clenched teeth. "Get some plastic bags and start getting these things into the freezer."

I had no intention of counting them; I didn't want to know. But Mary Beth decided the same number should go into each bag, so she kept a running tally.

Turns out they caught well over two hundred decent-sized squid. I have mercifully blocked out the exact number. But I was happy later that summer. Each time we pulled out a bag for pasta with olives and calamari, fried calamari appetizer, stuffed calamari, I knew that day's work was worth it.

And the next year I was ready. From the first of June, Mary Beth and I waited for that big calamari swarm to head into the harbor.

Like Gertrude the swordfish, it never happened again. The local kids would occasionally catch a few I could buy off them, and I'd run a special or an appetizer. But the whole time we ran the Allen House, there was only that one true Summer of Squid.

Fried Calamari with Spicy Remoulade Sauce

1 pound calamari, cleaned and cut into rings
1 cup buttermilk
½ cup all purpose flour
½ cup corn flour – NOT cornmeal.
1 teaspoon salt
1 teaspoon black pepper
1 teaspoon paprika
½ teaspoon garlic powder

Mix together dry ingredients.
Dredge calamari in buttermilk, then in flour mixture. Deep fry until golden brown and drain on paper towels. Serve immediately with remoulade sauce.

Remoulade sauce

1 cup mayonnaise
¼ cup zesty cocktail sauce OR chili sauce
2 tablespoons grainy spicy brown mustard (such as Grey Poupon or creole mustard)
4 teaspoons MILD horseradish sauce
2 tablespoons extra virgin olive oil
1 tablespoon Louisiana hot sauce, or to taste
2 tablespoons fresh squeezed lemon juice
1 teaspoon Worcestershire sauce
2 medium green onions, very finely chopped
½ teaspoon chili powder
1 teaspoon seasoned salt (such as Zatarain's or Tony Chacheré's)
½ teaspoon cayenne pepper
2 tablespoons finely chopped fresh parsley OR teaspoons dried parsley flakes
1 garlic clove, minced OR 1 teaspoon garlic powder

Section IV.

Island Provisions

South Side of the Annex

Chapter 30
About Town

Cuttyhunk is one of those New England places run by that most venerable of institutions, the town meeting. For those who have never attended one, this is a method of government where once a year, all the people who have both legally and illegally attached themselves to the permanent resident voter rolls come together in one place (in this case the Town Hall on Cuttyhunk) to decide matters of town importance for the coming year.

Cuttyhunk is actually only one of several islands that make up the town of Gosnold, but the other islands are privately owned. Since these islands have a greater landmass, and receive few town services, their representatives are naturally interested in how their tax dollars are spent.

And in the Town of Gosnold, interested means vocal.

My first full season on Cuttyhunk was a state election year. Since I hadn't stayed in one place long enough to vote in a state election for years, I decided to vote in Massachusetts. That meant registering on Cuttyhunk and listing it as my permanent address. This delighted my father, who had been forwarding my mail all over the country for seven years. This also made me a Cuttyhunk Island resident and eligible to vote at town meeting, which delighted Leon and Enna and Steve and Jan, who felt the more people the Allen House had on the voter roll, the better off we'd be when we wanted to request something.

Town meetings would have been acrimonious even if only actual year-round residents had made up the voter rolls, due to the splitting of islanders into family camps. More trouble came when a number of people with summer homes on the island felt they should have a say in how things were run, and over the years, changed their voter registration to list Cuttyhunk Island as their permanent address.

This annoyed the year-rounders no end, and motions were made every meeting to stop the practice. One required you have all your mail sent to your Cuttyhunk address if you were registered as a year-round resident (a motion that was soundly defeated each year by the postmaster and her large extended family.)

Other motions brought forth over the years were found to be impractical, illegal, or impossible to enforce. Nonetheless, the question of what exactly constituted a town resident and who should be allowed to register to vote was brought up at town meetings every year like clockwork.

It was one of those items on the agenda you could count on, a chance to go to the bathroom or get a quick snack while the debate raged. Although going to the bathroom didn't automatically preclude you from entering into the discussion. There was one memorable year when Alan debated an issue from inside the men's room, shouting at the top of his lungs while attending to other business. Town meetings could be rather informal.

Another hotly debated issue was the Cuttyhunk school system. As the Cuttyhunk school only runs through eighth grade, island kids have to move off for high school, either to boarding school, relatives, or in some cases to live with a parent who must also move off. All this costs money, and the people from Naushon, Nashawena, and Pasque islands whose children went to school on the mainland by way of a private ferry were not too keen on paying taxes for this purpose. Neither were many of the residents who didn't have school-aged kids. And as there were, at any one time, maybe five children in the school system, this was most of the voter roll.

But the state decrees that a town must provide schooling for its school-age children, and so, year after year, came the debate on just how much money the system needed, and where it would come from. This was another good opportunity to take a break from the close quarters and hard wooden seats. The trick to making it through a town meeting was to spend enough time inside the Town Hall and vote often enough so that you appeared to be a concerned citizen, while really biding your time until the issue or issues you were interested in came up.

Unfortunately for the Allen House, ours were usually at the end of the agenda. We were interested in the price of things, such as electricity, water, gasoline, propane, and fuel oil. We didn't really care *who* ran the powerhouse or managed the well or the gas dock. We wanted someone to pick up our trash every day in season, but we didn't really care who that was either. Nor did we care who the harbormaster was as long as the docking and tie-up fees didn't get so high that they drove boaters away.

Everyone else cared very much *who* did *what*. Although income was important, these jobs were as much about prestige and power as they were money. The more island services your faction controlled, the bigger power base you had. And just like any small town, the less there was going on, the more important relatively unimportant issues became.

You could hear a town meeting going on clear across the island. At first I found it a little scary when at times it seemed people might actually come to blows. As the years dragged on, it became clear that we would never get a liquor license; (one of our main reasons for showing up every year.) The old guard died off and their sons and daughters took their places, meetings became quieter, more boring, and in the end, less important, at least to us.

Real politicking, we discovered, was done behind the scenes. Issues of importance were often decided by convincing two of the three selectmen that what we wanted was either good for the island, or worth a favor to be repaid later. I stopped going to town meetings except to vote for the selectman most likely to agree with our needs. I stayed registered on Cuttyhunk, though, and continued to vote for political candidates by absentee ballot, or using the island's quaint wooden ballot box with its manual crank and ivory number plates until I left the island for good in 1997.

I have been registered to vote in a number of small towns, but voting on Cuttyhunk was by far my favorite experience. Voting, as with most public events, took place in Town Hall. Two registrars and the town clerk were paid $25 each for a two-and-a-half- hour shift just to make sure no funny business took place. These jobs were highly sought after. Aside from making money doing nothing, they were a great excuse to sit and gossip. My sister usually signed up for two shifts.

The prospective voter walked in and the registrars noted the name and crossed it off a list of eligible voters. Then the voter got a long paper ballot folded lengthwise in thirds, with official Massachusetts and United States seals on the front. They also got an official pencil (in case they had some sort of trick pen up their sleeve, I suppose) and went to a table set up in front of these steely eyed registrars to mark their ballot. The ballot was handed to the town clerk, who slowly fed it into the top slot of the ballot box.

This box dated back at least seventy-five years, maybe more: a beautifully detailed wooden cube roughly two-and-a-half-feet square with brass fittings and a brass crank on one side the clerk turned, which pulled the ballot down into dark, untouchable officialdom. As the crank completed its circle, a bell dinged and the ivory number plates on the front clicked over to show another vote cast. There were only three number plates on the box, so only nine hundred and ninety-nine people could vote on the island. I don't think that ever proved a problem.

Only about a third of people registered on Cuttyhunk ever actually voted there. At any one time, the rolls were padded with summer people from between ninety to one hundred names. Summer people rarely came on-island to vote in state or national elections, relying on absentee ballots. The town clerk sent out a huge number of absentee ballots every year I lived there.

I am not claiming the Allen House was blameless in this matter. Steve encouraged Higgins to register to vote her second year on the island. We were still pushing for a liquor license then, not realizing this was a dream that would never come true, and we hoped every vote would help. Higgins was quite amenable to this. As she spent more and more time on-island each year, she came to think of herself as a Cuttyhunker who unfortunately had to go off-island to find work in the winter, as opposed to a mainlander who worked summers on Cuttyhunk. One November, she found herself in Boston and caught a ride to the ferry with another summer voter to actually cast her vote in Town Hall. On the drive back to Boston, the two began discussing politics and discovered that they had, in fact, cancelled each other's votes in every race. Higgins suggested she call him every election year to compare votes. If they cancelled each other out, the two of them could save time, money, and paper ballots just staying home.

Chapter 31
Neither Fish Nor Ferry

Cuttyhunk had a ferry dock and a fish dock. The Alert was the only boat that regularly tied up for more than a few minutes at the ferry dock. Boaters could tie up briefly, but only to refuel at the gasoline and diesel pumps located on the dock.

Any barge carrying heavy equipment or large loads of construction material docked there to load or unload because the water was deeper, the dock larger, and there was a block and tackle available, but they rarely stayed any length of time.

The ferry dock was manned (or womaned) daily during the summer from eight or so until around five. This was considered an extremely cushy job, as all you had to do was pump gas for power and sailboats and sell an occasional block of ice. Most of the time, some member of the Jenkins family had the job, but occasionally they would hire an island kid to fill in. We would see that kid stretched on a lawn chair in a bathing suit, reading a book or listening to music as we raced down to the dock to retrieve a forgotten grocery item or a guest's luggage, and we would burn with envy.

The ferry dock was also where the big parties took place. It had all the right qualifications. There was electricity if you opened a window in the Coast Guard house and crawled in, so there could be lights and music. There was a large firm surface on which to dance. Most importantly, it was far enough away from almost everyone's house to soothe the irate summer people who usually complained about noise. Unfortunately, the town decided its liability was too great for kids to use the dock unsupervised, and parties on the dock became special events held three or four times a summer.

There were parties on the beach, of course—bonfires almost every night when it wasn't raining, but these were impromptu get-togethers. Dock parties were real parties that gave the girls a chance to dress up and everybody a chance to dance. Even adults came down to the parties on the ferry dock.

The fish dock was a curious mixture of a working dock and a tourist trap. There was a line of small connected shacks on the dock that split the fish dock in half lengthwise.

These shacks were rented out for a nominal sum to fishing guides, lobstermen, and shell fishermen who had slips at the dock and were, theoretically, used to store equipment. But their close proximity to the public slips and to the dingy dock offered a business opportunity too good to pass up. Seth served his Raw Bar platters of clams and oysters, shrimp cocktail and seafood dip out of his shack. Bruce and Carolyn sold their lobsters there. Bruce also sold fish, mostly imported but occasionally ones that had wandered into his traps and been caught.

And somehow, by virtue of being one of the oldest families on the island and having past fishing guides in the family, Bonnie, who ran the Island Bakery, managed to hang onto one of the shacks. Her shack didn't even pretend to hold boating or fishing equipment, just T-shirts, ice cream, sandwiches, and baked goods.

The fish dock was a nice bit of additional income for these people, and very convenient for those boaters who didn't wish to walk up the hill to the store or the Allen House. I suppose it didn't really cut into our business, especially after we put in public bathrooms and showers. But never a summer went by that we didn't wish there was some way we could finagle a shack on the fish dock.

Chapter 32
Dinner by Candlelight

Here's a copy of an old notice sent out with the electric bills well before my time. Somebody found it recently in the town hall offices and sent it out as a "joke" with the year's electric bills.

RULES REGULATING THE USE OF ELECTRICITY

Rule 1.
Sandwich toasters, grills, heaters and stoves of any kind shall not be used at all.

Rule 2.
Toasters and coffee percolators are to be used only between 7a.m. and 12 noon.

Rule 3.
Flat irons can be used only between 8 a.m. and 12 noon: except Monday when they can be used until dark.

Rule 4.
No single light bulb shall be over 60 watts; clusters of 2 or more bulbs shall not exceed 80 watts.

Rule 5.
All lights except those absolutely necessary must be put out at 10 o'clock or at a signal from the Power House.

Attention
Always put out all lights when not in use; do not waste your power. If everyone will co-operate and follow rules faithfully, electricity can be furnished at a moderate cost, and it will not be necessary to pull the switch at 12 noon and 11 o'clock evenings in order to keep the rate reasonable.

Caution
For any infraction of the above rules the Commission may at any time cut off supply of electricity at Power House or lines of party breaking the said rules.

Per order of the Electric Light Commission
G. Francis Jenkins John A. MacKay Carlton Veeder Alpheus P. Tilton Herbert A. Stetson L. Winslow Hall John L. Stubbs

The powerhouse wasn't quite that bad when I worked on Cuttyhunk, but it was far from the heavily muffled, modernized building packed with new generators we have today. Dave ran the powerhouse when I first came to Cuttyhunk, and had done so for a number of years.

And powerhouse Dave was a much different Dave than our jack-of-all-trades from Worchester; this Dave was the head of an old island family.

He and his wife ran the gas dock as well, and the fuel oil truck that supplied the oil furnaces on Cuttyhunk. All island fuel was brought over by barge from Martha's Vineyard, but unlike the Vineyard, Cuttyhunk produced its own power.

This came in very handy during nor'easters and hurricanes, as most of the power lines were underground and thus far less susceptible to damage. But the powerhouse wasn't exactly a model of efficiency at other times. There were four ancient generators Dave seemed to keep running with baling wire, duct tape, and probably a bit of magic thrown in. Later, a fifth, newer Cat diesel was added, but it was considered more of a back-up, an auxiliary generator to be run only at times of heavy need.

Dave alone determined the nature of the word "need."

It didn't matter so much in the off-season. We were used to our electric clocks running fast or slow. If you really needed to be somewhere on time, there were wind-up clocks. I always set two alarm clocks while I worked at the Allen House to make sure I woke in time to set up breakfast.

Electricity was our constant variable. Sometimes the power would go out without warning, but usually there would be a series of brownouts first, lights dimming and flickering, refrigerator motors groaning under the strain.

This happened most often in spring and fall, as Dave did his balancing act trying to decide how many people were going to use how much power at any given time. We burned the motors out of several electric appliances each year, and always kept hurricane lamps and candles at the ready.

In summer, Dave kept all four main generators running to accommodate the people who filled the summer houses. The fifth generator was reserved for times of heavy use down at the dock when powerboats pulled into slips and proceeded to plug in microwaves, fans, even air conditioners. There wasn't a single air conditioner on-island at the time, but down at the dock you could hear their constant hum.

As this was well before the days of cell phones and pagers, Dave could be a hard man to reach. He had a pay phone at his house, so *if* you could get to one of the other phones, and *if* it was working, and *if* Dave's phone was working, and *if* anyone was home, sometimes you could call him and tell him the power had gone out. Because unless he was watching TV, listening to the radio, or it was dark enough to have the lights on, he might not *realize* the power had gone out. If he were outside gardening or fishing or working on a boat or pulling lobster traps, he'd have no idea at all.

So chances were, if you reached Dave at his house he already knew, and was about to climb on his three-wheeled ATV and head down to power up the Cat diesel. But if he didn't answer, he could be down at his boat or delivering fuel oil, or just visiting with somebody who didn't happen to have their TV or radio on. Even with the truly astounding efficiency of the island gossip line, it could sometimes take as long as an hour to find Dave and get him to the powerhouse.

An hour without electricity when you are trying to run a business can be a long time. In a small kitchen poorly ventilated to begin with, an hour becomes a very, very long time when those exhaust fans stop running.

Once we'd been at the Allen House a couple of years, Higgins and I sensed a pattern in these summer blackouts. They came most frequently on Friday and Saturday nights in July and August, usually starting with what we called, after the first year, the annual Fourth of July weekend blackout. Every one of the six years Higgins worked at the Allen House, the power would go out during a dinner service July fourth weekend.

After a while, it became a running joke, at least as much of a joke as working in the dark in 110-degree heat can be. Nina found these cute little flashlights for the gift shop that we called "squeeze me's" because they lit up when you squeezed them between your thumb and fingers.

The bass guides discovered you could squeeze them between your teeth, leaving both hands free to bait a line or unhook a fish on a dark night. That was, as long as you didn't bite down too hard. We quickly adapted this strategy for blackouts in the kitchen, and it became a mark of island pride to be able to claim you had cooked a dinner by "squeeze me."

When we expanded the kitchen for the second time, fixing it up as closely as we could to our version of the Massachusetts fire code, our power problem worsened. Now it wasn't just a matter of sweltering in the heat, or creatively cooking without using the broiler, whose electric ignition rendered it useless in the event of a power outage. Now we had the hood and its state-of-the-art, up-to-code Ansel fire-extinguishing system with which to contend. A series of pipes hung over the stove and fryers, each pipe capped with soft lead designed to melt at a certain core temperature. When the caps melted, the whole system went off, covering the kitchen in foam and destroying everything it touched. This was a system we did NOT want to set off.

We had no idea what the actual melting temperature of these caps was, nor did we care to find out by example. So when the power went off, even though the fryers were gas and we could have kept them running, they went off as well. This pissed off a great many customers, especially on Friday nights when the special was fish and chips.

Our customers had no idea what lengths we went to in order to serve them when the power went out, and we tried to keep it that way. They sat at their candle-lit tables and made jokes about how hard it was to read the menu.

Back in the kitchen, we were telling the waitresses not to offer ice cream for dessert unless it was specifically requested, as each time the ice cream freezer was opened, we came a few degrees closer to losing the whole of its contents. We had towels tucked inside our shirts and wrapped around our heads to minimize the chances of sweat dripping into a customer's plate. One of our first waitresses claims that I told her during these blackouts I drew grill marks on the swordfish with a Sharpie before cooking it in the gas oven. I can assure you I never stooped so low. Higgins and I did, however, become quite proficient with a wire coat hanger and a large blowtorch the plumber left behind one spring.

Chapter 33
The Truth About Dogs and Cats

The best known of the animals passing through the Allen House annals was "Jesse the dog." She was re-named that by Higgins's first child whose best friend was named Jessie. She wanted to make sure everyone knew the difference. Jesse the dog came onto Cuttyhunk Island as an eight-week-old shelter puppy. Her rescuer brought the puppy as a present for her parents so they wouldn't be lonely. Unfortunately, her parents were actually delighted at being empty nesters and planned to use the opportunity to travel.

Ginger heard about the puppy, and knowing Nina and I discussed the idea of getting a dog every year, set out to make sure this adorable shepherd/collie/chow mix puppy did not end up back in the pound. It wasn't a hard sell, despite the fact that Nina and I both worked sixteen-hour days in the summer, it was already June, and utter madness for us to try to train a puppy. I was actually the voice of reason, an unusual position for me. At least for fifteen minutes.

That summer, puppy caretaking would have been impossible without the volunteer help of staff and houseguests. Luckily Jesse was cute, easy, and learned quickly. We tied her out in the yard behind staff housing where everyone who walked by could see her, and hung a leash on the wall next to a sign reading PLEASE WALK THIS DOG.

I rarely found Jesse on the tie-out, and I know she slept at night as if exhausted. The good part of this raising was that Jesse acclimated to people of every age and description. The bad part was that she quickly became an "anybody's," with very little loyalty to Nina or me.

Her second summer, she became known as the Allen House dog. A tag was made proclaiming her Cuttyhunk's official tour guide, and she wore it proudly. One of my favorite memories is seeing Jesse walking up from the beach with a family of tired, sandy children. Then she would spot another family heading down to the beach and do an about-face, abandoning the old family for the new. After all, beach time was beach time!

By that third summer she had moved in with one family for July and another for August, deciding they were more fun than I was. These families had small children who were delighted to lavish attention on an adorable dog during their stay on Cuttyhunk, especially one fed and housed by someone else. There was no way I could compete.

Each night after dinner service, I went to the appropriate house and politely requested my dog. I'd have to leash her to get her home, and she would be gone as soon as I opened the door in the morning.

After Labor Day, Jesse would more or less become my dog again. She didn't care for other dogs, and cats she generally disliked, and would chase out of *her* area. The exception to Jesse's cat rule was Tom, of Cheryl Wheeler fame.

When I met Tom he was an old but still extremely handsome and authoritative, gray-and-white tomcat. I assume that's why he was named Tom. I didn't ask at first, and by the time I did, there was no one left who remembered. This happened far too often. Most of the elderly island residents passed away in the time I was on island, taking with them an enormous store of anecdotal information and well as, I am sure, some great Allen House history.

Stories about Tom were legend.

He was supposed to be:

A. prescient;

B. not really a cat at all but some sort of island spirit;

C. holder of all the souls that had died on Cuttyhunk in his lifetime;

D. all of the above and then some.

I never found him spooky, although he did have an uncanny way of turning up precisely when you were talking about him.

Tom belonged to no one, but he'd been fed by Mildred during her tenure as landlord of the Allen House, and by Lucille Allen before that. He might originally have been Lucille's cat. He was old enough.

Tom didn't come to us for dinner on a regular basis. He still caught most of his food when I first knew him, not that it was particularly difficult to catch a mouse or baby rabbit on Cuttyhunk.

Tom was exceptionally particular about his food being fresh and raw. If he came by the kitchen door for a snack and you offered yesterday's fish, he'd simply walk away. It had to be today's catch. He was partial to cod and striped bass, but would eat tuna if it was straight off the boat. Tom's real weakness, one he shared with Jesse the dog, was smoked fish. I might not see him for a week, but the moment I fired up the smoker, he was there. Although he didn't care for fresh bluefish, he adored it smoked. I would come around the back of the building to see if the smoker needed more wood, and there would be Jesse, lying on the ground in front of the bucket of wet wood chips, and Tom stretched out on the stone wall right above her.

Jesse had quickly learned that Tom was Lord and Master around the Allen House property, and not a cat to be trifled with.

By most people's calculations, Tom lived to be somewhere in his twenties. He became thin and ratty-looking toward the end of his life, but everyone agreed it would do more harm than good to try and take him off-island to a vet. He had trouble mousing, and came more regularly to sun himself outside the kitchen, waiting for someone to cut fish into small pieces for him.

Occasionally, Jesse would join him there and they would sun in companionable silence. It was hard for Tom to haul his arthritic body upright, and several times I saw Jesse pick him up in her mouth and gently move him from the shade to another patch of sun. The first time I saw it no one believed me, but after several staff witnessed it, we decided this was simply one more example of Tom's powers. And just like no one ever actually saw him coming until he was there, no one actually saw him die. We just noticed one day that we hadn't seen him in a while, and then it was a while longer, and a while more. And that was that.

How to Smoke Bluefish

Dissolve 1 c. salt and 1/2 c. sugar in 1 gallon water.
Add 1/3 c. lemon juice and 1 T. black pepper corns.
Pour over bluefish fillets until they are covered with the mixture.
Refrigerate for at least 2 hours and up to two days.

Soak hickory, mesquite or alder wood chips in water.
Place bluefish in smoker over indirect heat.
Add woodchips to heat source and repeat as necessary. Smoke until the
fillets are firm,
2-5 hrs depending on the amount of heat your smoker produces.

Section V.

Wedding Dishes
and Menu Specials

View of the Allen House front door. (Note: no staff housing yet.)

Chapter 34
Skewered

The first big wedding Nina and I catered at the Allen House was, at every step, a millisecond from disaster. That we pulled it off at all is somewhat due to our absolute ignorance of what we were getting into but mostly because our staff, especially Higgins, was far better than we knew.

Davey was Dave's son. Powerhouse and gas dock Dave. His family and the island went way back, but I barely knew Davey. He had a house on the island, but he was in the Merchant Marine, and the house was rented most of the time.

Laylie's family were summer people, and Laylie met Davey on the island. Her family didn't seem too happy about the match, but Davey and Laylie were in love. This happened more often than you'd think, summer girl and island boy, and neither set of parents ever seemed very happy about it.

The wedding's biggest problem was not that it was planned for two-hundred-and-fifty people, or that we had never attempted anything near this scale before, or even that it fell right in the middle of our busy season. No, the biggest problem was me. I had worked with Laylie when I first came on-island, and thought of her as a friend.

To be fair, I don't think that Laylie considered what she was doing as taking advantage. I believe this sort of behavior comes naturally. It is a country-club attitude, *us* as opposed to *those people who work for us*. My mistake was in thinking I was an "*us*."

The bride's family pays for the wedding. Although Laylie's family was comfortably off, she felt it necessary to drive the hardest bargain she could. At that time, I was impossibly naïve, and when we first spoke, gave her my honest-absolute-rock-bottom price for what she wanted. Naturally, she took that as a starting point, and as the weeks wore on and the wedding got closer, she kept adding items without seeing the need to re-adjust the price.

Nina, who was thoroughly disgusted with me for taking on the wedding in the first place, begged to relieve me of this part of the planning. But I clung to the notion that Laylie was my friend and couldn't possibly be trying to screw me, no matter what Nina said. After all, Laylie must have priced these things out on the mainland. She must know how much things cost. Mustn't she?

Nina finally broke when I agreed to do Laylie's rehearsal dinner for one hundred people on the beach as a lobster bake based on a design Laylie found in a Martha Stewart cookbook. Even though Davey's parents were paying for this and gave us a decent budget in addition to supplying all the lobsters and shellfish, the addition of *Martha Stewart* into the mix pushed Nina right over the edge. I was removed from all further planning and restricted to the kitchen for the remainder of the wedding near-fiasco.

Martha's lobster bake called for a series of wooden boxes with screened bottoms which, after much persuading, Davey agreed to build. These boxes were to be filled with layers of food based on cooking time: potatoes and corn, then lobsters, then sausage, and finally shellfish on top. Each layer had its own boxes and each box was covered with seaweed. A deep pit was to be dug in the sand, lined with rocks, and a fire built inside. After the fire died out, the boxes should be layered on the coals and hot stones. The whole was covered with more seaweed and finally a tarp, and left to steam merrily away while the guests ate appetizers, drank beer, and danced on the beach.

Or so *Martha* claimed. None of us had ever tried this particular stacked-box method, and it seemed to leave a lot, especially cooking temperature, up to chance. But this was how Laylie wanted things done.

Nina's boyfriend, Dennis, graciously assumed charge of the lobster bake, as the rest of us were frantically preparing for the wedding. There was no money in the budget for overtime (hell, there was no money in the budget at this point for *food*), and so the tasks of assembling and cooking everything fell to salaried employees and whatever friends and family we could coerce into helping.

I still have occasional nightmares in which it is three a.m. the day of the wedding and I am assembling hundreds of chicken and swordfish kebobs with two other tired and angry people in the dim cold of a walk-in refrigerator.

Dennis was a Rhode Island boy and no stranger to lobster bakes. He had his own serious doubts about the workability of *Martha's* plan, but he followed it to the letter, collecting seaweed, digging the pit, lining it, and building the fire.

At two forty five p.m; (*Martha* specified two hours cooking time but Dennis had decided to give it an extra half-hour), we carried the carefully packed boxes out to the van, and Dennis drove off to the beach with a sixteen-year-old dishwasher as his allotted helper. They were immediately forgotten by the rest of us.

By some sheer fluke of luck it had occurred to me to close the dining room for the night. We were literally up to our elbows in preparations for the wedding when the worried dishwasher showed up at the kitchen door at five forty-five.

"Dennis asks if one of you could come down," he said. "He thinks there might be a problem."

Dennis was a theatrical stage manager by profession, and not one to panic. If he "thought there might be a problem," something was terribly wrong. Higgins and I washed the pasta salad off our arms and jumped in the van. We parked at the edge of the beach and ran down the sand to the party.

Dennis had uncovered the top boxes of clams to check their progress, only to find them stone cold. A little worried, he pulled back more of the tarp and began unstacking boxes. When he got down the lobsters and found *them* only slightly warm, he suggested the dishwasher might want to go get someone with a bit more authority.

We tore apart the clambake, grateful that it was some distance away from the rest of the party. *Martha* had failed us miserably. Three hours under the tarp and not a single section of the clambake was cooked through. Higgins pulled the van as close as possible without getting stuck in the loose sand. I sent the dishwasher running back to the kitchen with instructions to fill all the big pots and deep pans with hot water and haul them onto burners or slide them into cranked-up ovens, anywhere there was heat. Higgins, Dennis, and I carried those wet, slippery boxes across sand and rocks and stuffed every inch of that van with lobsters, corn, sausage and shellfish, all dripping with seawater and covered in sand and seaweed.

Then we raced back up the hill to the kitchen. Higgins jumped out of the van, yelling, "Everybody out here NOW!" while Dennis and I loaded each employee with as many boxes as I thought they could carry, and we hauled everything inside.

Higgins dumped lobsters into pots on the stove while I shoveled corn and sausage into pans in waiting ovens. We filled every pan, every pot, every oven. And then we waited.

We'd sent Dennis racing back down to the beach on the scooter with instructions to cover the hole with the tarp and place rocks around it as if there were still a clambake inside, and try to stall the hungry crowd as long as possible. We waited. There was nothing else we could do.

I have no idea how long that food took to cook, but finally, everything was ready.

With the faint notion we might pretend to have accomplished the lobster bake the way Laylie wanted, we piled all the food back into *Martha's* boxes and carried them, steaming and dripping, back out to the van.

Dennis, who we thought had been anxiously watching for the red and white van to appear, seemed to have vanished. I unloaded the boxes into Higgins', and the now thoroughly confused dishwasher's waiting arms, and they ran, cursing as hot water and steaming seaweed dripped down their arms, across the beach to where the tables had been laid out.

I don't know if anyone at the party noticed what was going on. I don't know that anyone cared, as they'd been drinking since four o'clock. All I know is somehow we pulled it off.

Higgins stayed behind to serve the food, and the dishwasher and I drove the dripping, stinking van up to the Allen House. I told him to hose the van down inside and out. Then I walked inside to survey the damage.

The tiled kitchen floor was awash in three or four inches of sandy seawater. There wasn't a clean pot or pan in the kitchen. Every surface was covered in sand, festooned with seaweed, and sticky with the runoff from cooked seafood. Every employee I had and most of my relatives were busy, either down at the lobster bake, or prepping food for the wedding. My only helper was washing out the van, which would be sorely needed tomorrow to transport guests. With a sigh, I went to get the mop.

The rehearsal dinner having come so close to disaster, could the wedding be any worse? Stupid question. Laylie's paring down of the budget had already ensured we wouldn't make a profit. Now we were trying desperately just to get the wedding done. Maybe we would break even, maybe not.

At that point it didn't matter. There were two hundred and fifty people to be fed the next day, half of them islanders. If we screwed this one up so early in our management career, our chances of making the Allen House work didn't look good.

The menu was ridiculously elaborate at any price. Four kinds of skewers (my previously mentioned nightmare), swordfish grilled to order, chowder, salads, roasted vegetable platters, passed hors d' oeuvres . . .

Nina was right. I was nuts. I should be committed, shot, drawn and quartered, dragged through the sand, and absolutely *never* let near another customer. At one point, I was so panicked even Davey's mother, Betty, noticed and asked me if I was all right. I confided I was afraid there wasn't going to be enough food. Laylie kept adding guests but refused to budge from the price we'd set. Betty was a dear, telling me to buy what I needed and she would cover the cost.

And then there was the cake.

I was making the cake. Of course. Just because I'd never made a wedding cake in my life, or even a three-tiered cake, and certainly not a cake for two hundred and fifty was no reason to refuse Laylie's request. She wanted my carrot cake, so carrot cake it would be.

Once again Higgins saved the day. She'd done a brief stint in a bakery in high school and was able to give me two life-saving tips.

1. You don't actually make a cake for two hundred and fifty people. You make a pretty tiered cake for seventy-five at most and then you make sheet cakes, however many you need, to feed the rest of the guests. Everyone gets cake; no one notices which cake it came from.

2. Use your surroundings. It is not necessary to pipe basket weave around three layers of cake when there are pink and white beach roses and purple beach peas in bloom. People pay big money in cities for cakes decorated with edible flowers, and decorating a cake with flowers takes half an hour as opposed to hours and hours of piping work.

I wish I could tell you about the wedding. Really I do. I wish I could describe the day, what the bride wore, the music –

But honestly, my clearest memory of that wedding is our three a.m. stint in the walk-in, putting together shrimp, chicken, beef, and swordfish skewers, exhausted, our hands cold and greasy with marinade.

And I remember the cake. The second cake. The one Betty made after we pulled off what everyone agreed was a brilliant wedding and recovered from the aftermath. Higgins and Nina lured me up to Betty's house one afternoon with the promise of a surprise guaranteed to please. There on the dining room table was a cake Betty had made. It said **JUST SAY <u>NO</u> TO LAYLIE.**

Martha Stewart's clams.
(Davey and Laylie's rehearsal dinner fiasco.)

Recipe for Carrot Cake

2 cups cake flour
2 teaspoons baking soda
2 teaspoons cinnamon
1 teaspoon salt
4 eggs
¾ cups oil
2 cups sugar
2 ½ cups shredded carrots, tightly packed
1 cup walnut pieces, roughly chopped

Grease and parchment paper two 9 inch round pans. Preheat oven to 350°.
Sift dry ingredients together. Beat eggs, mixed with oil and sugar. Mix wet and dry ingredients together. Add carrots and walnuts. Scale batter into pans. Bake at 350° for 30 to 35 minutes.

Carrot cake frosting

8 ounces cream cheese
2 ounces soft butter
1 pound powdered sugar
1 teaspoon vanilla
Zest of one lemon.
1/3 cup walnuts, finely chopped

Cream together cream cheese and butter, add sugar and beat until light. Add rest of ingredients and blend well.

This recipe for carrot cake became an Allen House favorite. I was forced to make it three or four times a week. Gourmet magazine wrote three times asking for the recipe because people wrote asking for it. Of course I graciously consented, hoping they would feature it in their letters column, but they never did. Perhaps because it was actually so simple. I would love to take credit for this recipe, but I found it in the back of an old cookbook in the Providence public library at the end of my first season at the Allen House. I picked this recipe because it did not contain canned pineapple or raisins, which I detest, and because all of the ingredients were measured in even increments and therefore easy to remember. I can't remember what cookbook it came from, but it must have been an old one, because the recipe calls for baking soda only. Most modern recipes call for either baking powder or combination of the two. Remember, because there is only baking soda in the recipe you have to get the cake into the oven as soon as you mix the wet and dry ingredients.

Chapter 35
Parsonally Yours

The dining porch was L-shaped. We numbered the tables starting at the long end of the L, closest to the annex. This made table nine, in the corner with its cross-ventilation and equidistant stationing from the kitchen doors, the best table in the restaurant. At least that's how most dinner guests saw it. There was cross-ventilation around every porch table when the fans were running, which was every hot day during the summer. As for the bustle of the restaurant, most people were desperate for any distraction after being cooped up on a boat or in a tiny rental house with the same people for days. And it never ceased to amaze us how many people insisted on certain tables for "the view" when it was clear it would be full dark before they even got their order in.

But people are strange, and table nine somehow became prime real estate. Guests waited for it, passing up other tables, which could wreak havoc on our dinner reservation system. Sometimes they could be persuaded to accept another table. Usually not. We found their hostility and insistence level was usually in direct correlation to how important they thought they were.

The people *we* considered important were our regulars, the ones who returned every year. They were pleasant, courteous, infallibly gracious, and would have taken any table we gave them. *They* were given table nine.

Of all our gracious guests, I would have to say the Parsons were everyone's favorites.

There were actually three sets of Parsons, the older Parsons, the younger Parsons, and the "kids." The older Parsons, who owned a house on the island, were in their late seventies when we first became acquainted. The younger Parsons, who lived on a boat in the harbor most of the summer, were close to sixty, and the "kids," who only showed up a couple of times a year, must have been in their forties.

The elder Parsons ate with us several times a week. They came right at six p.m. but liked to sit for a while before they ordered. The waitstaff loved them, and always made sure their table was set and waiting for them with a glass of unsweetened iced tea for Mr. Parsons.

The younger Parsons ate at seven-thirty unless they were dining with their parents and always brought a bottle of red for him and a bottle of white for her. When the kids visited, they ate at seven-thirty with their parents and always brought a bottle of wine for me.

You remember the good ones.

During the middle of our first season, Higgins and I felt bold enough to make some menu changes. There were several dishes Steve served those first years that Higgins and I disliked. One of the dishes we really hated was Steak Mornay. This was a dish Steve invented to use up the meat in the tips and heads of the beef tenderloins after the prime fillets were cut out. It was still the same lovely meat as the filet mignons, just too thin or oddly shaped to make a decent eight-oz. cut. Steve had cubed it, sautéed it with onions and peppers marinated in Italian dressing, and topped it with a Mornay sauce. Yuck.

We tried out a number of different dishes that summer, rotating a few that proved most popular. Three of the four Parsons ordered the steak tips with Dijon mustard sauce every time it was offered. (The elder Mrs. Parsons usually picked at a dish of broiled scallops. She was a small, frail woman who ate very little but loved to go out.) Towards the end of that summer, the Parsons men began ordering the dish even if it wasn't on the specials list, requesting we just make the sauce and pour it over a filet. The younger Mrs. Parsons would request the sauce over shrimp and pasta. Higgins and I decided we'd discovered our new menu item.

The next summer our reprinted menus read:

Steak Parsons – *cubes of filet sautéed with mushrooms in a Dijon mustard sauce over rice pilaf*

People still occasionally stop Nina on the island to reminisce about the dish and ask her for the recipe.

Steak Parsons

6 oz. filet mignon
2 tsp. butter
mushrooms
¼ cup white wine
1t. Dijon mustard
heavy cream
salt and pepper to taste

Sauté 6 oz. of cubed filet in a small amount of butter. Add a handful of sliced mushrooms as the meat begins to brown. Deglaze the pan with ¼ cup white wine, and add a tablespoon of Dijon mustard to the mushroom and meat mixture. Add a pinch of salt and pepper, and finish with a splash of heavy cream. Let the mixture cook until desired doneness of meat is achieved. Serve over rice pilaf.

Dining Room

Chapter 36
Musical Interlude

The exception to our table nine rule was the Chisholms, a lovely couple who were a fixture for years until ill health prevented their return to the island. They rented a place Memorial Day through the Fourth of July and, when they came, always requested table thirteen.

This was considered the worst table in the restaurant. It was at the end of the short leg of the L and the only table with a view of the kitchen door instead of the harbor. The Chisholms claimed they liked it because they could watch us cooking. I believe they found Higgins and me amusing. God knows we found ourselves amusing.

The kitchen door was often left open to give the waitstaff an extra entrance and us a bit more cross-ventilation. Even when it was closed during dinner, the door's glass upper half made it easy to see what was going on inside.

Let us just say Higgins and I did not always comport ourselves in a dignified manner. We both felt that if you had to do a job, you might as well have fun at it. We joked, we laughed, we sang, sometimes we did little dances. We were determined not to let ourselves get bored during the slow periods. And since the Chisholms generally came in May and left before July, most of their meals were during slow periods.

The Chisholms loved to eat out. In the mornings they would come in for breakfast, even though breakfast for them usually consisted only of toast and coffee. I asked Mrs. Chisholm once why anyone would go out for toast and coffee when it was so easy to make at home. She replied that she had cooked for fifty years and she was done with it. Never again.

So they came, and they watched. And I hope we entertained them.

An old boyfriend of Higgins' sent her a mix tape of songs from the sixties and early seventies. It was a bizarre mix but one of our favorite tapes as it had "Build Me up Buttercup" on it. For some unknown reason, we loved that song and when it came on, we would sing it at the top of our lungs. Eventually we got the whole kitchen doing it. This was good, as Higgins and I have terrible voices. The only problem was the old boyfriend had an odd sense of humor. The next song after "Build Me up Buttercup" was by the dead kennedys, and was titled "If You Don't Want to F--- Me Baby, Baby F--- Off." So as soon as we heard the ending notes of "Buttercup" someone had to lunge for the radio and shut the volume down.

It is positively amazing what seems amusing on a slow day in June.

Another of our not-so-private joys was making up lunch songs, taking any popular song and replacing the word love with lunch. It's surprising how well this worked, but then, it was the eighties. Everything from "Lunch, Lunch my Lunch is Blue" to "Lunch Hurts" to "I'd Love to Lunch You Baby." No song was sacred. These songs were also shared with the rest of the kitchen, usually at the top of our voices and accompanied by little dance steps as we put together tuna plates and grilled burgers. Higgins and I shared a secret fantasy that someday we could get Cheryl Wheeler to make the album.

And speaking of lunch, long before Davey and Laylie got married, Davey and Higgins had a brief fling. It ended acrimoniously, and I always thought Higgins got the worst end of it. I made this assumption because I remember one spring lunch the waitress came into the kitchen and asked "Is Davey's order ready?"

Higgins, who was working the broiler, turned around and looked at the waitress.

"Is this Davey's lunch?" she asked.

"Yes," the waitress replied. "He's here with his brother and some guys, and they're in a hurry."

Higgins nodded and turned back to the broiler. "It'll be ready in just a second," she said calmly over her shoulder. In one fluid motion she flipped vegetables off the grill and onto the floor, then bent down, scooped them up on her spatula and threw them back onto the grill. After less than two seconds she flipped them off.

"Now it's ready," she said.

Higgins looked at me as she pushed his lunch toward the waitress. "Don't worry," she said. "I've never done this before, and I never will again." She motioned the waitress out the door with her hand. "But that bastard deserved it."

(Higgins says this is one of the few incidents in the book she actually remembers and she would never drop anything over a fling with a guy, but dropped the food because Davey had gone on his honeymoon without paying his wedding bill. Who knows which version is true. Probably hers.)

One of the sweetest things that ever happened in that kitchen was something the Chisolms, unfortunately, never got to see. Wilfred was a small, elderly islander, who looked a little bit like a jolly elf. He was a hermit, rarely going out and almost never socializing. He'd been quite talented as a potter, going off-island to the Rhode Island School of Design, and coming back to open a small pottery using local clay. He hadn't always been a hermit, cultivating a large garden in front of the pottery that everyone stopped to admire as they walked by. We still went there in the spring to gather his rhubarb wild in the weeds. But now Wilfred stayed home almost all the time.

Almost, but not always. If he had drunk just the right amount of vodka, the spring or fall night was warm enough, and we didn't have too many guests, he might show up at the kitchen door just as we were cleaning up. He'd stand just inside the doorway, chat for a few minutes about nothing in particular, and then leave.

One night we were cleaning up to a tape of jitterbug music. Nina happened to be in the kitchen and, being no mean dancer, started to jitterbug. Suddenly Wilfred swept her up and began to dance with her. It turned out he was an amazing dancer, and they must have jitterbugged for twenty minutes. It was a wonderful thing to see. Then he bowed to Nina and left.

Wilfred didn't come back often, but when he did we always called Nina to the kitchen and put on that jitterbug tape.

Chapter 37
Anyone for Cocktails?

Cuttyhunk was (*and still is*) a dry island. No alcohol can be bought or sold legally anywhere on the island. No liquor stores, no bars, no wine or beer sold in restaurants.

Rumor has it the island voted itself dry after WWII, when the antics and noise at the Coast Guard Houses got to be too much. I have heard some great stories about legendary parties while the Coast Guard was stationed on Cuttyhunk, but I have no way of knowing how much truth there is to them. I do know at least three of the longtime marriages on the island were matches between military personnel and island girls.

Cuttyhunk is the wettest dry island you can imagine. Just watch the ferry on boat days and you will see almost as much liquor and beer being off-loaded as you will food, especially in summer. In fact, more liquor stores than grocers deliver to the boat.

It was no better and often worse when I was working at and running the Allen House. This was the eighties, and people seemed to have much looser ideas about what was acceptable in regard to underage drinking, and to heavy drinking in general. Maybe it was because you really couldn't get into trouble on the island if you had too much to drink. Driving drunk in a golf cart wasn't liable to do much damage.

My staff, few of whom were even 18, nevermind 21, all seemed to have accounts at New Bedford liquor stores. It wasn't until near the end of our tenure at the Allen House, that stores required an employee to come in person to open his or her account. Everything was handled over the phone.

Even when restrictions tightened, all that was needed was one person of legal age to establish an account, and a blind eye was turned to the fact that this person routinely ordered ten bottles of assorted hard liquor a week, in addition to a dozen cases of various brands of beer.

I remember many a tough July or August night, with dinner service finally over, that Higgins or I poured a glass for each staff member of the jug wine we kept in the walk-in and lined them up on the counter. It was just a way of saying "Good job, we appreciate it." Anyone who didn't want a glass of wine got a free dip into the ice cream cooler.

That jug wine wasn't kept just for cooking. We advertised ourselves as a BYOB restaurant and charged a few dollars for corkage and wine glasses or set-ups for mixed drinks. A lot of people, especially those off boats, didn't read, didn't listen, or simply didn't feel the rules applied to them. We kept a couple of bottles of slightly better-than-average jug wine so we could send a glass or two out to a difficult table "with our compliments." This usually placated the angry boater who was "damned if I am going to trudge all the way down that hill and up again just for a lousy bottle of wine" but was willing to make his waitress or waiter miserable because he didn't have it.

We'd make sure our staff told the customers they really weren't supposed to provide this service and couldn't do it again, but just this once . . . so the customers didn't expect the same service every time they came in. Oddly enough, as with the laundry, those types of customers were almost always male.

I kept a few bottles of decent wine on hand from my own private stock, for the odd boaters or houseguests who truly didn't know the island was dry and didn't ask for anything more than the means to set up an account on the mainland. This was fairly difficult, requiring a deposit by boat or mail, and few guests were around long enough to make it worth the trouble. In those cases, I would (if I really liked them) graciously offer a bottle of my own free of charge. I never asked for anything in return, and I never failed to receive within a few weeks a bottle equal to or greater in value than the one I had freely given.

Alcohol was a serious moneymaker, and so every year we applied at town meeting for a liquor license. Every year we were refused.

Nina and I narrowed our request to just beer and wine, only after six p.m., only with a full meal, two glass maximum. Still the answer was no. I suppose the town was afraid once they opened that door, they would never be able to shut it again.

Since my first trip to the island, I had thought of Cuttyhunk as a place lost back in time, divorced from rules that governed the mainland. Massachusetts had dozens of laws stricter than the ones I was used to in Tennessee, from health inspections to waste disposal, vehicle inspections and gun laws, rules that really didn't apply or were not enforced on Cuttyhunk. A frontier, if you will, of the not-so-wild East.

In the late eighties, liquor laws tightened on the mainland, and we felt the pinch even on the island. We gave lectures about buying beer for underage staff, and no longer let them keep cases in the walk-in cooler. We stopped giving wine to staff, although we never went so far as to actually card anyone in the restaurant. And we stopped, finally, trying for a liquor license at town meetings. Bartenders on the mainland were being sued for allowing people to drive drunk. The last thing we wanted was a lawsuit brought by someone hurt by a drunken boater we'd served.

The noose around the last frontier tightened a notch.

Chapter 38
Musical Fare

We had always wanted music on the porch. Hard plywood floors and that long stretch of windows made the room extremely noisy, and didn't all fine dining establishments have music in their dining rooms? We always strove for a fine dining establishment tone, even if we did constantly have to remind our customers to put on shirts and shoes.

Every attempt I made as the resident electrician failed miserably. The only place we could put an easily accessible tape deck was the front desk. By the time the current traveled up the wall, across the ceiling, down the length of the ramp and passed through five speakers, there was barely enough juice left for a whisper, even with the speakers turned full volume.

At least that was the professional opinion I gave Nina. The fact the speaker system was cobbled together from three different cheap stereo sets and the tape deck/tuner cost $30 at Kmart might have had something to do with the problem. In any case, the result was the same. If the volume was correct in the gift shop, it was inaudible at the far end of the dining room, even if the dining room was almost empty. If you could hear the music in the dining room, it blew out the speaker in the gift shop. I knew that for a fact. That's why our system had five speakers instead of an even six.

Our musical savior appeared in the form of an old friend of Nina's who arrived in the fall of our second year to wait tables. Bobby was a *real* sound technician, not someone like me who'd hooked up a microphone or two. He bought some kind of signal booster and rewired the speakers in a manner which made absolutely no sense to me but perfect sense to the speakers. Suddenly, we were in business.

I had a number of jazz and classical tapes I thought would set just the right tone for our dining room, but as we tried them out we discovered most musical pieces had serious flaws when all you wanted to do was put a tape on and forget about it. Classical music, especially, has a tendency to get very loud and then very soft.

This may well be important to the composition of the piece, but it renders it entirely unsuitable for dining room music. Jazz tapes were a bit better. Vocals were generally useless, although my old re-mastered monotone recordings of Billie Holiday worked out well. Unfortunately, there wasn't much recorded in mono. But we found a handful of tapes that seemed to work okay.

Once we got the speaker problem sorted out, I retreated to the sanctity of my kitchen and put the matter out of my mind. If I couldn't hear it, why worry? The dining room was, after all, Nina's venue.

By doing so, I missed some interesting changes taking place. We'd managed to train most of our customers to make reservations, but we couldn't seem to make them understand that if they made a reservation for six p.m. we would very much like to seat another party at that same table two hours later.

They didn't understand, that is, unless *they* were the party waiting to be seated. Getting tables to turn over was a very tricky endeavor.

You didn't want to piss off the party you needed to vacate the table. You didn't want the party you needed to seat angry either. We had a lot of repeat business, and word of mouth travels at the speed of light in the boating community.

The real problem was there was nothing else to do on the island at night. Of course the party sitting at the table wanted to sit there and drink their wine or coffee and linger over dessert when the alternative was to go back and sit on their boat. And the party waiting to be seated was hungry, and didn't want to eat on their boat, or they wouldn't have made a reservation and walked up the hill.

Or so Nina was constantly reminded.

After we'd picked out a stack of the most appropriate tapes, Nina left the selection of the actual music for that night to the front desk person. This was the person who would have to listen to it over and over, and Nina felt they should have some choice in what drove them crazy.

As July wound into high gear, Nina noticed an odd pattern. Some nights she couldn't make the customers leave no matter *what* she did, and she wasn't above trying anything, including allowing the waiting party to get within sight of their prospective table and stare at the guests who wouldn't vacate.

Other nights the tables turned over quickly and beautifully, and she could even seat walk-ins who showed up without reservations.

At first Nina thought it could be specials. Maybe people didn't like certain appetizers and were ordering only entrées, which made them finish their meals faster. Or maybe they weren't ordering dessert?

Nina tried keeping notes of fast and slow evenings, what the weather was like, what the specials were. There appeared to be no correlation. To anything. Nothing connected or made sense. Nina checked the schedule and saw that the same employee was on the desk most of the quick nights, and asked *her* if she'd noticed anything.

It was, of course, the music she played. For unknown reasons, certain music made people want to linger for hours, eating slowly, chewing each bite deliberately. Other music made them order faster, eat faster, even talk faster. And they left faster. We never understood why some tapes had this effect and others didn't, but we went through a quick process of trial and error and soon had a pile of tapes we unceremoniously called chew and screw music. These we saved for nights when we were booked to or beyond capacity, and I am pleased to report they rarely failed us.

Chapter 39
Employee Fare

During my first three years, most Allen House employees were friends or relations of Steve, with a couple of summer island kids thrown in. When Nina and I took over, we wanted to increase the business. More business means more employees. More employees mean more problems. Lots more problems.

Of all the hassles I encountered running the Allen House—deliveries by ferry, bad weather keeping boats and new customers from entering the harbor, islanders who wanted to make life difficult for the "newcomers," power outages, using a public phone as a business line, the repair and maintenance of several one-hundred–year-old buildings, everyday dealings with the public, both famous and those who only thought they were – every problem Nina and I dealt with paled in comparison to what we had to go through to keep the Allen House staffed.

Our first and most vital piece of new business was housing. Unless we exclusively hired teenagers whose parents had summer homes on the island, we had to provide accommodations. And when Steve left, his extended family, which lived fairly uncomplainingly anywhere he told them to, left with him.

There weren't nearly enough teens of the right age and temperament that summered on the island to provide even half our staff. And that's without throwing in competition from the store, the bakery, the dock, mowing lawns, or cleaning houses.

Even if we *had* been able to hire the cream of the teenage crop, many of them spent only a month on-island. None of them spent more than two. That left the Allen House, with our mid-May to mid-October season, in a serious and never-ending employee bind.

The state of the shack that comprised the majority of our housing kept us from being able to hire anyone over the age of 18, which limited our selection and its consequent maturity level.

The shack had originally been constructed as a cook shack, then hastily remodeled to temporarily house Mildred's newlywed daughter.

The shack was decrepit—two dark-paneled rooms with a small bathroom in between holding a tiny sink, a mildewy tin shower stall, and an ancient toilet. The shack's two other rooms were equally un-attractive. At least five different layers of carpet padded the springy floor, and what furniture there was obviously had been purged from guest rooms by virtue of age and battered appearance. I couldn't imagine anyone who changed their underwear more than once a week even considering sleeping there. Yet we housed three girls and four guys there.

Nina and I did our best to spruce it up. We tore up all the old carpeting, painted and sealed the plywood floors, and put newer carpeting down. We spread thick coats of Navajo white over the old paneling, and added as many extra lamps as the ancient electrical wiring could take in an effort to lighten the place up. We replaced the old moldy mattresses with slightly newer, not quite as moldy mattresses and covered them all with plastic sheets. But there was nothing to be done to disguise the fact that the shack was a poorly constructed, 40-or 50-year-old wooden building that was literally falling down.

Three mattresses on the floor of the main house attic comprised the area used to house our slightly more mature female staff. The emphasis was on *slightly*, as it was hot and cramped, and they had to descend a steep ladder to get to a bathroom shared with houseguests. They also had to be very quiet, as they were directly above rooms two and three.

We couldn't hire married couples, or anyone with kids. We couldn't hire anyone who couldn't get along with other people in cramped, close quarters, or anyone who was claustrophobic. We did, after all, live on an island 14 miles from the mainland. It always amazed me how much that bothered some people.

As our business grew, we found ourselves going farther and farther afield in search of help. Come spring we'd be calling in favors and calling friends we hadn't talked to in years, trying to convince them to come out for a month or so. Nina's boyfriend was in the theater, so he had contacts with unemployed actors and technicians as well, even more than I.

We could usually manage to get the place open with these people and islanders who didn't have much to do until the real season started mid-June. And then around the middle of August, we'd be pulling out our personal phone books again, as staff that had promised to stay through Labor Day suddenly decided they needed an extra week or two to get ready for college.

Even if we managed to keep them until Labor Day, they were gone on that last boat, leaving us with an inn to run for another month and a half. One season we even had my soon-to-be-brother-in-law washing dishes for us for a week. He was arguably our best educated dishwasher (an almost PhD working on his dissertation in French literature) if not the most observant. He sliced his leg open on a piece of glass sticking out of a trash bag, and had to be treated by Ginger. Unwilling to be sewn up by her, he suffered her to close the wound with 19 butterfly bandages, and limped down the wedding aisle with my sister Lisa a week later.

We limped along too for another couple of years, expanding the business, using more and more part-timers in an effort to give our staff enough time off. One family with a summer house had five children and we employed every one of them at one time or another. Even the mother took a few wait shifts when her daughter wanted to go off island to a cousin's wedding.

We had a saying that if you could reach the sink standing on a milk crate, you were old enough to wash dishes. I think the youngest kid we ever employed was eight. He could only manage an hour-and-a-half shift, but he was a hell of a worker.

Cuttyhunk had no child labor laws. If your mom said you could work, you could work.

Chapter 40
Who Did What to Whom

For the first few years, ninety percent of our employees seemed to arrive because they knew someone who had worked at or was somehow connected to the Allen House.

When Steve was here he had his nephew, Jimmy, his niece, Barb, her boyfriend, Keith, and his sister all working with him. I remember at least one other nephew as a temporary dishwasher. There may have been more.

I was the queen of finding spring and fall replacements. My friend, Mary Sue, was still working in the theater and had a number of contacts who were usually unemployed at some point. Mary Sue came out every spring. After my first full season as an employee, I had come up with a deal Steve agreed to.

I could bring people out and they would work a half-day, and have the rest of the time to themselves. We would feed them and house them in return. It cost us very little as we weren't open yet, and they got a mini-vacation on the island. In return, we got five hours of cheap, available labor every day.

Some people were more skilled than others. My mother's friend, Lynn, painted houses throughout college and he was invaluable for reaching the high peaks on the main house and annex with an extension ladder no one else wanted to climb. Even if you had no skills as a painter, or carpenter, you could clean. Mom brought Lynn and his partner, Ron, every spring. I brought Mary Sue, and she brought anyone she knew who was out of work and available.

And the employees themselves formed linked chains. I found Higgins, and she brought her brother, Bill, and her sister, Laura. And of course she brought Christopher.

Katheryne was the daughter of a longtime girlfriend of my father's. She came, and the next year brought her friend, David.

I coerced Gretchen, the daughter of my old high school guidance counselor. Nina persuaded Cordelia, the girlfriend of a man she'd met working at the New Orleans World's Fair. She also brought Bobby, of dinner music fame. Bobby brought several acquaintances over the years when he came to work those crucial two months in the fall after all college students left us. Nina reunited with Leslei, an old childhood friend. Leslei brought her sister, Mary Lee. Zane came up from my father's country club in Tennessee. Tasnima was the daughter of a man Nina had worked with in Washington, DC.

Mary Beth had been visiting the island for several years on her boyfriend's boat. He brought her up for an interview, and we hired her as a prep cook. She later became my partner. When she went to Vermont to work for the winter, she brought back Pelky and Moe. Later, when we were desperate in the fall, she brought up her friend, Sara, from Florida. Sara stayed with us for years after Mary Beth left.

We had brother-and-sister teams, mother-and-daughter teams, mother-and-son teams. We hired little sisters after big sisters, little brothers after big brothers, and friends of friends. You didn't have to know someone to get a job at the Allen House, but if you did, we probably hired you.

Even in those earlier, easier days, we had to set rules of behavior for the staff. Many of them were the brothers and sisters or friends or roommates of kids who'd worked for us at one time or another. For a lot of them this was their first time away from home on their own. So to speak. So every year around Memorial Day, we would have THE MEETING.

Nina and I would gather the staff in the inside dining room and try to explain just how different living on Cuttyhunk and working at the Allen House was going to be from their previous life experiences. We needed to teach them about the islanders who helped us. To many of the kids, Alan, in his hard hat and overalls, riding through town on his tractor and trying to teach them about propane tanks and refrigeration units in his thick Maine accent, or Hunter, with his torn, stained clothes and beat-up, old, blue truck that always seemed to break down in our driveway, or Dave, who looked like Santa gone bad driving along in his three-wheeler, his long while hair and beard streaming out beneath his straw hat as he traveled between the gas dock and the powerhouse, were figures of fun, caricatures of the "normal" people they were used to. We tried to explain that people often came to live on Cuttyhunk *because* they wanted a certain lifestyle, and that people here could not be judged by the way they looked.

As these were just three of the people who lived on Cuttyhunk that might be classified as "not your everyday, small town, main street type of folks," it was important to us the staff respect the islanders, and realize that living on an island, far from being a lazy way of life, was something only a special type of person could handle.

The we-all-have-to-get-along lecture ended with Nina's admonition, "All the bass guides who work out of the Allen House are either married or in committed relationships. No matter *what* they tell you." And that segued directly into the sex lecture. Nina left that one to me, because *I* insisted we have one. I felt strongly that a bunch of teenagers cooped up in a small space, away from home and thrown up against the same people twenty-four hours a day, was a recipe for possible big trouble.

I was determined not to send anyone home pregnant who hadn't been that way when she got to the island. Nina always left the room, so I don't think she ever knew my sex lecture went something like this:

"Nobody gets pregnant on my watch. This is a condom. Ginger sells them at the store. Use them. Does anyone need a demonstration how?" At that point I would hold up a condom and a banana. Usually everyone declined the offer, but occasionally some smartass would say yes. I got very good at putting a condom on a banana.

Section IV.

Sometimes a Great Notion

Allen House Walkway

Chapter 41
Shit on a Shingle, Island Style

The economy had begun to slow by the time Nina and I became comfortable with all aspects of running the Allen House as it was, and we had to decide whether to shrink the business back down or widen our net to attract new customers. When we made our fateful decision to expand the business, we knew that soon we would have to come up with some better way to house our staff. The shack was full, as was the attic. The apartments across the street we'd rented were crammed to the limits with beds, and the rent was skyrocketing. Every other idea we could come up with was costly, inefficient, or both. We were out of space.

We'd kicked around the idea of building staff housing the year before, and I had talked my way into a construction job off-island that winter, hoping to pick up a few new skills. I'd become something of an expert in re-hanging one hundred-year-old windows, patching horsehair plaster and stripping floors, but new construction was beyond me. I learned a number of invaluable lessons that winter, but most of them had to do with never working on a wharf in Boston with a bunch of guys from the North End again.

Nina and I spent the next summer discussing ideas, trying to patch together the best use of money and space into a coherent plan. We finally decided to rip the roof off the gift shop/shower/laundry area and build up. We thought we could do this without destroying anyone's view, which was a major concern on a vacation island. We planned a simple structure fifty feet long and eighteen feet wide, running as a second story along the length of the gift shop addition. There would be two bathrooms just inside the entryway, conveniently hooking directly to the hot water heater for the public showers and laundry, thus bypassing the ancient inn furnace entirely.

The addition would be over the gift shop so inn guests would not be bothered by noise. There would be a series of rooms opening off a central hall running the length of the building, simple rooms, each with a single doorway and window. The first two rooms would hold two bunk beds each, and the other rooms would each house two single beds. One room would have a double bed in case, as was happening more frequently, we had a couple apply for jobs together.

A simple, elegant solution. At full capacity we could hold twenty. We hoped, with judicious hiring of island kids, this would be enough space. Murphy's Law, or somebody's, states that employees expand to fill the space allotted them.

Whoever he was, he was one smart guy.

The actual building of staff housing was one of those stories that's a nightmare while you're living it, but even then you can see that it's going to make a great comic story some time in the future. Far in the future. I'm still waiting.

Even though I had learned next to nothing that I needed to know working in Boston, I decided that I would do most of the work myself to save money, with two island "carpenters," A.P. and Roland, to guide me.

I thought we could complete construction easily by spring, even given the probability of several weeks of mostly bad weather. After all, A.P had built or helped build half the older homes on the island. Okay, so he was in his eighties. They were very young eighties. And he hadn't missed a poker game Dot let him come to since I'd been on island. And Roland had been working on houses on the island most winters for the past 15 years or so. True, he was a fishing guide in the summer, and a retired motel owner, but he was damn handy when he was sober. And he had stayed pretty sober most of the summer. I figured with a real project to oversee and a deadline, he would step up to the plate, so to speak. And he assured me this was the case.

What a nightmare that turned out to be.

The project started out innocently enough. As soon as we closed for the season, Nina and I got to work. We hired some old ski buddies of hers, construction workers from New Hampshire, to help with the initial tearing off of the old roof and framing and roofing the new second story. They had initially come on-island to build Leon and Enna's house, so we knew they were good carpenters and familiar with the foibles of the island.

After those tasks, the guys would go back home where they had work waiting, and I would finish the job, watched over and ably assisted by Roland and A.P.

I went-off island to make a quick trip to Tennessee during the first part of the demolition and construction, leaving Nina in a panic. She would have to cook for the guys every night, and these guys could *eat*. Nina had learned how to make a mean gumbo and jambalaya during her stint at the New Orleans World's Fair, and how to operate a still at the Knoxville Energy Exposition. But cooking anything else had been someone else's provenance up until then. Mary Beth was coming with me to Tennessee, and Nina refused to let us leave until we had written out explicit instructions on how to roast a turkey, bake a ham, make a roast, or pot roast. What seasonings, in what amounts, and exactly how long things had to be cooked. I bought her a meat thermometer, gave her my copy of the *Joy of Cooking*, and wished her luck. I still have a few of those recipe cards in Mary Beth's handwriting. I was going to print one here, but I certainly don't want to embarrass Nina. Let's just say it had four lines and started with: Rub roast with Toney's. Put on rack in pan.

The first half of the project went off without a hitch. A.P. had actually built the gift shop addition fifteen or so years earlier. He was the only one not surprised when the roof came off and it was discovered that all the cross-pieces and trusses were made out of driftwood, tree branches, or reclaimed wood from the dump. There wasn't a single board foot of new lumber in the entire construction. As A.P. put it, "Why buy new stuff and have to pay to haul it over when there was all this perfectly good stuff already on-island?" Hunter would have been proud.

A.P. shrugged and gracefully accepted my pronouncement that I wanted to use new wood constructing staff housing. It was my money, after all, and if I wanted to throw it away. . .

The guys from New Hampshire had the roof off, the plywood flooring laid, the structure framed, and the new roof on within two days of their one-week timetable. This was probably a Cuttyhunk record. I returned just as they were capping the roof, and managed to talk Roland into including the guys in our discussion of exactly how much of each item (sheetrock, plywood, nails, shingles, insulation, etc.) we wanted to purchase and on what schedule we would have the ferry bring it out. Storage space was at a premium, but we didn't want to get held up by bad weather, needing supplies we were unable to get. Construction was a delicate balancing act on Cuttyhunk, especially in winter.

When I was satisfied that between Roland, A.P. and me, we pretty much had things covered, I saw the real carpenters off with an effusive amount of thanks. Nina, I am sure, saw them off with an equal amount of relief. Now we could go back to our typical hummus and chips or cold cereal winter dinners.

Hummus and Chip Dinner, Winter Island Style

Open a container of hummus. Open a bag of chips. Carry both to table in front of TV.
If you feel the need for vegetables, open a jar of salsa as well.

A.P., Roland, and I started off at a fine pace. The weather held cool, clear, and even slightly less windy than a usual Cuttyhunk fall. We set up staging, nailed plywood on the frame, wrapped it in Tyvek® sheeting, and began shingling. As soon as we had all the shingles on and the place was watertight, Roland said, we could begin insulating and sheet rocking the rooms inside. This was where I shone. I could insulate, sheetrock, tape, and mud with the best of them. I had learned to tile floors, and Roland said he could handle the plumbing and wire the place right up to the end connections, as both were simple, straightforward jobs.

Somebody, maybe A.P., might have had a contractor's license. Maybe not. It wasn't a big deal in those days. Things that got built on the island stayed up during storms and didn't burn down, and that was really all that mattered.

Yes, things were going along splendidly. One of the fondest memories I have of these days is sitting next to A.P. on the wooden scaffolding, trimming shingles and handing them to him as he fitted them effortlessly and expertly in place. As we worked A.P. would tell me stories of construction in the old days, of tearing down one building so you could put up another, of whole houses that had been floated over on barges from the mainland, still bearing their street numbers and front door letter slots.

Then the impossible happened.

A.P. died.

Roland, whose problems with alcohol were legendary, but who managed to stay in control for the first part of construction, fell apart. Completely. I was left with a shell of a building, plans drawn on the backs of a set of placemats, and a contractor who showed up drunk when he showed at all. To make matters worse, Roland had been ordering the building supplies from some friend of his on the mainland. I had no idea who this guy was, or how much Roland had already ordered from him.

I was left hanging without a clue as to what was supposed to happen next.

Growing up, I'd become an expert in denial, especially where alcoholics were concerned. Roland kept assuring me it would be all right, that he would pull himself together, that he would get the job done. I needed that to be true, so I believed him.

Fall stretched into winter. I finished shingling the west wall with advice from a couple of islanders who took pity on me, and decided that since the last wall faced south and was protected, I could start work inside until Roland sobered up. Fortunately, he'd ordered the insulation and some of the sheetrock already and we'd piled it in the gift shop downstairs. Insulating is something anyone can do, although it is a nasty job. I insulated the walls of the dorm rooms, but the bathrooms had to be left as empty shells, since the plumbing had to go in before anything else could be done. Plumbing was not something I wanted to tackle myself. I was pretty cocky in those days, but I wasn't stupid.

It was getting colder. We'd borrowed a couple of kerosene heaters at the start of the job, but they hardly made a dent in the temperature inside that shell. The insulation I had put in was to muffle noise more than anything else. The structure as never designed to be used past the first week in October. And it was now the end of December.

I started to panic. We had enough sheetrock for three rooms piled downstairs in the gift shop, if I didn't make any mistakes at all. There was no tape, no joint compound, and I wasn't sure of the drywall screw situation. I was under the impression that some summer person had part of a box of the sort of screws we needed stuck away in their basement they were going to sell us, but I hadn't seen the box, and couldn't remember whose basement it was.

After a couple of weeks of mourning A.P., during which I insulated and prayed for deliverance, Roland started showing up a couple of mornings a week, hung over and half drunk. He would drill a few holes in the studs for the electrical wires, leave for lunch, and never come back.

Someone, I wish I could remember who, stepped in and did the simple wiring the rooms required, two outlets each and an overhead light with a switch by the door. The hallway was even simpler, with three overhead lights and a wall switch at either end of the hall. All the wires ran across the hall ceiling, ending in a tangle at the far end of the hall, waiting for a real, licensed electrician to wire up the box and run a cable to the transformer.

I started hanging sheetrock on a freezing cold, windy day in January. Roland sobered up enough to help carry some of the sheets up the outside stairway and lean them against the studs of the hallway wall. We should have started with the ceilings, but he didn't feel up to it, so he showed me how to sheetrock two walls of one of the small rooms. I thought I remembered that you should stagger the sizes of the pieces of sheetrock used, so you didn't have giant seams but Roland said that was pretty much bullshit and anyway it didn't matter as it was only staff housing. He was right in that respect, but for five years I couldn't look at those bulging seams without cringing.

I began the laborious task of sheet rocking each of the rooms, trying hard not to make a single mistake or waste a scrap of material. Daily, I went down to Roland's and asked him about more material. He swore to me the very next morning he'd get it together. Finally, one day I went down and banged on his door until he came out and said he'd be right up. Several hours later, I saw his ATV coming slowly up the road. He staggered into the phone booth on the corner, dialed a number, and began reading a list off of what appeared to be a crumpled napkin. I stood on the top of the staff housing steps and watched him. I had never felt so close to bursting into tears.

I called Nina that afternoon from the corner phone booth and explained what was happening. She had gone skiing with the carpenters from New Hampshire, who worked winters as ski patrol. I had been in only sketchy communication with her, not wanting to admit I couldn't handle the situation on the island. Nina told the guys what was happening and they promised to come back and help finish up whatever wasn't done as soon as ski season ended.

On the next boat, which miraculously showed up despite predictions of a nor'easter, was a truckload of sheetrock, joint compound, tape, and screws. I have never been so happy to see anything. After a tough day of hauling stuff up the hill and stowing it away, I got down to serious work. It was almost February, and time was running out. Nina would be back soon but wouldn't be able to help much, as she would have to begin the huge pile of spring tasks alone: brochures, staffing, bookkeeping, ordering for the gift shop—a thousand and one tasks we usually began together before March first.

Roland and I developed something resembling a routine. He would show up sometime in the morning, and we would hang sheetrock in silence till noon, then he would go down to his house for "lunch," and that would be the last I'd see of him. I would return to the achingly cold structure and tape and apply joint compound until my arms would no longer obey me.

It was just too cold. The heaters we had could barely keep the compound from freezing, never mind get the rooms warm enough for the stuff to dry. Until the first coat of compound dried, I couldn't sand it and put the second coat on. Things were looking grim.

Then the cavalry arrived. The guys from New Hampshire came down and took charge. By that time, strong-willed and stubborn as I was, I would have let Barnum and Bailey Circus take over if it meant getting help. The guys showed me how to hang plastic over the doorway of the room I was working on, and blast the space heater at the walls. Hunter jumped in and showed me the Cuttyhunk method of drying annoying wet spots of compound by focusing a hair dryer on them, and how you could use a moist sponge on some of the seams between coats, saving hours of sanding and breathing dust.

It was an extremely tight race to get the bathrooms finished before the plumber from the mainland came in to install the copper pipes, but by the end of March, we were finishing the final coats of paint, hanging inside doors, and hauling furniture up.

With no time to put in the sound-proofing carpet I'd wanted, or anything else for that matter, Nina and I painted the plywood sub-flooring with leftover dark grey from our annual porch painting and created a splatter effect with all the colors we had hanging around in the basement. By the end of the first season, the splatter pattern had completely worn off, I'd had to patch half a dozen holes knocked in the walls, the bathrooms had proved themselves entirely too small, and three staff members had moved back into the attic. Just like old times. It took me a year, but I even forgave Roland. Mostly.

Before the new staff housing was built, our main worries were whether an employee would agree to be housed in the shack and whether they could last a couple of months on the island. With the new staff housing complete, all the other employee problems moved closer to the top of the "hassle list."

Section VI.

More Employee Fare

Fourth of July at the Allen House.

Chapter 42
Dishwashers á la Carte

In most restaurants, the hardest employees to find and keep are dishwashers, so they tend to be treated relatively well. It's a thankless job, and when you find someone willing to do it well, you want to hold on to him or her. Surprisingly, we didn't have as much trouble getting dishwashers on Cuttyhunk as I've had in restaurants on the mainland. There was usually somebody's little brother anxious to get away from home, or a friend of a guy who'd worked for us last year, or a former guest who wanted his or her son to learn the meaning of work before going off to college.

One year we had the sixteen-year-old son of a fishing guide wash dishes for us. Joey was the originator of one of my favorite lines. I had asked him to wash the van, and he started complaining: it was too hot, he'd planned to go to the beach, he was tired. Finally, I got mad.

"Forget it, Joey," I said. "Just forget it. I'll find someone else to do it."

He looked at me in utter shock. "Oh, no, Margo," he said. "I'll do it. Of course I'll do it. I just gotta piss and moan about it first."

Joey was also the cause of my now-legendary tantrum, the one time I truly lost my temper while running the Allen House.

In my defense, if there is any defense for behaving that way, events conspired to construct a sequence of worst-possible moments. We were in the middle of a major luncheon for Howland Lodge, a job we'd had since Steve's first year. Thirty to forty elderly men came out on a special Alert run. They spent the afternoon playing cards and eating hors d' oeuvres before consuming a hearty early meal and heading back at five, leaving us just enough time to set up for dinner service. Howland Lodge ordered the same menu every year. Lazy lobster, swordfish, or filet. And French fries. Baskets and baskets of French fries, served family-style to each table. As we began preparation for the meal, I dropped a basket of fries. They didn't bubble when they hit the fat. Then the flames under the pots on the stove began to flicker.

"Joey," I yelled. "Didn't you check the gas this morning? Change over those tanks, NOW!"

Joey ran outside, but was back in less than two minutes. "They're all empty," he said. "What do I do?"

"Get a new one, dummy," I said. "Get one full one on each appliance. We can worry about the others later. I have food to put out here!"

Joey backed away from me. "No," he said. "I mean they're *all* empty. All the tanks out there. I guess I forgot to keep an eye on them."

I got right up in his face.

"You forgot?" I said through clenched teeth. "Forgot? Haul your ass down to Horseplay and grab a tank off it for the fryers. I want them running again in less than five minutes. I don't care if you have to carry it up on your back!"

Joey hurried away. I told one of the waitstaff to get Nina to try and raise Alan on the marine radio and tell him we needed propane urgently. Then I ran outside to start unhooking empty tanks in preparation for full ones.

Only there weren't any. There was one extra tank on a cabin that was half full we could sneak away temporarily. The other two cabins were dangerously low on gas as well, and we had guests who were apt to expect little niceties like hot showers.

Grimly, I rolled the half-full tank Joey had brought me off the handcart and handed him a wrench to hook it up. I yelled into the kitchen to relight the fryers the moment Joey was done and keep going on the dinner. Then I ran across the street (in full kitchen whites, my apron still on, towel hanging from my waist and a large crescent wrench in one hand; I must have made quite a sight) to the building where we rented apartments. Luckily George, bass guide, part-owner, and semi-caretaker, was home and just waking up after a late night fishing trip.

"I need a propane tank, George. Now! I'll replace it later!"

George, of course, had several full spare tanks. I, of course, had neglected to bring the handcart. I tipped one over and rolled it away from the others, toward the side of the house. Then I ran back to the Allen House where Joey was still trying to hook up the tank. These hook-ups were tricky things, made of soft copper wire, and you had to get the nozzle into the opening just right to get a proper seal. Not an easy job under the best of circumstances, and with your boss on the warpath and a dining room full of hungry customers, damn near impossible.

"I'll take over," I yelled. "Get the tank from the apartments. Hook it up to the stove, then get me some tanks!"

The kitchen was organized chaos, the rest of the food damn near ready but no French fries. And there would be no French fries for at least ten minutes, as the oil had to be brought up to temperature again before we could even start.

Nina had been unable to raise Alan on the radio, so Joey set out in the van to track him down. Meanwhile, I continued with Howland Lodge, sending the waitstaff out to say we would begin serving the entrées and the French fries would be along in just a minute. And I continued to simmer, pulling up every mistake Joey had ever made: late arrivals, half-cleaned pots, anything he'd ever done wrong. By the time he drove back up the driveway, I had achieved just short of a full boil.

Joey came inside the kitchen looking like his world had collapsed. "Well?" I demanded.

"I went down to the docks," he said. "Alan's boat is gone. Someone said he was headed toward the mainland."

That was it. Something snapped inside me. I don't recall all the words, just the image: standing an inch from his face, screaming about what a fucking loser he was, how could he do something so incredibly stupid. And so on. Not one of my proudest moments. When I finally ran out of steam, Joey was trembling. The rest of the staff who had been unfortunate enough to witness me let him have it right in the middle of the kitchen were absolutely silent.

Then Higgins suggested I step outside for a moment, that they were handling the meal just fine. She told Joey to take a couple of hours off and come back at dinner.

By then my emotional firestorm had passed, and I was deeply sorry and ashamed. I knew I had a temper, but I had controlled it for so long I'd assumed I had outgrown outbursts of that sort. Somehow I had let all the built-up frustrations of our first year of innkeeper/managers out on poor Joey.

Sure, it was an irresponsible thing to do to let the gas run out. It was his responsibility. But he was also only a sixteen-year-old boy, and someone should have been delegated to double check. In any case, there was absolutely no excuse for what I did.

Joey seemed to take his dressing down in stride. He showed up at dinner, accepted my apology, and went back to work. He had a hot-tempered dad and was, I suppose, used to being yelled at.

I, on the other hand, can remember that day as clearly as if it happened last week. Even though Alan was furious when he came back because the tank we had borrowed turned out to be one of his competitor's, and even though he gave me an earful similar to what I'd done to Joey, *my* part in that day remains the clearest in my mind. Many things happened in the years after that which drove me crazy. Stupid things, irresponsible things, even dangerous things. But I vowed I would never again lose my temper like that. And I never did, not at the Allen House, and not now, more than twenty years later.

Over the years, we had countless dishwashers. Some of them actually stick in my mind. I picked up Schuyler while working in Newport one winter. He had prep school manners and an attitude to match, but he was wonderful with customers and could make anyone laugh. In no time at all, he was promoted from dishboy (yes, that's what we called them, and it was intended to be belittling and demeaning in a funny way. Almost every staff position had a belittling nickname, lest any employee decide his or her position was better than anyone else's) to an intern position, and allowed the run of the place.

Then there was Boy Lee, a diminutive nickname for a diminutive young man who could, when he wanted to, move faster and get more done than anyone I knew. The key phrase: when he wanted to. Boy Lee's problem was that he started each summer with amazing enthusiasm, but tended, like most sprinters, to burn out early in the race. We hired him two years in a row, but by the third, decided we needed someone a bit slower and steadier. Lee wrote me a letter several years later thanking me for not hiring him that third year, thus forcing him to move on.

We got a lot of interesting letters from former employees, some many years later. My favorites, of course, were the ones that started, "I never realized what a good thing I had at the Allen House," or "I never realized what great employers you and Nina were until . . ."

Another dishwasher who I'll never forget was brought to the island by one of our early cooks, who'd met him during the winter. I won't use names here, because he was a great guy and I don't want to embarrass him, wherever he's ended up. He was older than our usual dishwashers and planned on spending a year on the island which meant he'd be available the whole season. A full-season dishwasher! And he even had a place to stay.

He turned out to be pretty handy as well, and it was lovely to be able to give him a wrench and say, "Go tighten the faucet washers in the upstairs bathroom sink," and know it would actually get done. The only problem we had with him was that he was extremely slow in putting freight away, and in taking things down to and bringing things up from the walk-in.

Sometimes when I'd send him down for rice, he'd be five minutes bringing it back. For a while we suspected he was downing a quick beer in the walk-in, or swiping a piece of cobbler, but we never found anything missing.

As high season approached, this lingering habit of his annoyed me more and more. It wasn't just the wasted time. It was that I felt he was putting something over on me.

Finally, I'd had enough. When I sent him down for rice one day, I quietly followed him. It had just taken him ten minutes to find some cooked lasagna noodles I wanted for staff dinner, and I wasn't about to wait ten minutes for rice. Sure, the walk-in was crammed full and almost everything was in an opaque plastic fish tub or ricotta cheese container, but most of the shelves were labeled, and I insisted that every item be carefully labeled and dated.

Like most of the dishwashers, he wore a walkman with head-phones to block out the noise and help keep boredom at bay. This made it hard to get their attention (hence the time-honored tradition of throwing cherry tomatoes at dishboys to get their attention) but easy to sneak up on them. I waited until he'd had time to go into the walk-in and then followed. Most employees didn't shut the heavy door all the way behind them. Even though you couldn't lock yourself in, the sound of that heavy door thudding closed was a bit scary. This dishwasher was no exception, and it was easy for me to pull the door open unheard.

His back was to me, and I stood and watched as he opened each container and peered inside, then carefully closed it and put it back exactly where it had been before moving on to the next one. When he was two containers away from the rice, I closed the door and slipped back upstairs.

I'm sure my face was burning. Yet another lesson in prejudging people. I never spoke to him about it. It wasn't like I had the time or the ability to teach him to read. What I did do, instead of getting pissed off when he took a few extra minutes to find something, was start decorating the container labels with little pictures. And he picked up on the idea, although neither of us ever said a word. I would go down to the walk-in and find a couple of grains of uncooked rice on the container holding that night's pilaf, or a baby carrot on top of the cake holder containing the carrot cake. Nothing else was ever done or said, and he moved on sometime that winter. Too bad. He was a helluva dishwasher.

Higgins's 16-year-old brother, Bill, was easily bored and even more easily distracted. Containers placed on the edge of a certain counter were supposed to be automatically carried down to the walk-in by dishwashers whenever they were sent to the basement for something. This container of blanched broccoli had been sitting there for one-half hour. Bill made at least three trips to the walk-in in that time. Finally, I could not stand it any longer. I side-armed a cherry tomato at him.

"Bill," I said. "Label and date the freaking broccoli and get it into the walk-in. Do you think if you ignore it long enough it's going to grow feet and walk down by itself?"

Maybe an hour later I was down in the walk-in, checking inventory. There was a container of broccoli on the already prepped shelf. The label read:

7/2-BROCCOLI, COOKED (no feet).

"Broccoli no feet" became Bill's Indian name. People tried to outdo each other with creative labels for things. My personal favorite was Christopher's *FRENCH SILK PIE (dinner, dancing, maybe a movie?)*

Jim did the end-of-season dish shift the last year Higgins was with us. They were together by then. Neither of them would admit their relationship was anything serious; although, it was hard to ignore the fact that Jim practically lived in room four. The inn just wasn't that big.

When the wealthy man who owned the Avalon moved off-island, Jim's cooking job went with him, and Jim was at loose ends. He was also pretty broke after two years of school. We didn't have an end-of-season cooking job, as Higgins and I handled that between us, but we did need a dishwasher.

Jim spiced up our slow nights. He was a musician in addition to his many other artistic talents, and after he'd cleaned up the mess we'd made during the afternoon shift he'd experiment with placing pots on various surfaces in the dish room to get the best tonal quality.

With those, the stainless steel sink and the steel dishwasher, he could produce the effect of a full steel band in the dish room. When that ceased to amuse him, he began the extremely serious job of turning the dish room into an Elvis shrine, using found objects. Life in the kitchen was rarely boring that fall.

One of our hardest-working and best dishwashers was also a perfect example of one of the major problems of running an island business. He was a great guy when sober, but he drank. And when he drank, he drank a lot, and became rather belligerent. He never hurt anyone, but he would lose his temper and yell, and several times he punched holes in the thin staff housing walls.

Had I been running a restaurant on the mainland, this behavior would not have been my problem. In fact, I doubt I would ever even have known he drank, as he never missed a day of work, never showed up visibly hung over or even late for work. He was always cheerful and never complained about even the dirtiest jobs. But he was housed in the same building with ten teenaged girls, and they were afraid of him.

I had no choice but to let him go after they voiced their concerns to me. I called him in and asked him if he thought he could quit drinking. He replied that he didn't think so. I explained to him that I was very happy with his job performance, but I simply couldn't let him scare the young women.

I gave him a great reference and promised to bring him back in the fall when we had a more mature staff that would be better able to cope with his outbursts. He thanked me, and promised to patch the holes in the walls before he left, which he skillfully did. I brought him back in the fall, as promised, gave him his own room in the now half-empty staff housing, and asked him to confine his partying to the beach. He worked as hard that fall as he had in the beginning, and we parted ways on a good note.

Over the years I worked at or ran the Allen House, I would venture to guess we hired well over a hundred dishwashers. Those were just a few of the ones I remember.

French Silk Pie

9" chocolate pie crust
(ready made or make your own with 1 ½ cups crushed thin mint cookies, ¼ cup granulated sugar, 3 tablespoons melted butter. Mix all together and press into pie pan. Bake at 350 for 5 minutes.)

Filling:
3 ounces unsweetened chocolate
1 ¼ cups sugar
6 ounces softened butter
4 eggs
¼ teaspoon almond extract.

Melt chocolate in saucepan and let cool slightly but not until set. Add almond extract. In a separate bowl, cream butter and sugar until very light and fluffy, then add eggs, one at a time, into mixture, beating at medium speed 2 minutes after each egg. Make sure each egg is incorporated into the mixture before adding the next one so the mixture does not break. Fold in the cooled chocolate mixture, pour into pie crust and let set overnight in the refrigerator.

We had to stop making this when MA law banned the use of raw eggs in restaurant menu items. When you make it at home, just be sure you buy local eggs from a farmer's market or someone you know, and you will enjoy a classic dessert you can't get anywhere else.

Blueberry Cobbler

5 quarts frozen blueberries
½ cup sugar
¼ cup lemon juice
1 tablespoon cornstarch
4 cups white cake mix
2 cups water

Pour blueberries in a 2 inch deep hotel sized pan. Mix together sugar, lemon juice, and cornstarch. Add mixture to blueberries, mixing in well. In separate bowl, mix cake mix and water. Pour over blueberry mixture, spreading evenly. Bake at 350° for about one hour or until browned evenly.

When we began making the blueberry cobbler, a recipe I sort of re-invented from a cranberry cobbler recipe, we made our own topping. We often had problems with the topping being too thick or too thin. Finally, Higgins noticed that all we were really making was a white cake batter. We began to use a boxed white cake mix for the batter on top and never had another problem. This cobbler was one of the three signature desserts at the Allen House. I never understood why people liked it so much, but they insisted it always be on the dessert menu.

Chapter 43
Demented Desk Delights

The front desk person is the most important employee a house-guest meets. He or she can set the tone for an entire experience. This meant that, unlike most of the rest of our staff, they needed to be presentable at all times. They didn't have to balance a tray, do laundry, or learn how to stack a dishwasher, but they did have to look nice and act nicely.

Okay, so they had to unplug the occasional toilet, and Nina did assign them the tasks of cleaning the bathrooms and showers and laundry nightly. The hardest thing they had to do was smile and be pleasant, no matter how many times they were asked the same question or how many outraged dinner guests were tired of waiting for their tables. Personally, I'd wash dishes or do laundry any day.

I would say ninety percent of our desk people over the years were young, female, and cute. We had one woman in her thirties who worked two seasons for us on the desk and she was wonderful. She'd been an executive secretary, and was looking to change her life. But in general, we hired younger people because they were the ones applying. In general, we found the personalities of young women more suited to the desk than those of young men. Most young men, it seems, have shorter fuses.

I don't know why they were all cute. It just seemed to happen. And you can't even blame me for it. Nina hired them.

Front desk people answered the phone, took reservations, checked inn guests in and out, and sold T-shirts, souvenir items, and shower and laundry tokens. They rang up restaurant checks and made sure the public bathrooms were clean and working properly. They could get very, very busy and there were certain shifts when we needed two people behind the desk. But there are also slow times, when the front desk could be a very boring place. There were only so many T-shirts to refold, so much inventory to count, so many times a rug could be vacuumed. And they could never be more than a couple of steps away from the phone.

Some desk people read surreptitiously, their books held under the counter. Some learned to knit or crochet. One year, there was a staff newsletter created primarily at the front desk. Another year our van driver, a budding film student, created a staff video consisting primarily of front desk staff going wild, choking tourists who asked too many questions, and throwing them off a cliff. That same year, they developed a list of the most frequently asked annoying questions. I reproduce it for you here:

1. What's with the big fan on the island? (the windmill)
2. At which church is the AA meeting?
3. Where are the bathrooms? (While standing in front of the sign.)
4. What's wrong with the phone? (Everything.)
5. Is the liquor store still open?
6. What island are we on?
7. Could I get some glassware to go? Silverware?
8. Is there really an amusement park at the West End? (Yeah. Right next to the mall.)
9. How big are the lobsters?
10. And the perennial –What do you kids do for fun?

But in real life, the front desk people were some of our most well-behaved employees. One year, we did have those two that fought over the same island guy, and the one who had to be let go for teaching sex education to twelve-year-olds. And the one who only lasted three weeks before we found her wandering the front lawn in her nightgown. But something tells me she had problems before coming to the island.

Other than those few, Nina got pretty lucky.

I don't remember most of them well, as they were under Nina's purview, but one story still sticks with me.

Susan worked the front desk for three of those earliest years, when Steve was still running the place and Higgins and I were kitchen peons. She lived in the attic with Higgins and two other young women who waited tables. Susan had the bed directly over room three (often referred to by employees as the honeymoon suite), and she had a habit of filling us in at breakfast every time we had a couple of amorous houseguests. She felt that if she "wasn't getting any," as she so delicately put it, she should not be forced to listen to other people who were "getting some."

One hot August afternoon, she cracked. We had a couple in room three we'd barely seen since they checked in. They appeared briefly for occasional meals, but that was it. The housekeeper was told to "just leave the towels outside the door." I was, as usual, in the kitchen when it happened, but it wasn't long before the report reached me. Susan had placed her stereo speakers on the attic floor pretty much where she imagined the bed in room three to be, and then turned on Ravel's "Bolero" with the volume up high. Nothing happened immediately, but the staff did report seeing the couple outside their room a great deal more frequently after that.

"Bolero" has never been the same for me. I used to like that piece.

Privacy on Cuttyhunk was a rare and fleeting thing. The original illegal extension from the phone booth had been to Mildred's office. This tiny combination office/storage area was built into one of the inside dining room closets. It was so small that when I went in to talk to Nina, I had to stand behind her desk chair and talk over her shoulder as she worked.

Enna had sweet-talked the phone guy into running another illegal extension up to the front desk in order to be able to take reservations more easily. With this extension, however, came a new responsibility.

The moment the inn opened for the season, we were message central for the island. If you wanted to get in touch with anyone, you called the Allen House and left a message, which was then posted on a note board at the bottom of the ramp near the phone booth.

The upside was you were able to communicate with people off-island. The downside was everyone read the message board.

Most people read it daily, even when they were sure there was nothing for them, on the premise that you never knew when you might find out something interesting. There was a constant flow of foot traffic in and out of the porch door every morning. Not to eat, or buy something in the gift shop, or even just use the restrooms. Everyone came to read the board.

Some people stood there and scanned the messages as if looking for something with their name on it, then shrugged their shoulders elaborately and walked away. Others were more candid. They came to find out if there was any good gossip and they didn't care who knew it. I liked their style.

Chapter 44
Housekeepers Diablo

In the beginning were the girls, Peggy, Ann, and Jenny. During Steve's first years they not only waited tables but performed the duties of housecleaners as well. It had always been that way at the Allen House. You served breakfast, then went and made beds and cleaned toilets, came back and served lunch, finished the rooms and served dinner. It wasn't as bad as it sounds. The Allen House was essentially a boarding house, and the only meal open to the public was dinner. And considering that dinner was first-come, first-served and the menu invariably ran to fish and chips on Fridays and hot dogs and beans on Saturday, the load could be handled by the three young women.

I arrived for the end of Leon and Enna's second-year campaign to turn the Allen House from boarding house to fine dining establishment with attached charming inn, and that required a few more employees, preferably a staff that inn guests didn't see cleaning their toilet right before serving them lunch. I remember numerous attempts to find a full-time housekeeper. But I don't recall anyone lasting in the job. What I remember is Jan cleaning rooms, me cleaning rooms, Enna cleaning rooms, Jimmy cleaning rooms, Steve's sister, who also cooked one year, Steve's nieces . . .

By then I was busy learning to cook, and only came out of the kitchen when I was really needed elsewhere, like the annex on a Sunday when we had a complete turnover of guests and the whole building had to be cleaned and ready between eleven and three. I try to remember this when I want to check into a hotel room early and the desk person tells me my room won't be ready until the stated check-in time.

Yes, housekeepers. We had our share of bad ones, and a few that were priceless. The first year Nina and I ran the Allen House, we hired Cordelia, the girlfriend of a friend she'd met at the New Orleans World's Fair, to housekeep for us. The main thing I remember about her was sitting at a gift shop table listening to her complain how the guests treated her as if she wasn't there. "They see me when I bring them towels, they see me cleaning the bathrooms, and they look right through me," she complained.

Christopher was standing next to the table, and in his usual fashion he exclaimed, "Honey, don't you get it? You're the **maid!**"

Cordelia left soon afterwards, but that phrase lingered for years.

And there was the woman we hired through the New Bedford employment agency as end-of-season help after the college students had gone. She *loved* the island, she told us, she was going to rent a place and stay for the winter, and she would be available to us for the whole season the next year. She even arranged to put her son in the Cuttyhunk school. We were still green enough to take that statement on face value.

Then came Hurricane Bob. By then we'd learned what weather the Allen House was capable of withstanding, and we gave our employees the option of leaving or staying. We planned to stay and keep the Allen House open for houseguests and anyone in the harbor who needed a place to stay.

Our housekeeper was totally freaked by the idea of staying on-island during a hurricane, and insisted she would not put her son's life in danger, even though we told her she'd be safer on the island than on the mainland, at least based on our experience. She promised to return as soon as the hurricane passed, but, not surprisingly, we never saw her again.

Although we were short a housekeeper, several of the employees who shared an apartment with her were quite relieved, for she had a rather carrying voice and a tendency to wake everyone in the morning with an extremely loud cry of, "**How's my sweet baby boy? Wake up, sweet baby boy.**"

We had two young women one season who worked as a team, and that worked out well for everyone. They didn't mind getting half-pay each, and enjoyed the extra hours off. But we didn't really have enough housing to hire two people for one job so that was the only season we tried that approach. I think Nina would agree that the best housekeeper we ever had was a young woman from Smith College. She cleaned rooms in leotards, diaphanous skirts, and ballet slippers. She was extremely attractive and well spoken and probably earned more in tips than she did in salary that year. Of course I may be prejudiced, because she later became my lover for a short period. But I don't think so.

I traveled quite a bit in the mid-eighties, spending parts of most winters wandering around the United States. Everywhere I went, if I got decent service at a restaurant, I'd tuck a card under the tip with a note on the back saying *call me if you want a summer job.* We got a couple of calls but nothing ever came of this ruse, although we did anger the manager of my father's country club in Tennessee by stealing his best waitress for a season. I guess we ruined her, for she'd never been out of Tennessee before, and after a season with us decided that perhaps working at the country club for the rest of her life was not what she wanted to do. I'm not sure the manager ever forgave my father.

What I thought was my crowning achievement in hiring across country turned out to be a recipe for disaster, and spelled the end of my "Let's hire gay and lesbian people out of the blue just because we can" phase.

I was spending the winter in Santa Fe, New Mexico and met a lesbian couple who were not particularly happy in their present circumstances. I called Nina and told her I was going to hire this couple as housekeeper and van driver/jack of all trades.

Nina was a bit skeptical about me hiring for two such important positions on such a short acquaintance with these women, but I persevered and after a short argument, she gave in.

She should've argued longer. On Memorial Day weekend, the woman we'd hired as van driver/jack of all trades slid down the hill in front of my father's house and broke her leg. As they had given up their apartment in Santa Fe and moved north to work for us, we had no option but to keep them on and find someone else to do her job.

This meant another employee we had to house, and a housekeeper who spent more time taking care of her partner than actually cleaning the inn.

Nina was not amused. She was even less amused when a few days before Labor Day, the housekeeper announced that her work was simply not fulfilling and she was not happy. She and her partner (still on crutches and supported all summer by us) had decided that they would leave Labor Day weekend and not come back.

Once again, we were left scrambling for end-of-season help.

One thing that never failed to amaze us and our succession of housekeepers was the condition in which people left their rooms. It's true that the rooms were not furnished with antiques and fine linens, but we did our best to keep them bright, cheery, clean, and in good repair. Often that wasn't easy.

We got used to the array of stones and driftwood, even the occasional fishing net or lobster buoy guests left in rooms. It seemed people just couldn't resist picking up ten or fifteen pounds of beach stone and driftwood during their stay and decorating their windowsills and bureaus, only to decide these items were too heavy or bulky to take home. This happened so often that the staff began to refer to these collections as housekeeping tips.

And then there were the towels. People used our towels for everything from wiping off lipstick to cleaning muddy shoes and lubricating fishing rods. They took our towels to the beach, wiped chocolate off their kids; carried home stinking sea treasures in towels tied in knots. Then these same wet and dirty towels, along with soaked swimsuits, were tossed onto their beds.

After the first couple of years, we placed notes in every room, asking people not to misuse towels, to throw out any sea treasures they had collected but decided not to take home, and generally respect the rooms as we had only one housekeeper. We also tried having the housekeeper introduce herself to any houseguest she saw, on the theory that if you met the person who was cleaning your room, you were less likely to destroy it. These things helped a bit, but never a season went by that we didn't trash at least a hundred towels, and haul several hundred pounds of treasure back to the beach.

We had, it seems, at least a hundred housekeepers over the years. Some were better than others, but it was a difficult job at best, and I thank all of them for giving it a try.

Chapter 45
Chef's Choice

Cooks. It seemed as if I was *always* hiring cooks. Their turnover rate was worse than housekeepers, dishwashers, or waitstaff.

There's something about the people restaurant kitchens attract that's just a little bit scary. I feel I'm justified in saying this since I've been a cook/chef for thirty years. We are all a little crazy. You have to be. I don't have that much of a problem with my own craziness. I'm used to it. But some of the cooks I hired . . .

The first one who comes to everyone's mind when we talk about Allen House cooks is Manuel. Perhaps that's because he seemed so normal. In fact, he seemed to be dealing with the island quite well right up until the moment he went down to the walk-in for scallops and just kept going.

After ten minutes, it occurred to me that he'd been gone quite a long time, and I went down to the walk-in to look for him. There was no sign of Manuel. Not in the walk-in, the storeroom, not in his room upstairs in staff housing. I questioned the staff. No one had seen him, no one knew where he had gone.

Finally, the van driver, returning from a run to the ferry, told me he saw Manuel getting on the boat. I called down to the Ray, the ferry captain, on the ship-to-shore radio and asked if Manuel was there. He checked, and reported that Manuel was indeed on the boat, in his kitchen whites, with no luggage. Ray asked me if I'd like to speak to Manuel. "Not particularly," I said "Just ask him if he's planning on coming back."

Ray reported back that Manuel said to tell me he *would* be coming back, he was just tired, and needed to go off for a couple of days.

The boat was sailing any minute, and with Manuel gone we were shorthanded in the kitchen. I couldn't afford the time to go down there and interrogate him myself, and conversations over ship-to-shore radio are notoriously difficult.

We called New Bedford and found someone to meet him when the ferry docked and see if they could find out what was going on. Manuel repeated the same line to them. He was tired, he was stressed, and he needed a few days off. Of course he was coming back; he'd left all his stuff.

We believed him because we wanted to, and because he'd seemed so together. Yet, in keeping with a long line of past Allen House employees, he wrote a week later and asked us to put his things on the boat.

Then there were the breakfast Bobs. The first one couldn't seem to handle being a breakfast and lunch cook. Higgins made an unfortunate comment to him, something along the lines of, "It's not like it's important, Bob, you're just scrambling eggs."

Bob got more and more depressed as the days went by, and any time he was asked a question or for an opinion he would reply, "Don't ask me, I'm just here to scramble eggs."

No matter how hard we tried to explain to him that was not what Higgins had meant, it didn't seem to sink in. After another month of muttered "I'm just here to scramble eggs," he was gone. His replacement, oddly enough, also was named Bob and so was the replacement after that. Higgins gave up. "I'm just going to call them all Bob," she said. "The breakfast Bobs."

The name stuck. Perhaps it wasn't the best thing for these guy's egos, (and at least they were all guys) to be told the moment they stepped into the kitchen that their name was now Bob. But when you worked with Higgins and me, you had to have a sense of humor or you just wouldn't last. Being called Bob was a litmus test.

The breakfast Bobs continued, one after another, for two years. It is exceptionally hard to find a single person (we had no real housing for married couples) skilled in cooking breakfast and lunch who isn't just a bit too odd to be housed in the same structure safely with a bunch of teenage girls. I don't mean to offend any breakfast or lunch cooks out there, but when we were hiring it was hard to find one who was willing to come and spend the summer on the island who didn't have either a criminal record or some sort of oddity. Basically it seemed to boil down to, if they were willing to come, generally we didn't really want them to. Higgins was gone by the time we found Tex. Too bad. They would have gotten along famously.

Tex was a big, tall, good old boy who'd come to New England from Texas looking for a change. His résumé showed work at a tire store, as an odd-job man, and automotive store clerk. Tex was applying for the van driver position.

Nina and I liked the guy, but we weren't sure we wanted him to be the first Allen House representative most houseguests met on the island.

We asked him if he knew any other way he could be useful to us. He didn't want to wash dishes, and I couldn't blame him, as our other dishwashers were sixteen and seventeen year old boys and Tex had to be thirty.

Finally, he mentioned that he'd worked for a little while in a Waffle House. Nina jumped on that.

"Doing what?" she asked.

"Just flippin' eggs," he said dismissively.

"Did you work anyplace else flipping eggs?" I asked.

"A couple of places," Tex answered.

"Why didn't you tell us? We're dying for a breakfast/lunch cook."

"Aw," Tex drawled. "I don't want to cook, I don't much like it."

"Come on, Tex," I said. "We really need a breakfast/lunch cook. And that's the only position we really have for you."

"Well," he answered. "If that's all you got, I guess I'll take it."

Tex stayed with us for three years. He wasn't as fast as I would've liked; he seemed to have one steady pace that never varied. But he showed up, he was always on time, and he did his job competently. That made him worth his weight in gold.

I hired Mary Beth as a prep cook our first season and she stayed with the Allen House until our personal relationship broke up. We weren't a perfect match in the first place. And I have to interject that I never consciously chose to date an employee, at least not while they were still working for me. But Mary Beth fell in love with me, and made it clear she wasn't going to take no for an answer. I finally gave in when she stayed up all night cleaning the kitchen after one of our broiler fires so that I would not have to deal with the mess first thing in the morning.

Anybody who would do that was worth chancing a relationship with. Mary Beth made the best osso bucco I've ever had, and came up with a stuffed striped bass recipe that was a hit with everyone on the island. It was a great loss to the kitchen when she left. Before she went though, she gave us one of the best presents we'd ever get. She brought her friend, Sara, up from Florida to help out for the end of the season.

Sara was a gem. I made her work the fryer until the end of the season, which she did almost graciously. I told Sara I'd give her anything I could if she would come back the next year. She said she never wanted to work the fryer again, and would I please let her bake as well? Sara really wanted to be a pastry chef. She'd met Mary Beth at Johnson and Wales, where she fell in love with baking.

Sara stayed with us for three years, only leaving when she was offered a position teaching baking and pastry skills at New England Culinary Institute. They sent us a chef and a sous chef in return, but they got, by far, the best of that bargain. Sara cooked special meals for my mother whenever she visited the island. Although my mother invariably sent at least one portion of her meal back to the kitchen when I was cooking, Mom never complained about Sara's food. And Sara worked through eight different versions of a German chocolate cake recipe to try and duplicate the taste I remembered from my childhood birthday cakes. Sara never got mad, and she never complained. She was amazing.

After the first couple of years, Nina and I gave up on placing ads in newspapers for cooks, and went directly to the sources. We placed ads on the bulletin boards of Johnson and Wales Institute, Culinary Institute of America, and New England Culinary Institute. We had graduates from all three places, all with varying skill levels. In the end, we discovered that it wasn't the school that made the cook, it was who the person was before he or she went in.

There was one year we seemed to have nothing but trouble with cooks. Tex had moved on, and we were once again searching for someone to cook breakfast and lunch. That awful year, we had our first problem with thefts. Money and beer were disappearing from staff housing. I realized that for the first time in the history of the Allen House, we were going to have to put locks on doors. I was devastated. The doors in the main house and the annex didn't even have locks, their keyholes long since drowned in paint and the keys missing for who knows how many years. I put locks on the staff housing doors, but I knew that was just a temporary fix. I had to find the thief before he or she moved on to stealing from the guests. Cuttyhunk, and by association, the Allen House, had a reputation for being a place so safe you could leave your wallet in the middle of the road and all that would happen is that someone would move it to the side so it wouldn't get run over.

Finding the thief took a while. I was looking for a drunk because large amounts of alcohol had been stolen, and beer was continuing to disappear from the walk-in, which had to be left unlocked during the workday.

In the end, it turned out to be a cook with a cocaine habit. He was using the stolen money to buy drugs, and alcohol to smooth himself out, which is why I hadn't noticed any excessive drinking. We caught him when he paid for something at the register with a twenty-dollar bill. The desk clerk recognized the bill as one stolen from her room. She had pinned it up on her bulletin board because it had something written on it, and she wasn't sure she wanted to spend it.

The cook broke down and confessed, we put him on the next boat, and the thefts stopped. With a sigh of relief, I unscrewed the locks from the staff housing doors.

The last breakfast/lunch cook I personally worked with was Dick. He was older than previous breakfast/lunch cooks. He'd been in the Navy and was married but seemed to have no problem leaving his wife for six months and just visiting her on his time off. We never could understand what a guy like Dick saw in the island, or why he wanted to work for us, live in staff housing, and flip eggs. But he did, and we loved him for it. He was extremely easy-going, with a great dry wit. He stayed with us even after I left the kitchen to work the front of house with Nina, taking the transitions that followed in stride.

Margo's German Chocolate Birthday Cake
that Sara Perfected

½ cup + 3 tablespoons Cocoa
1 cup boiling water
3 large eggs
2 ¼ teaspoons vanilla
2 ¼ cups sifted cake flour
1 ½ cups sugar
1 tablespoon baking powder
¾ teaspoon salt
1 cup softened sweet butter

Mix cocoa and water, add 1/3 mixture to eggs and vanilla. Beat together. Sift dry ingredients into mixing bowl and whisk together on low. Add rest of cocoa mixture. Add butter, whip 1 ½ minutes. Add egg mixture in three stages on medium speed. Pour into 2-9" round pans. Bake 25–35 minutes at 350.

Cool and slice each layer into 3 pieces.

Icing for 6 layer cake

1 cup butter
2 2/3 cups heavy cream
1 cup brown sugar
16 egg yolks
3 cups toasted coconut
3 cups chopped pecans
1/3 cup corn syrup

Melt butter, cream and sugar together over low heat. Temper egg yolks into butter mixture, cook, stirring constantly over low heat until thick. Add rest of ingredients into mixture and let cool.

It is easier to ice the thin cake layers if you freeze them first.

Thank you, Sara.

Chapter 46
Waiting for Summer

Our waitstaff was a problem category all its own. Nina usually hired them, and when they were in the dining room, they were her responsibility. But when they were in the kitchen, they became mine.

Nina trained them to wait tables; I trained them to communicate information. Preferably to me. This doesn't mean I wasn't interested in how they behaved in the dining room. If the customer didn't like the waitstaff, the customer generally didn't like the meal. And above all, we wanted the customers happy.

In the early days of the Allen House, it was much simpler to keep control. The menu was smaller and so was the waitstaff. Peggy, Ann, and Jenny waited tables for us for three years during the main season. Liz came on for the last year they were there. Around them, first spring and fall, and later throughout the season, were Barb and Keith, Jonathan, and Kathy, Becky's older sister. But I remember the island girls.

There was, of course, Peggy's famous baked stuffed lobster story. And shy Jenny, who one night had to wait on a large table of fishermen. Everyone fought not to take those tables. Fishermen might tip well, but they were often real pains in the ass. Sometimes literally, as a couple of them had trouble keeping their hands to themselves.

Jenny approached this table with mild trepidation. Putting on her best attitude, she smiled sweetly and said, "Hello, my name is Jenny. I'll be your waitress tonight." She recited the two specials for the night, took drink orders, and as she was leaving, she said, "Remember if you need me for anything tonight, just call me. My name is Jenny."

She got perhaps four steps from the table when one of the men called out, "Yo, sweetheart. Come here."

Jenny came into the kitchen so angry she was practically in tears.

"I told them my name," she said. "I told them my name at the beginning, and I told them my name again right when I left. What part of Jenny sounds like yo, sweetheart?"

I tried to assure her that they were oafs and Neanderthals and not worthy of her anger. Privately, I was burning, too. If I could've gone out and given them a lecture on feminism—hell, even a lecture on manners—I would've done it. It drove me crazy that all I could do was tell a waitress to ignore it.

And then there was Liz. Liz once asked Nina if she could please not be scheduled for any lunch shifts. She was willing to take breakfast shifts instead, which everyone hated because they didn't make any money. Surprised, Nina asked Liz why she didn't want to work lunch.

"Oh," Liz replied, "between ten and two are the peak tanning hours. I hate to miss them."

One night Liz had a huge table of fishermen in the inside dining room. Twelve of them in all, grouped around our largest table. Liz actually liked large groups of fishermen and was willing to put up with a great deal for a big tip.

Most of the fishermen ordered lobster, and as Liz was carrying an over-laden tray from the kitchen, the balance shifted just enough that two of the boiled lobsters slid off their plates onto the floor. Without missing a beat, Liz set the tray down on an empty table, snatched up the two lobsters, and put them back on their plates. She turned and smiled sweetly at the table of fishermen.

"Isn't it a good thing those bad boys come in shells?" she asked.

Liz proceeded to unload the tray, smiling and making small talk with each of the fishermen as she placed his plate in front of him. Their eyes were on Liz and no one noticed who got which lobster. And no one complained.

Christopher could take up an entire chapter on waiting tables by himself. Along with his famous collection of bowling shirts (for which he made up a different personality according to the name embroidered on the front), he had somewhere acquired a pen that attached to a large rhinestone pin. The pen pulled out from and slid back into the pin, sort of like a tape measure. Christopher called it his Flo pen, after the waitress in "Alice Doesn't Live Here Anymore."

Whenever he wore the pen, he tried to imitate a 1950s diner waitress. Being well over six feet tall with bright red hair and a beard, this was not an easy order to pull off. But Christopher put his heart into it, like he did everything else.

The Coast Guard trained its new recruits in Connecticut, and part of the training was to have them sail a boat up the coast with stops in various harbors. Cuttyhunk was part of a rotation of harbors and they generally docked there every three or four years. That is, until Nina and I took over the Allen House.

The first year we ran the Allen House was a year that the Coast Guard docked in Cuttyhunk Harbor. Several of the young recruits came up to the restaurant for burgers, and word quickly spread that on this tiny island were a number of young, attractive women. Moreover, these women seemed to be impressed by the Coast Guard recruits who were mostly male in those days. After that first summer, somehow the Coast Guard schedule was re-written, and Cuttyhunk became a permanent stop every year.

I found it embarrassing. Nina found it amusing. The rest of the island agreed with Nina. The moment that sailboat entered the harbor, even before it hit the dock, word flew around the island in that odd, almost eerie way places without telephones seem to disseminate information, and someone would walk into the Allen House and say with a grin, "The Coasties are here."

I argued that it didn't become us for our staff to be known as *those girls who went out with the Coast Guard*, and that we should nip the problem in the bud before it got serious. Nina told me I was being a puritan and a hard ass and to get over it. I later found out that she had gone out with the Coast Guard captain several times. The only one who seemed to agree with me was our dishwasher, Joey. Nina came upon him sitting glumly on the staff housing steps the second time the Coast Guard was in the harbor. She asked him why he was so down.

"Goddamn Coast Guard," he replied, "comin' in here, stealin' all our women."

The Coasties continued to come to the island every year until we sold the Allen House. Then their schedule mysteriously changed again and now they are back on their old rotation.

With our kitchen expansion and the new staff housing, we got busier. And busier meant more waitstaff for me to keep an eye on. One year, it became apparent even to me that leggings were the new fashion rave. I hated them. I thought they looked like the woman had forgotten to put a skirt on and was walking around in tights.

We didn't have much of a dress code for our waitstaff. It was, after all, a casual island. But we wanted our staff to dress one step up from the customers at all times. We believed it garnered them more respect.

So we had certain no's. No torn or cut-off jeans, no sleeveless shirts, no shorts or jeans at all at dinner. On weekends the waitstaff wore black and white. Preferably black on the bottom and white on top, although we allowed the occasional innovation. I put up with a lot of argument from the staff about what did and did not conform to the dress code. I was much more of a stickler than Nina.

One Friday night, Kim came down from staff housing wearing leggings and a slightly oversized shirt belted around the waist. I happened to see her stand up after staff dinner, well before the customers began to arrive. I walked over to her. The staff dining table got quiet as they waited to see what was going on.

"I believe you forgot something," I said to Kim. "Your skirt."

Kim tried, she really did. "This is the fashion, Margo," she said. "Look in any of the magazines. Everyone is wearing leggings."

"That's very nice, Kim," I said. "It's very nice that you're in fashion. I'm surprised. I never really thought of you as a trendsetter."

A soft chatter started up again at the staff table. Obviously, nothing was going to happen.

"But," I continued, "*I'm* really not much of a trendsetter. And it's my say over yours as to what is worn in the dining room. That shirt barely covers your ass. Go upstairs and put something else on."

Kim started to say something. I cut her off.

"Look," I said. "This is not a democracy. It really doesn't matter what you think. I want you to put on some more clothes. So you will put on some more clothes."

Kim stood there for a moment, frustrated. I gave her "the look" and she sighed and went upstairs to change.

For a while there, we employed the Frame family. Seemingly all of them.

Maura came to us first. She was an amazing waitress. She could handle twice as many tables as anyone we'd ever hired without blinking an eye.

The next year, we employed her sister, Kate, as well, and that's when we found out how good Maura really was.

Kate was the exact opposite of Maura. She was as spacey and easily distracted as Maura was focused and right there in the moment.

And Kate had this amazing habit of walking out the kitchen door and disappearing. Literally. Time after time that summer, we would watch Kate walk out the kitchen door. I would walk out that door a moment behind her and find she had vanished. She wasn't in the dining room, she wasn't in the gift shop, she wasn't in the salad pantry and no one had seen her. Her food would come up, and Maura would grab it and take it out to Kate's table. A few moments later Kate would reappear.

When I asked her where she'd been, she would look at me as if I were crazy and say, "In the dining room, of course."

I could swear she hadn't been. A number of times that summer, I asked Kate where she went when she disappeared. I would explain to her that I had come out the door a moment after her and that she was nowhere to be found. She insisted she had no idea what I was talking about.

But I knew Maura was handling at least half Kate's tables as well as her own. Maura said she didn't mind, she had plenty of time. And as her work never suffered, I just let it go. But the next year, instead of hiring Kate, I hired the youngest Frame sister, Anne.

I hear Kate became a lawyer. I wonder if she still disappears.

I made up a lot of dessert recipes while on the island. Or rather, I took old recipes and tinkered with them, trying to make them more interesting. Of course, then I'd have to re-name them. I've never been creative when it comes to naming dishes. I usually just use the first three or four non-standard ingredients. The waitstaff hated this, because the names tended to be long and hard to remember. Their object of least affection was the bittersweet chocolate bourbon cake. They claimed it was impossible to say while naming the list of desserts. I told them I really didn't care what they called it, they could call it Fred if they wanted, as long as the customer knew what he was getting.

Christopher had to be different, so he decided he hated the chocolate chip pumpkin walnut cake. In the kitchen he called it the chocolate chip horseshit cake. I don't know what he called it in the dining room. But he sold a ton of it.

Chocolate Chip Pumpkin Walnut Cake

2 cups flour,
 2 teaspoons baking powder
One half teaspoon salt.
1 1/2 teaspoon cinnamon
one quarter teaspoon ginger
 2 cups sugar
4 eggs
1 pound pumpkin
1 cup oil
2 cups All Bran cereal
6 ounces chocolate chips
1 cup chopped walnuts

Stir together dry ingredients. In large bowl, beat eggs until foamy. Add pumpkin, oil, and cereal. Add rest of dry ingredients and mix only until combined. Stir in nuts and chocolate. Spread into greased bundt pan. Bake at 350° one hour and 10 minutes.

Turn out onto rack and dust with powdered sugar when cool.

Chocolate Bittersweet Bourbon Cake

5 ounces bittersweet chocolate.
One half pound butter.
1 3/4 cups coffee.
One fourth cup bourbon.
2 cups sugar.
Two eggs.
2 cups flour.
1 teaspoon baking soda.
One half teaspoon salt.
One quarter cup cocoa.

Melt together, chocolate, butter, coffee, and bourbon. Cool slightly, and pour into good-sized bowl. Beat in sugar. Let cool completely. Beat in eggs. Sift flour, soda and salt together. Beat well into the chocolate mixture. Pour into a greased and cocoa'd bunt pan. Bake at 375° for 10 minutes. Turn oven down to 275° and bake for one hour. Let cool 15 minutes. Turn onto rack and let cool completely. Can be glazed or dusted with powdered sugar to finish.

Section VIII.

Stormy Weather

Cuttyhunk Winter

Chapter 47
I Will Survive

It was the beginning of October, 1985. We were gearing up for the last two weeks of our first season as managers, our staff pared down to bare minimum, the inn rooms booked mainly with fishermen. The weather had been very accommodating that fall, and we hoped to end our first season as managers with a bang, going out with a strong and profitable Columbus Day weekend.

Ha.

We got a fair amount of warning, as hurricanes go. The first reports came in three days ahead of the storm, warning there was a good chance that Hurricane Gloria would run up the East Coast without veering off to sea or making landfall farther south. Old-timers such as Hunter and Roland advised us on how much plywood to order from the mainland, which windows to board and which to tape, what needed to be brought inside or tied down.

Nina got on the phone and cancelled any reservations that hadn't already called to cancel. And we insisted any guests that had already arrived leave. I was surprised how many didn't want to go. But we were worried about liability and wouldn't back down.

Higgins and Christopher were pretty much it as far as staff went. Our housekeeper from New Bedford left at the first storm warning and never returned. My ex-girlfriend, Annie, was still around working at the store and helping us out some, although we were no longer together. Everyone wanted to stay, and as we needed the help closing down, we didn't argue.

We filled the cellar with lawn chairs and picnic tables, turned off and lashed down propane tanks. We nailed boards over screen doors to keep them from blowing off, boarded up the porch windows facing the ocean, parked the van in the narrow space between staff housing and the kitchen, tied down the bulkheads, and waited.

Gloria came in right on schedule. Nina and the rest of the staff went to George Isabel's rear-facing, ground-floor apartment for a hurricane party.

Not me. I spent the storm on my bed in room two, alternately staring at the pages of a science fiction novel about humanoid elephants and going to the windows to look out. Somehow I believed that by staying sober and staying in the Allen House, I could prevent any major damage. When the eye of the storm came and the rain slackened, I put on a slicker and went outside. There was storm debris all over the front lawn, tree branches as thick as my arm tossed around like sticks.

I could see the ocean washing up over the lower road. The beach on that side was completely under water. A cursory look around showed no real damage to the inn so far. I was headed across the street to George's to see what was happening there when the wind picked up again. I saw a couple of four-wheelers head down the street and decided whatever they were doing, I'd rather not know about it. I went back to the Allen House to resume my vigil.

After the storm, I found out George had thrown quite a party. The traffic I'd seen heading downhill was a drunken foray first to the dock to "check" the boats, then to the top of the hill, where people took turns trying to stand up while other people held onto their legs to keep the wind from tossing them over.

After that, the party continued until pretty much everyone had passed out. Higgins confessed she passed out so early she missed the hurricane entirely.

I, of course, had single-handedly held the Allen House together by sheer force of will.

Aside from a number of missing roof shingles (and I was getting pretty expert at replacing those), our casualties were limited to a screen door on Horseplay and a soaked porch runner from water driven in through the leaky porch windows.

Everyone on the island got off lightly, partly because anything big that could have blown down had already done so over the years, but mostly because the islanders were pros at this sort of thing. They knew how to tie down and board up, what to move to higher ground, and the best way to position a boat in the harbor.

We lost one boat that storm—a sailor on his way to Nantucket who had tied up to a piling in the harbor and ridden out the storm in the Town Hall, as I found out many had done over the years when a hurricane caught them unawares. A small shack had been moved off a private pier and placed up at four corners crossroads, and by the next morning, courtesy of Higgins and Christopher, it lay atop a pair of stuffed black-and white striped stockings and red, high-heeled "ruby" slippers.

We had survived Gloria. Now what?

We had a kitchen stuffed with food for the expected busy weekend. We had freezers full of fish and meat, cases of lettuce, peppers, and mushrooms, bags of onions and potatoes. We had sent away all of our houseguests, and reports on the radio spoke of carnage in the mainland harbors, boats tossed and broken like matchsticks. There would be no more traffic that year.

In fact, Cuttyhunk Island seemed to have survived the hurricane better than just about anywhere else in a hundred-mile radius up and down the coast. In New Bedford, boats were smashed against bridges, driven up onto shore, or sunk. Power was out all along the coast, and not expected to come back on for three to five days. My mother in Rhode Island did not have power. Martha's Vineyard did not have power. Several docks had been crushed there, and a number of boats lost.

We had power. We even had a functioning restaurant. What we didn't have were customers, or the hope of any before our food spoiled. The four of us put our heads together and brainstormed.

The next morning signs appeared down at the dock, at the general store, and at the post office.

FRY FOR ALL

Below the headline we gave the time, five p.m., the date, which was the next day, and the place, the Allen House front lawn.

This was our grand scheme: Cuttyhunkers loved fried food, so we would fry everything in the reach-in and walk-in. Nina and I could take the frozen meat and fish to our apartment and use them all winter. We would batter every vegetable that could conceivably be fried, and turn the rest into coleslaw and salad; cut the leftover desserts into small slices and put them out on paper plates; set up an ice cream bar with the leftover gallons of ice cream. We would prepare a blow-out unlike anything the island had ever seen. Nina and I decided to charge $8.00 for adults and $4.00 for children over six. We might make back at least some of our loss, but most importantly, the food would not go to waste.

We had our plan. Now all we had to do was put it in motion, and pray that someone would show up.

Higgins and I cut up sword and cod into chunks, sole into strips. We cut onions into rings, potatoes into fries, peppers into slices, and zucchini into cubes. We shredded cabbage and carrots for coleslaw.

Christopher made huge bowls of salad, and he and Nina worked out the logistics of how and where everything would go: the cold food, the ice cream bar and desserts, plates and cups and bowls for the leftover clam chowder. They charted the easiest course between the fryers in the kitchen and the tables on the front lawn. Annie came over and helped Christopher clear the debris and branches from the sidewalk and lawn.

By the next afternoon, we were as ready as we were going to be. We had dragged long tables outside, pushed them together, and draped them with our signature blue table cloths. We pulled a number of chairs out and placed them under the trees for the elderly. Everyone else, we figured, could stand, or sit on the newly cleaned lawn. Higgins and I laid the different food out around the fryers in a semi-circle, deciding which foods would go in the wet fish fry batter, which foods would go into the dry, crunchy, scallop batter, and which foods would do best in the dry, fluffy clam batter. We had egg wash, flour, and large bowls of batter at the ready. Christopher and Nina set out pitchers of iced water and tea on the tables, and weighted the paper goods down with beach stones.

By four-thirty a few Islanders were straggling in. Nina sat outside at the head of the table with a cashbox on her lap. By four forty-five there were probably twenty people milling around, drinking iced tea, and waiting. Nina sent Christopher in to tell us to start frying. Then he brought out the salads and the coleslaw. Within ten minutes we had baskets of food ready to go, and, it seemed, the entire island on our front lawn.

Higgins and I were fry-maniacs. The second that one basket came out of the fryer, another went down. We fried clams and cod and sole; zucchini, mushrooms, potatoes. We fried our own handmade onion rings. We even fried swordfish, a first for me.

Christopher never stopped running for a solid hour, hauling full baskets out to the waiting customers and bringing empty ones back. He would shout out to us, "More cod, more clams, more onion rings, hold off on the french fries for now." He was so busy it was left to Nina to bring out the desserts and set up the ice cream bar. But that was okay, because after fifteen minutes she could abandon her cashbox. Everyone still on-island was on our front lawn.

People ate damn near everything in the house. What they didn't eat, if we'd already cooked it or prepared it, we made them take home.

At the end of an hour, Higgins and I were covered in grease and three types of batter. The kitchen around the fryers looked like a battlefield. But we had done it. The reach-in was empty, and the walk-in held a few lonely buckets of vegetables. And what was even more important, the islanders were pleased. Really, really pleased. Higgins and I, of course, saw nothing but the inside of the fryers. But Nina was happy to relate how she had seen people on the same lawn that she had not ever seen together. Everyone was there, everyone was eating, and everyone was talking and laughing. And we had made this happen.

(A footnote: When we were looking at pictures taken that day, we spotted Mark, Nina's future husband, at the edge of a crowd. It would be another year and a half before they would actually meet.)

Beer Batter

Full recipe that will get you through a Friday night fish fry.

10 cups all-purpose flour
1 cup baking powder
¼ cup Tony Chacheré's salt-free seasoning
10 eggs
Four cans cheap beer
Water

Mix together flour, baking powder, Tony's seasoning. Add beaten eggs and beer. Add water, stirring, until you achieve proper consistency. Proper consistency is when the batter sticks to the fish without peeling off when the fish hits the hot oil.

Chapter 48
Just Call Them All Bob

By the time Hurricane Bob came along in August of '91, Nina and I felt we were old hands at nasty weather. We'd had several close hurricanes, and some nor'easters during winter months that were as bad as any hurricane to hit the island while we were there. Through them all, the Allen House stood like a rock, losing a few roof shingles here and there and the occasional cracked window, but that was it.

Even our mother had stopped worrying about us "all alone" out on the island, as her hometown of Providence usually got hit a lot worse than we did. Our electric lines ran underground; our phone cable ran underwater to the mainland but storms didn't seem to affect it in the least. The cable usually went down once a summer in good weather for no reason at all. Our harbor was designated a Coast Guard-approved harbor of refuge, and everyone on the island who had a boat knew how to tie it up to properly ride out a storm.

On Cuttyhunk, most any tree that was going to go down already had. We'd lose a big one or two in a really wet storm, and that was always a shame. But anything that was going to blow away pretty much had, over the years.

This time the forecast was for a big one, and it looked like it was going to hit us straight on. We no longer automatically sent staff off-island during storms. For one thing, the island had proved a pretty safe place to be. For another, most of them had no place close to go, and if they went home chances were they wouldn't return. Hurricane Bob came in August, and we were determined not to lose the rest of the season's business. Not this time. Many local boaters would pull their boats for safety, we knew, but we hoped this early in the season, they'd put them back in the water after the storm had passed. We really hoped that.

We didn't have as much lead time with Bob as we'd had with Gloria, so after we'd carried all the porch furniture into the annex basement, and tied down the gas tanks, and moved the van and the scooter into the shelter of the nook between the kitchen and the L of the house, I had two people board up the front windows and sent the rest of the staff around the island to help other people get ready.

We carried stuff from the houses closest to the water up the hill and stored it in garages, outbuildings, and people's basements. Hurricanes were one time when everyone pulled together, differences put aside for the moment. Billy even agreed to let his competitor store his propane bottles on Billy's concrete pad at the top of the hill, out of danger.

In previous storms boaters caught on-island had sheltered at the Town Hall, which wasn't the most comfortable place to be with its hard wooden chairs and bad ventilation. It could get damn hot and stuffy when you packed a lot of bodies in there, as we knew from countless town meetings.

This time we had given our houseguests the choice of staying or leaving, and most of them chose to stay. Our staff decided to make over the gift shop area into the waiting-out-the-storm room, as it had easy access to the bathrooms, a large open space once the racks and shelves of gifts had been moved back against the wall, and most importantly, a gate you could close at the top of the ramp, thereby containing everyone in a single space. No need to worry about people wandering around and possibly getting hurt. Some smart staffer thought to bring down the TV and VCR from staff housing, and we borrowed a selection of Disney videos. We made pitchers of iced tea and lemonade, and piles of tuna and peanut butter sandwiches. As word spread, more and more stranded boaters showed up, especially the ones with kids, until finally we had to set a limit on the number of people we could handle. At the height of the storm, I believe we had sixty.

We didn't have TV reception up in the gift shop. I doubt we had it in the TV lounge, but we had a weather radio on, and it sounded like the coast was getting hit pretty hard. Nina and I fielded several calls from anxious mothers of staff members who needed to be reassured their son or daughter truly was all right.

I was making the rounds, checking for leaks or problems, and just happened to be in the gift shop when the phone rang. The young woman manning the desk picked up, assuming it was yet another worried friend or relative. It was The Weather Channel®.

The actual Weather Channel of cable TV fame. Someone's mother had called them, concerned that there was nothing on the news about Cuttyhunk, and on a whim, some anchor decided to try and call the island and see what was going on. I guess they thought it would make a good color fill-in, something to break up the shots of men and women in raincoats standing on coastlines and saying, "Yup, it's pretty wet and windy out, Jim."

There was no separate section for the six Cuttyhunk phones in the phone book then, but the Allen House was the first one listed if you called directory assistance. I assume that's how they got hold of us.

"This is The Weather Channel," a voice said.

"Yeah, right," our desk person replied, assuming someone was making a prank call.

"No, it really is," the voice said. "How are things there on the island?"

"I'll get the manager," she said and called out for me immediately.

I picked up the phone. "Yes?"

"This is The Weather Channel," he repeated. "How are things out there?"

"Well, let's look out the window," I said. "The rain's blowing sideways and the building is rocking. About usual for a hurricane, I'd say."

"How hard is the wind blowing?" the voice asked.

"Well, to know that I'd have to go outside and measure it," I replied, "and you see, we're in the middle of a hurricane, so I'd rather not do that."

The man laughed. "If I call you back in ten minutes, would you like to go live on The Weather Channel and tell us what it's like out there?"

"Sure," I said. "That will give me time to call my sister down south and have her tape it. Just hope the phone cable doesn't break between now and then."

Word spread quickly around the room that we were going to be semi-famous for about three minutes, and people crowded around the gift shop counter, waiting for the phone to ring again.

Almost exactly ten minutes later it did.

I am sure the weatherman, or assistant producer, or whoever he was introduced himself at some point, but all I remember is the voice, so that's how I've always thought of him.

"Still there?" he asked when I picked up the phone.

"Yep," I answered.

"Now, I am going to ask you some questions, and you answer them, then I will tell you we are going live and I'll ask the same questions. Answer them anyway you please, but remember we are on national TV."

"So if I want to swear, do it now, huh?"

He laughed.

After a short rehearsal, he said, "Ok, ready to go live?"

"Ready."

I held the receiver away from my ear so that several people could hear the exchange.

"We are live on the line with Cuttyhunk Island, a small island in the heart of the hurricane. If you look on the map, you will see it circled."

I wished we could look on the map.

"I'm speaking with the owner of the Allen House, an inn and restaurant on the island. What's going on there? How bad is it?"

"Well, let's see," I answered. "We've got about sixty people here in the gift shop, which has the smallest area of window space and so was the easiest to board up. We have staff, houseguests, and some people who were on boats in the harbor. The kids are watching a Disney video; we have iced tea and lemonade and sandwiches, and some board games. We've got a hand-held ship-to-shore to keep in touch with the rest of the island. All told, it's not so bad."

"How hard is the wind blowing?"

I repeated my earlier statement and he laughed dutifully.

"Aren't you afraid, being on a tiny island so far out to sea?" he asked.

I gave him my Cuttyhunk spiel, how an island so isolated learns to take care of its own, how the power lines were underground and we didn't build anything that couldn't withstand a storm like this one. "We're better off here than the mainland," I ended. "Wait and see. I bet you fifty bucks we'll open for dinner."

The voice laughed again and said something like, "Well, that's it from Cuttyhunk Island, where they seem to be doing just fine."

Then he went off air and thanked me.

"No problem," I said. "You kind of livened things up around here for a minute."

The eye of the storm passed overhead about a half an hour later, and several of us went outside to check the damage. It seemed minimal, and we hurried back inside as the wind picked up again. The south end of the storm was mercifully shorter, and by four p.m. we were out pulling plywood off the windows and mopping up water.

And yes, we opened for dinner that night. A limited menu, as we had almost no prep time. But by god we were open.

Peanut Butter Sandwiches for a Hurricane

40 slices of bread
5 pound tub cheap peanut butter
1 economy size jar raspberry jam

Take whatever sandwich bread you have, and spread forty slices with the peanut butter you keep for satay sauces. Spread another forty slices with the raspberry jam you use to fill the middle of birthday cakes. (hey, it beats opening 50 or so jelly packets.)
Put slices of bread together and cut on diagonal.

You already have the tuna dressing recipe.

Chapter 49
Practically Perfect in Every Way

Storms in winter are often worse than named hurricanes. In fact, a nor'easter is basically just a hurricane in winter, except it comes in faster and more unexpectedly. Nor'easters (named for the direction the come from) can change the entire shape of an island, move sand from one beach to another, fill or clear out a channel leading into the harbor.

There was a hurricane in the fifties that almost destroyed the spit of land going out toward Mel Dorr's house. Mel owns a roundish chunk of land at the tip of a peninsula that is actually one side of the channel. That problem had been solved by buying old wooden barges, filling them with sand, and ramming them up against what was left of the spit, creating what is now known as Barges Beach.

The barges are almost completely deteriorated now, and the government would never let something like that just get done because it needed to be done today. There would have to be studies and surveys and discussions that alone could take years.

That's what almost happened with the perfect storm, the one they wrote the book and made the movie about. Cuttyhunk Island lay almost directly in its path.

The perfect storm came the fall after Hurricane Bob. Bob had not been particularly destructive in terms of wind, but the waves and tidal surges were brutal. Part of the spit that made up Barges Beach washed completely away, and the part that was left was less than a quarter as wide as it had been. Mel Dorr's land was officially an island.

I remember heading out toward Barges Beach after Hurricane Bob to check out the damage. There were seagulls everywhere, and seaweed piled high as my thighs and thicker than I'd ever seen it. The seagulls seem to be playing in it, but I knew seagulls don't play. They don't do much but eat, caw hoarsely, and defecate where you don't want them to. As I got closer, I saw the seaweed appeared to be moving.

But it wasn't the seaweed that was moving. It was what had washed up with the seaweed. Live fish, mostly tautog, and lobsters. That's what had attracted the seagulls. Some rogue wave must've dredged them from the bottom of the ocean.

I ran to the house to get a bag, and by the time I got back to the beach, it was filled with islanders, shoving the live fish and lobsters into bags and dropping them into buckets. It was like Poseidon had paid us back for taking part of our island.

The cut through Barges Beach greatly worried the Army Corps of Engineers, the Coast Guard, and pretty much anyone who had anything to do with conditions on Buzzard's Bay. Cuttyhunk Island's harbor was considered a safe harbor, protected enough so that boats could moor there in stormy weather. With the cut through Barges Beach and deterioration of the spit, the worry was that the channel would slowly fill up with sand and rocks, and in time become un-navigable. Committees were formed, studies were commissioned; we must have had eight or nine different groups of people come out in official boats to check out the situation firsthand.

They needn't have worried. Just as the committees were really heating up between those who wanted to dredge and try and rebuild the spit versus those who wanted to let nature take her course, nature took her course. The perfect storm, nor'easter extraordinaire.

And by the time those three days of wind and waves were over, the cut to Mel Dorr's was filled in and Barges Beach looked almost exactly as it had been before Bob happened.

Chapter 50
It's not exactly the QE2, but

Remember that chart in the library showing the hundreds of wrecks, the ship names, the year, and approximate position of each wreck? After certain northeasterly storms you could still find pieces of saltwater-petrified ebony logs washed up on the shore between Barges Beach and the West End from a wreck in the 1600s carrying ebony from Africa to America. But this was the twentieth century. There were up-to-date charts available, especially to commercial ships, as well as loran, radar, depth finders ...

We expected a few sail and power boaters to go aground each summer, as many of the folks who sailed these waters barely knew what a chart was, let alone how to read one. But a cruise ship?

The Pilgrim Belle went aground on a reef off Cuttyhunk. These reefs were famous in sailing days for the number of shipwrecks that occurred on them. It was a small cruise ship, maybe eighty passengers plus crew, doing a New England coastal cruise. Somehow the captain took a wrong turn; and around dusk a Mayday went out to the Coast Guard. They radioed the island, and all available fishing and sport boats went out to help ferry the passengers to shore. We were well into the middle of dinner service when one of our selectmen came to the front desk and announced there were eighty mostly elderly people holed up in the Town Hall waiting for a boat from the mainland to come pick them up. The Shumanche, a ferry that normally went from New Bedford to the Vineyard, was slated to come, but the crew had to be assembled from their homes and the boat readied, and it was going to be a while. Could we feed these people anything?

Nina came into the kitchen to relay the news. We had a full dining room that night, and every reservation space was booked. Higgins and I looked at each other. Then, in that symbiotic sharing of a single brain cell that made our work together so effortless, she went downstairs to the walk-in while I checked the freezers and the upstairs refrigerators. Higgins came back up. "Cod," she said. "Plenty of tuna and bread. Five gallons of chowder."

"Clams." I answered. "Salad. Ice cream."

Higgins turned to Nina. "Tell them yes, if they accept these menu choices. They can have baked cod, fried clams or clam roll with fries and slaw, a tuna sandwich with chips, chowder, salad, or any combination of these. Coffee or tea. No substitutions. Menu price. Ice cream for dessert. That's it. Where we gonna put them?"

I continued to put out dinners for the dining room while Higgins and Nina went into action, figuring out logistics. They decided the castaways could be brought down to the gift shop in groups of sixteen and seated at the coffee shop tables, which were usually reserved for walk-in dinner guests on busy nights. We would attempt to feed them up there, with Nina and the young woman at the desk running food up the ramp while the waitstaff attended to their customers in the dining room who hopefully would not notice anything amiss.

Astoundingly, the caper went off like clockwork. Not only did we feed almost every person from the cruise ship, we also sold out of our entire stock of medium, large, and extra large sweatshirts, an added cash bonus. And the waitstaff told us that ninety percent of our customers didn't notice anything at all different that night.

After we'd fed the last of the cruise ship passengers and sent them on their sweat-shirted way, and the final few dinner tickets were hanging in front of us, Higgins and I looked at each other, and again, without a word, she took two beers out of the fridge and cracked them, handing one to me. We clanked the beers together in an aluminum toast. Just another crazy night on Cuttyhunk. When Nina came in to tell us the last of the passengers had left the gift shop, and that the captain had come in to personally thank us, she asked, "Forget about anyone? I did."

Higgins and I looked at each other blankly.

"About halfway through the gift shop melee," she said, "I was rushing down the ramp with an order and a bus bucket of dirty dishes when I just happened to look over into the salad pantry." She waited.

"Oh, my god—Dennis!" I said.

Nina's boyfriend had offered to make salads that night to cover for a sick employee. Nobody had thought to inform him that he would have sixty or so extra customers.

Nina smiled. "I stopped and started babbling how sorry I was, and how I had forgotten he was working, and did he need someone to help him, and he just laughed."

"I've stage-managed circuses, rock concerts and two world's fairs," Dennis answered. "A few extra people aren't going to throw me." And with that he waved her off and went back to mixing up a new batch of blueberry vinaigrette.

A well-oiled machine, indeed.

Blueberry Vinegar

Makes one gallon

Place 3 cups frozen blueberries in glass gallon container.
Fill container with hot cider vinegar.
Let sit for at least 24 hours or up to six months.

Blueberry Vinaigrette

Makes one gallon

1 1/2 quarts blueberry vinegar
4 tablespoons Dijon mustard
4 tablespoons white pepper
9 bay leaves
1 cup chopped parsley
7 cups orange juice
1 1/2 cups blueberries
1 1/2 cups corn oil
2 tablespoons salt

Shake thoroughly before each use.

Chapter 51
My god, it is the QE2!

Mary Lee came into the kitchen. "Wow," she said. "There is the biggest cruise ship I have ever seen out there."

We were used to seeing the lights of cruise ships pass by at night; several lines sent ships out of Boston and we saw them as they came around the back of Martha's Vineyard heading south.

"Yeah, yeah," I said. "If I can't be on it, I don't want to know about it."

"No," Mary Lee said. "I mean really, really huge."

Sara and I went out into the dining room to look at the *really, really* huge ship. It was enormous. It looked half the size of Martha's Vineyard.

"Damn," was all I could say.

Nina's response was "I'll go get Mark. He'll know." That was her response to anything involving boats or the ocean.

Sara and I went back to cooking dinner, and I, at least, thought no more about it.

But later that night, while I was sleeping, Mark, along with almost every other boatman on the island, and anyone else who could beg a ride, was out at sea.

Around eleven o'clock word spread via the island grapevine (and marine band radio) that the QE2 had run aground on a rock just off the island. It was just a bit south of the reef where the Pilgrim Bell had gone aground.

This was the largest cruise liner afloat. Surely they could have figured out a way to navigate around a rock?

Nina decided it wasn't worth getting out of bed to see, so Mark picked my dad up and took him out for a look. As soon as it got light, it seemed as if every boat in Cuttyhunk Harbor and another hundred from Menemsha were circling the QE2, to snap a picture or just get a close-up look. They looked like sharks circling for a kill.

The next morning the QE2 was the only topic of conversation in the kitchen.

"Wow," Mary Lee said. "If they can't get it to move, do you think they'll bring the passengers here?" Nina returned in time to hear that last statement.

"Be great for business," she said. "I've got a hell of a lot of unsold sweatshirts. This fall has been just *too* warm."

"Uh, Nina," I said "This is not the Pilgrim Bell. This is not eighty or a hundred people. This is something like five or six thousand, maybe more. That's more than five times the population of the island when the harbor is completely full!"

Nina shrugged it off. "We could handle it," she said.

Well, maybe we thought we could handle it, but obviously no one else did. Several large ferries were sent over from Newport, Rhode Island, and the passengers were evacuated there. We got all sorts of details from Cuttyhunkers who went to watch the show. It turned out they didn't evacuate everyone, just those who wanted to go. Which was probably a good thing because I'm not sure even Newport had six thousand available hotel rooms on a moment's notice. The main source of talk around Cuttyhunk was not that the QE2 had run aground, but how a ship with supposedly such experienced captains and so much expensive navigating equipment aboard that regularly ran from America to England across the Atlantic could manage to go far enough off course to hit that reef. Nobody ever explained it, at least not to me. When the next high tide came, they floated the QE2 off the reef and towed it into Newport for repairs. That was the closest Cuttyhunk ever came to becoming a cruise line destination.

Chapter 52
Tea for Two

I met Annie through my mother. Surprising, because I knew Mom still harbored hopes I would find a "normal relationship." Nevertheless, she arranged a meeting through a co-worker.

Annie and I had absolutely nothing in common besides the fact that we were both gay, and too shy to try and find other gay women in the Providence area. She had just moved back from the Midwest, had no job, and no reason not to come out to Cuttyhunk for my first season as manager. What better basis for a relationship?

I got Annie a job with Ginger at the store, so at least our fledgling relationship would not be burdened by a boss/employee stigma. Ginger was delighted to have an employee she didn't have to house and one over the age of sixteen at that. She promptly made Annie her assistant manager.

As the summer wore on, my relationship with Annie disintegrated. I couldn't understand why she didn't want to come help out at the restaurant after the store closed at five, why she would rather go out and party than hang around and watch me work. There wasn't much to the relationship to start with, and it wasn't too surprising to anyone but me when Annie told me in mid-August that she wasn't happy. Ginger offered her a room above the store, and she moved out.

Hurricane Gloria put an end to whatever hope I clung to for reconciliation.

Annie was a seriously practiced drinker. As was Tyler, Bonnie's husband. Bonnie, who ran the bakery and didn't care for me *or* the changes the Allen House was making to the island. At some point during the second half of the storm, Tyler and Annie drove to the top of the hill in his old blue pickup to see just how strong the storm was. There's a picture somewhere of Annie at the top of the hill, standing at a 45-degree angle, jacket blown straight out behind her, and Tyler lying flat on the ground, holding onto her legs to keep her from flying down the hill.

I guess you had to be there.

I wasn't, and he was. He had the same do-your-job-because-you-have-to-but-spend-the-rest-of-the-time-partying attitude Annie had. Tyler and Annie both loved to drink, fish, and just hang out and have a few beers.

Except for the minor details of his being a guy, married, and twenty-five years older, they were a perfect match. Within days after Gloria they were an item. A carefully hidden item, as Bonnie had a serious temper and the physical the strength to back it up. But on an island, especially one as small as Cuttyhunk, nothing stays secret for long, and Bonnie found out. She promptly threw Tyler out. It was, after all her house, her business, her island.

Tyler and Annie moved off-island to a small town on the coast where Annie opened a fish market. They may still be there, for all I know.

Bonnie even told me a few years later that she wasn't mad at me, it was a bitch having our partners run off together but hey, we were probably better off and life was a bitch anyway, wasn't it?

Section IX.

More Island Provisions

Back deck of the annex.
Obviously the north side was next in line to be painted.

Chapter 53
It's the Law

For as long as anyone could remember, there were no police on Cuttyhunk. The town constables, who were also the selectmen, did any law enforcement that had to be done. Since quite often at least one and often two of these constables were men or women over the age of sixty, you could correctly assume there was little crime on the island.

During the winter, any stranger coming on-island would be instantly noticed and identified as such. There are few places to beach a boat, as the shore is mostly rocks and boulders, so anyone wanting assurance that they could land would have to come into the harbor.

Town itself was inconvenient for an outsider, with ninety-five percent of the houses within hailing distance of one another. And anyone intent on mischief or mayhem would have to have a private boat because, in winter, the ferry only ran twice a week at most, less if the weather was bad. Kind of difficult to commit a crime and then wait around for the ferry to get you back to the mainland.

Few people who spent winters on the island were rolling in cash, and the richer summer people left nothing of value in their houses. On Cuttyhunk, you lived down if you were a summer person. You dressed down, drove an old golf cart, or later, an old truck. So chances were your house wasn't worth breaking into, especially if the thief had to carry his loot across island to the marina. It really wasn't worth the trouble. Besides, few people who didn't sail knew about the island. Even in New Bedford, if you tried to get directions to the ferry, half of the people you'd ask would have no idea what you were talking about.

So there really was no need for law enforcement in the winter.

Summers were a slightly different story. As the island got busier (and I freely admit the growth of the Allen House was partly responsible for this), there were not only more tourists, but also more teenagers around working the various island businesses. More young people meant more beach parties, which meant more drinking, and consequently more noise and the occasional stolen golf cart joyride or minor vandalism.

There was the odd moment of panic, like when Oscar insisted he had been attacked cutting across the Post Office lawn towards his house, his glasses knocked off, and an attempt made to strangle him. He of course could not recognize his assailant, as he was almost blind without his glasses.

Closer inspection of the crime scene the next morning found Oscar's glasses, slightly bent, under Ellen's clothesline. Upon questioning, Oscar admitted he might have had a few drinks at Bill's before heading home.

There was an occasional ugly incident, like hockey star Jim Craig getting drunk and wrecking one of the island's public phone booths. As it was one of the booths in an accessible place where you could stay dry if it rained, this was deemed an offense of the highest order. George and Joe, our off-island cops turned summer fishing guides, took care of that problem, but quickly got tired of being awakened at all hours to deal with guys like Craig, and hassles down at the docks in general.

The town met and decided to hire part-time police from Martha's Vineyard. Cuttyhunk would supply an apartment as part-payment, and the policemen could rotate week by week so no one would have to be posted to this desolate rock for all three months. It seemed like a great solution.

The main sticking point became apparent almost immediately. The guys they hired were cops. That meant they didn't just want to walk around in uniform looking scary and keeping kids in line. They actually wanted to enforce the laws.

Laws?

Like not riding four-wheelers or dirt bikes or, technically, even driving golf carts on state roads. Turns out Cuttyhunk *was* actually considered part of Massachusetts, at least by the Vineyard police, and the three paved roads on the island belonged to the state. They wanted up-to-date vehicle inspections, county stickers, license plates, a motorcycle license if you rode a bike, and helmets.

All this in a town where the only standing sacrosanct rule was that dogs and children in the road had the right of way and must be driven around, quietly if they were sleeping.

Then there were the problems concerning drinking. If Cuttyhunk *was* actually part of Massachusetts, it was illegal to walk outside in public with an open beer. *And* it was illegal for anyone under the age of twenty-one to drink. This put a terrible damper on beach parties. What good was a bonfire if you couldn't drink beer?

Few parents worried about their kids drinking on Cuttyhunk. If your kid got drunk enough to pass out, the worst that would happen is that he or she would wake up in the morning with a mouth full of sand, or sunburn if it was high summer. This was the eighties, too, when underage drinking didn't seem like such a big deal.

Big deal or not, it was illegal, and the policemen from the Vineyard had been hired to enforce the law.

After that first summer, and a lot of conferencing back and forth, some compromises were reached, and a few policemen found that were willing to concede Cuttyhunk might indeed be a special sort of place with special sorts of rules.

But a couple of years of even this lax sort of law enforcement proved to be too much, and the people of Cuttyhunk decided what they really wanted weren't actually state cops, just some sort of official presence that could be called upon in emergencies and ignored the rest of the time.

Enter Billy.

Billy was an island boy, who after his stint in the Merchant Marine had returned to the island to live. Billy was about 6"2' and at that time somewhere in the neighborhood of 300 pounds. He was familiar and competent with firearms, owned a number of guns, and had every gun license the state of Massachusetts would issue.

He had his own four-wheeler and use of a truck so the town wouldn't even have to get him a vehicle. And best of all, he didn't give a damn about vehicle stickers or a few beers on the beach. Billy just liked to break up fights. It seemed a match made in heaven.

And it was, for a while. Billy went off-island to take a month-long law enforcement class and returned with a certificate proclaiming we had an official law enforcement officer on Cuttyhunk Island. That and a buck would get you a cup of coffee at the store, but it was all we needed. After a couple of years, though, Billy's ideas of law enforcement grew slightly grander. He'd taken over the running of the powerhouse from his father, and started his own propane business to compete with Alan's. He ran a charter service with his boat, and was now a family man with a corresponding sense of responsibility. He asked the town first for an official police car, and then summer deputies, radios, and other equipment. He began to wear a uniform and tinted sunglasses in the summer. The town might have decided these were good ideas, and in fact by the time I left the island years later, they had adopted most of them. But Cuttyhunkers are a stubborn bunch, and they like innovations to come slowly and be their idea, not forced upon them.

So exit Billy, stage right. And enter the solution still in force today, a series of young island men who go off for initial training and then take a refresher course every summer. They call it cop school. They wear dark blue shirts and pants, and carry radios, handcuffs, and a gun that may or may not be loaded. They walk and ride around town and the beaches, making people aware there is a law enforcement presence on island. There are several of them so that they can continue their summer jobs and be on hand to back each other up. Recently, one of the fishing guides who worked off-island as a cop retired and moved to the island to take the harbormaster job. He is now also the official police chief.

It's a simple solution for a simple island, and it works just fine.

Chapter 54
Fire Drill

The volunteer fire department is one thing that hasn't changed much since I first came to Cuttyhunk. Sure, they have a newer engine now, courtesy of a mainland small town trading up. And the engine and pumper truck have actual garage space built onto the powerhouse, instead of being parked next to it.

But my first memories of a fire chief are of Seth, and he is still involved in the fire department today. Many of the older volunteers have retired from duty, moved off-island, even died. The core of the department is still a few young, strong, island men and women who live on Cuttyhunk year round. The names have changed, but not the ill-fitting coats and boots, the fire drills and the determination. These folks know that they are the island's *only* defense against the devastation an island fire can bring.

Every summer Seth ran a little recruitment campaign for extra fire department personnel among the summer folk, and he always seemed to target our staff. Most of them were curious enough to sign up, and since I required at least two people from every department to go through the CPR course, a little additional training looked like fun to them.

In foggy, cool June, that is. Fire drills in the July heat wearing rubber boots and coats, lifting ladders and rolling heavy cloth hoses up and down hills to fireplugs weren't quite such a lark. But Seth put on a demonstration for the town every July, and every summer he managed to come up with a fairly impressive-looking crew.

The thinking went like this: The more tourists we had on boats and on island, the more likely a beach or campfire or overheated BBQ grill was to get out of hand. Personally, I worried about fire in those two wooden buildings comprising the Allen House, and that took up all my time and energy.

Usually, those few grass or beach or dump fires every summer were quickly and efficiently contained. Except for a few notable examples.

It was a Fourth of July weekend that had magically gone by without a power outage. Just at dark, maybe three-fourths of the way through dinner service, the siren sounded. I came out onto the porch to see what looked at first like a typical bonfire on the beach.

Except it was on the wrong side of the jetty, and seemed to be in the tall beach grass there. I strained my eyes against the dusk as the siren sounded a second and then a third time. The fire was definitely over on the neck side of the jetty, a piece of land connected to the main island by Church's Beach and a small spit of land. They had no power over on the neck, those isolated homeowners relying on generators for power. Water had recently been run over there, but there was no hydrant close enough to the jetty beach for the hoses to reach.

My best dishwasher, a small but brawny young guy, came out of the kitchen. "I gotta go, man," he said to me. "I'm a volunteer."

I agreed of course he had to, and told him to round up the other volunteers and they could take the van as far as it would go, before the track became impassable for any vehicle without four-wheel drive. He took off, and I went back to the kitchen to check on the dinners in progress. I felt rather than saw a great deal of movement throughout the dining room, and when I went out a few minutes later, I saw why.

More than two-thirds of my staff that year was, it seemed, part of the fire department. I had a total of two waitstaff left, one of whom had to be dragged in because she was technically off-duty. I had no dishwashers. The housekeepers and all the front-of-house staff were gone. Nina was on the front desk, fielding questions from tourists and inn guests.

I returned to the kitchen and forbade any of the kitchen staff from leaving. I pressed one of them into service in the dish room, one as a sort of bus person/back-waiter, and went table to table, explaining to each one why their service might be a bit under the usual standard that evening. Most of them were watching the commotion out on the jetty beach through the porch windows anyway, so I told them to look closely and they might just recognize their waitperson down there.

The guests took the lack of service in stride with few complaints. Most of them just chalked it up to another unique Cuttyhunk experience, like dining with the power out or watching Jackie Onassis walk through the dining room barefoot.

The fire was soon out, but by the time the staff showered and changed, dinner was over. At least everyone pitched in cleaning up the dining room and dish room.

This fire had been started by boaters who had pulled their motorized dinghy illegally up on the neck side of jetty beach and proceeded to set off fireworks, which in turn set the dry beach grass on fire. Luckily, there was a good stretch of sand and rock between most of the fire and the nearest house, and the fire was relatively easy to contain with the water in the pumper truck.

Full responsibility for two one-hundred-year-old buildings meant I never grew used to the constant threat of fire. We were fourteen miles from the mainland, almost every island building was wooden, and a good many of them were old. The Allen House buildings were some of the oldest, and while attempts had been made over the years to update the wiring, most of the plugs weren't grounded, and hanging from the beams in the basement was a horrific tangle of ancient wires no one was sure had been entirely replaced.

The kitchen and new bathroom were the exceptions in the main house, strictly up to mainland code, which was almost unheard of on the island at that time. And, of course, as we built on, adding showers and laundry and eventually staff housing, we continued to replace and upgrade the wiring. But who knew what lurked inside those horsehair walls?

Having been an electrician in my past life, I knew the smell of an over-heated wire, and my olfactory instincts were on high alert the entire fifteen years I was at the Allen House. Any time I smelled more than a whiff of smoke at night, I'd not feel comfortable until I had located the bonfire producing it. Smoke during the day had me sniffing around the entire building until I could determine it was a coffee pot left on a burner, or the wind shifting on a day Hunter was burning the dump debris. I can remember countless times I would imagine I smelled burning insulation, only to trace the source to a spatula leaning against the side of the stove or an oven mitt touched by flame.

Even in an updated kitchen, the threat of fire is a real and constant presence. The application of heat is, after all, a vital element of the cooking process. Higgins and I found ourselves repeating that often in those first years, as we discovered quiches left to bake in ovens that were preset and not turned on, stockpots left overnight with no flame beneath them. It was enough to make you wish for the days when you couldn't afford any kitchen help and had to do it all yourself. Almost.

Amazingly, we only had three small fires the entire time I ran the Allen House. I don't count the first year when the breaker box for the gift shop blew off the wall and burst into flames, because technically Steve was in charge then.

And the last one was more of an *almost* than an actual fire, although oddly enough it was the only electrical problem we ever really had and involved brand new wiring. A houseguest sleeping in room two just over the kitchen woke an employee to say he thought he smelled burning wood. I ran around the back of the kitchen with a flashlight and discovered a small charred area behind where a flattop grill had recently been installed. We pulled off the shingles and found a crossed wire and some slightly burnt insulation. Easily fixed, and luckily for us, minor. That houseguest got his room and meals comped for the rest of his stay. It was a cheap price to pay.

No, the two fires that scared the hell out of me both took place during dinner in the height of the season and involved the broiler. This was a massive piece of equipment that came with the building. Technically called a salamander as the flames came from above and heated a series of grill bars below, it also had a huge bottom oven and a smaller "warming" oven on top of the flames. This "warming" oven actually stayed near seven hundred degrees when the gas was turned up high, and we used it to quickly finish food off just before service. The whole steel-and-cast-iron monster sat flush into the kitchen wall, and stuck out the back of the building about three feet. It was surrounded by its own little shingled hut and vented out the back of the warming oven by a handmade metal flue.

No matter what sort of tool you improvised, there was no way to really get inside and clean or even get completely down into the flue, which was a good seven feet off the ground. It was forty years of baked-on grease and a disaster waiting to happen.

It happened twice. The first time scared me the worst, even though it was the lesser of the two fires. It was the first time it had happened to *me*.

We often finished large trays of baked stuffed lobsters in the top oven because they took up so much space. If you left the door to the oven open, there was little chance of the butter on the pan getting hot enough to ignite. But the lobsters took much longer that way, and we were always in a mad rush during high season. I often risked it, closing the door for a few minutes to allow the heat to build up.

About once a week, I'd lift the door and see a small flame shooting up, which I would quickly smother with another pan.

One night, I wasn't quite quick enough. I opened the door, saw the flames, lifted the sheet pan of lobsters out and capped it. The flames were still there, the grease on the floor of the top oven having ignited as well. If I didn't get it out quickly, the whole flue could go up in flames. I turned off the gas, yelled for baking soda and a stool, climbed up and dumped one huge box of baking soda on the flames, then another. I couldn't smother the fire with a pan because air and heat were still coming up from the broiler below. Finally, three boxes of soda later, the flames were out.

Unfortunately, it was still the middle of dinner. Four steaks and several assorted pieces of fish in various stages of cooking were sitting on the grill covered with baking soda, and the whole area looked as if a fifty-pound sack of flour had exploded. Fortunately, I had a great crew that night. Within fifteen minutes we had all the soda cleaned off the grill bars and oven floor, new steaks and fish on, and complementary appetizers sent out to those guests whose dinners would be seriously late. We were back in business, if a little dirtier and more than slightly the worse for wear.

The second fire, a year later, was much worse and could easily have ended in disaster. It started the same way (some things we learn, some things we don't), and this time I was even savvy enough to take a second and pull the swordfish and filets *off* the broiler rack before I climbed up to douse the fire. I hit the flames with several boxes of soda, one after the other, but by the third box I realized this fire was different. The flames I could see were out, but I still smelled burning. I sent the fry cook outside to climb onto the stone wall, look into the back of the broiler hut flue and see if he could see flames.

He was back in moments, his face literally as white as his uniform.

"There's fire coming out of the back of the broiler," he said. "I can see it from the door."

Shit. I grabbed a fire extinguisher (the hell with baking soda, the hell with trying to save that night's dinner service) and aimed it upward through the top oven into the flue. It emptied in less than a minute and I ran outside to see if that had worked.

Flames licked the shingles of the broiler hut roof. I grabbed another fire extinguisher from inside the door (we always kept twice as many as regulations required) and headed around the corner. Mary

Beth followed right behind me with a third. I jumped up on the wall and began alternately spraying the shingles and the flue. I couldn't afford to let the fire spread from the broiler hut roof to the Allen House roof, but neither could I let the fire get a real hold inside the broiler. If that happened, with all those years of accumulated grease, I knew we'd be done for.

By the time the third extinguisher was empty, the fire was out. The Cuttyhunk Fire Department in the form of Seth Garfield was eating in the restaurant and so arrived rapidly on the scene, but it was all over but the trembling. Nina somehow gracefully cleared the dining room and sent the customers who were still waiting home, as the kitchen was literally covered in soot, ash, and foam from the extinguishers that had blown back in from the flue.

We cleaned most of the kitchen as best we could, and I sent everyone home, planning to come back at five the next morning and deal with the broiler.

Seth and I examined the outside damage by flashlight and concluded we'd been amazingly lucky, that after replacing a couple of shingles you wouldn't even be able to tell there had been a fire.

And when I arrived at five the next morning, I walked into a pristine kitchen, with the broiler as shiny and clean as I had ever seen it. Mary Beth stayed up all night working on it, because she didn't want me to have to face it in the morning. I didn't realize it that morning but her gift was not just that of an employee to employer, or even one friend to another, but the equivalent of a dozen red roses. Less than two weeks later she had moved in with me.

It was ironic that the worst fire I ever saw on Cuttyhunk occurred years after we'd sold the Allen House, and by chance on the first night I'd been back. In the winter, if you are on-island and you hear the siren blow, if you are capable of walking you head toward the fire. I was staying with Nina, and around two-thirty a.m., I woke to what my confused brain first thought was the sun coming up and my alarm going off.

It took only seconds to realize the glow was coming from outside and the alarm was the fire siren. I looked out the bedroom window just in time to see the roof of Pete's Place erupt in flames.

I raced into Nina's bedroom and shouted, "Pete's Place is on fire!" Unfortunately, this caused both Nina and Mark to jump out of bed and head to the window. I say unfortunate because they sleep nude. That was more information than I needed.

It was the middle of winter. We pulled on whatever clothes, coats and boots were handy and Nina and I raced down the hill, arriving moments before the fire truck with a few trained volunteers aboard.

Mark had taken his four-wheeler to round up the few islanders who lived farther out of town. Nina and I watched as the skeleton fire crew expertly set up, connected hoses, and began fighting the fire. Other islanders began collecting around the fire, some with thermoses of water and later, coffee for the firefighters. Some connected garden hoses and began playing water on the nearest buildings, scant yards away. Some helped manhandle heavy hoses.

Most of the rest of us ran around like crazy, stamping out flying pieces of burning wood and insulation. Kathy Olsen and I simultaneously noticed a house a few buildings over right in the wind's path with large pieces of burning foam insulation landing on its porch and roof. Kathy had the foresight to bring a broom when she ran from her house, and she began to sweep chunks off the roof while I ran after burning embers on the porch, stomping on them until they stopped glowing.

Every so often we looked over at the fire. We had a great vantage point from the porch of that house, and we watched as the firefighters gradually conceded the loss of Pete's Place and began playing their hoses over the nearby structures.

We were incredibly fortunate that night in terms of weather. A winter night without a twenty-five to thirty knot wind is extremely unusual. That night the wind blew less than ten knots, and in the best possible direction, with only a couple of houses in its path. Any other direction and we would have had to try and beat embers off of a dozen houses instead of only one.

The New Bedford paper ran a two-paragraph story a couple of days later, with a picture of the charred ruins where the building had stood. They mentioned the volunteer fire department almost as an aside. To my knowledge, this was the only winter fire on Cuttyhunk in a very long time. Certainly there has never been one in my memory.

But the volunteer fire department that night was far more than a two-line mention in a local paper. I don't think any professional fire department anywhere could have worked harder, or more efficiently, or with more determination and heart than they did that night.

Chapter 55
Hook, Line and . . .

People were always hooking up in the summer, and that was natural. You'd expect our staff to find the island kids exotic, and the island kids, most of who had grown up together, to see our ever-rotating staff as a constant supply of fresh dating material. Occasionally, a couple of our own staff members got together, but something about living, working, sleeping, eating, and especially sharing a bathroom with someone made further socialization less than appetizing.

This is not to say that our employees were angels and never dated one another. Many a long summer passed with two or more employees studiously avoiding each other because of breakups or love triangles. I remember one summer when two young women who started the season as best friends and roommates dated the same young islander. By July, they had traded rooms and were no longer speaking to each other. This caused some difficulties as they both worked the front desk, often overlapping shifts. It amazed me that two people could work in a seven-foot-by-four-foot area and never speak to or look at each other while still remaining perfectly pleasant to customers.

Then there was the employee we had to let go when an island mother complained her twelve-year-old son was being taught about sex in a way she considered quite inappropriate. When questioned, the young woman readily admitted she had been teaching not only him but several other young men as well. She was quite surprised that we found this a problem, as she explained she considered it a gift to make their first sexual experience a good one. We had to let her go, of course, but it was a pity. She was one of the best front desk employees we'd ever had.

Sometimes when we had to let an employee go, we would discover we were losing more than one. We fired one cook only to discover he was sleeping with a front desk person who promptly left with him. Another cook took a waitress with him. Nina felt she kept pretty well up-to-date on staff romances, but we still got surprised occasionally, and what we thought was a scramble to replace one employee turned into a bigger scramble to replace two.

We catered several island weddings over the years that were the result of two kids who summered on the island getting together, and I catered more after the Allen House closed and I was working on my own. Maybe it was just proximity. But for an island with a summer population of maybe four hundred and a winter one of around thirty-five, I still feel the number of unions the Allen House had some hand in verges on the amazing.

My own sister, Nina, fell in love with and married a man who had fished off Cuttyhunk since he was a boy. Mark moved permanently on-island after his divorce, and he and Nina have been married twenty-two years as of this writing. They still live on-island and Mark is Cuttyhunk's only full-time commuter. Their union is the one most special to me, but there are many others.

Billy, who grew up on island, and Anne, who came out to be our housekeeper, married several years after they met at the inn. I catered their wedding, and they lived for a number of years on the island before moving off to Maine. They have several children now.

Will was a carpenter on the island, building houses for Pete Lehner. Leslei was a childhood friend of Nina's we had re-connected with while driving up from Tennessee one spring. We detoured through Rehoboth Beach to visit with her, and a month later she was on island as our front desk person. She never left until she and Will moved off to the Vineyard when his oldest child was ready for high school.

Then there was Frank and Nicole. Frank moved on-island to re-build Mark's house when Mark made his summer home permanent. Frank found island life to his liking and, as a skilled carpenter, had more work than he could handle. He hooked up with Nicole, who came to the island as our kitchen manager after Higgins left. Nicole was the one who dragged Nina and me kicking and screaming into the twentieth century by forcing us to purchase a computer. I have a computer now and couldn't write without one, yet I still harbor a sneaking suspicion *that* computer generated more work than it saved us.

Of course, there was Higgins herself, a self-professed beer-swilling harlot, who met Jimmy when he came out to the island in pursuit of Mary Beth, not realizing Mary Beth was my girlfriend. Jimmy and Higgins fell in love on the island that summer. They have been married twenty-two years and now have five children.

Mark G. came on-island with his wife, who I had worked with several winters before in Newport. The marriage wasn't going well, and when his wife and child left the island to return to England, Mark G. stayed behind. He spent several winters on the island doing carpentry work, and summers waiting tables for us. That's where he met Jaime. She worked for us first as a waitress, then at the front desk. Although there was a sizable age difference between them (as seems to be the case with many island couples), they became friends and eventually fell in love. They married in Nantucket and moved off-island. They have one daughter, and still keep in touch.

Tessa grew up on-island, part of an old Cuttyhunk family. She worked for us off and on from the time she was fourteen. Tessa went off to college, but came back to the island and met Zac, who had just taken over the freight business on Cuttyhunk. They married here, and still live on-island with a couple of young sons as of this writing.

Duane's father grew up visiting and later boatbuilding on the island, and Duane returned to Cuttyhunk after high school to become a fishing guide. He is married to Lexi, who worked for us in the gift shop and at the takeout counter. They live on-island and have a boy and a girl.

To me, these couples show the make-up of the island changing. When I arrived in 1981, there were four of us almost the same age (twenty-five), living and working on the island. Perhaps as many as a half-dozen others were between the ages of eight and sixty-five. The vast majority of people on-island had lived out their lives there, or summered there and then retired. By 1990, at least twenty had passed on, and now almost everyone I knew when I first arrived is gone, and a whole new crop of young people have made the island their home. My sister and her husband, in their early fifties, are considered old-timers. As the islanders I once knew died off, it seemed for a time Cuttyhunk might soon become a summer place, with no real full-time community. I am happy to report my fears proved groundless. Life moves in a series of cycles, and the island is thriving now in a way it has not since before I knew such a magical place existed.

Chapter 56
Out of My Hands

Hunter died in my hands. Literally.

He was an amazing person. He'd initially come to the island with the Coast Guard. He fell in love with an island girl, married, and moved to Cuttyhunk permanently. Hunter was one of the few people I've known who lived his life exactly the way he wanted to. That may have been responsible, at least partly, for killing him in the end, but while he was here he lived his own life.

Nothing was junk to Ken Hunter. Everything had a use, a second use, and a reuse after that. His house and garage were piled high with treasures he rescued from other people's trash. Most of his clothing came from the dump, as well as most of his furniture, parts for his truck, and the thousands of bits and pieces he used to fix everything under the sun on the island. If you needed a window sash weight, 1972 Chevy pickup carburetor, a propeller for a fifteen horsepower Evinrude, you went to Hunter.

When Alan Potter retired as trash man, it seemed only logical that Ken Hunter would take over the job. He was the island's Mr. Fixit and he already spent hours at the dump. Picking up the trash and taking it there seemed a natural extension.

Among his many gifts, Hunter had an amazing ability to judge the exact height, width, and weight of an object. He could look at a refrigerator and a cellar door and tell you to a quarter-inch if one would fit through the other. And he was always right. Even when I'd measured both the door and the refrigerator and discovered that mathematically there was no possible way, if Hunter said it would fit, it would fit.

Conversely, even if the tape measure said there was plenty of room, if Hunter said you had to take a door off the hinges in order to fit a couch or bed into a room, you had to take the door off the hinges. It took several scraped doors and dented door jambs before I would accept what the islanders already knew. If there was a way to do something, Hunter knew what it was.

Hunter took care of everything on the island except himself. He lived on candy bars, Pepsi, and Lucky Strikes. The postmaster at the time, Ellen, had been a nurse before she moved, and she regularly took Hunter's blood pressure. It was always too high.

Everyone loved Hunter, and everyone at one time or another had talked to him about losing a little weight, about changing his diet, about cutting down on smoking. Hunter just smiled. And you didn't push Hunter. That was one thing I learned early on. No matter what it was, from borrowing his truck to take a load of old sheetrock from a ripped-out wall to the dump, to having him come over to inspect an appliance, fix a leak, judge a distance, whatever you wanted Hunter to do, if you treated him properly, he would do it. But in his own time. Nobody rushed Hunter, nobody pushed Hunter, and nobody pushed Hunter around.

The day Hunter died was a day like any other, at least in the beginning. I got the dishwashers together after lunch and we loaded an old broken dryer onto a handcart and hauled it up the steps from the basement. I sent one of the boys to Hunter's house to ask him to please come and carry the dryer to the dump. And he had shown up in his usual style, about an hour and a half later. By then, the dishwashers were long gone on their afternoon break and not expected back until dinnertime.

I suggested Hunter leave his truck and the boys would heave the dryer into it when they returned. But Hunter had come to carry the dryer to the dump, and that was what he was going to do.

"It's just air," he explained to me. "A dryer is just a metal box with a metal drum and a small motor. Everything else inside is just air."

And with that, he bent his knees, grasped the dryer from the bottom and straightened. I grabbed the back end of the dryer as it tilted toward me, and together we lifted it onto the tailgate of the truck. Hunter pushed the dryer a few inches back, then walked around toward the driver side door and reached in to get his smokes. Assuming he would finish the job when he felt like it, I went back to work. Not more than a minute later, someone came running into the kitchen.

I can't remember now who it was—the housekeeper, a waitress? All I remember is a female voice screaming "Something's wrong with Hunter! He's on the lawn!"

I ran out the kitchen door and around the corner and there was Hunter on his back. Maybe three yards from his truck, twitching, his mouth opening and closing silently.

Some things I remember. Some things I may have made up. Soon after his death, I wrote a poem about the incident, and now I am not sure how much I remember the actual event, and how much of what I remember is the poem.

But this is what I think I know. I yelled for someone, anyone to get Donnie. He was one of three emergency medical technicians who lived on the island, and closest to the inn. Someone yelled "get Ginger." The store held all the emergency medical equipment. I knelt beside Hunter and started telling him it was okay. That's all I said, over and over again. It's okay, Hunter. It's okay. I remembered from CPR class to make sure his airway was clear. So I opened his mouth and stuck my hand inside, tipping his head back, pulling his tongue forward. He was still moving when Donnie came running up the hill.

There were no doctors on the island then. Ellen, our retired nurse, was seventy years old. There were three EMTs, and three or four first-responders. Several of us had taken a CPR class. That was the sum total of the island's medical help. When Donnie saw him, he sent one of the group now huddled around Hunter to tell Ginger to call the Coast Guard before she brought the oxygen. Then, the Coast Guard's emergency helicopter was the quickest transportation to a hospital. But the Coast Guard helicopters were often slow in respond-ing. Sometimes they were busy, often the island was fogged in, or the weather was too bad to attempt a take off or landing.

Basically, we were on our own. I have never felt so completely alone as I did that afternoon.

Donnie started compressions on Hunter's chest, stopping every six to tell me to blow into Hunter's mouth. It became a mantra. One, two, three, four, five, six. Donnie would count, and stop, and I would pinch Hunter's nose closed, fit my mouth around his own, and breathe. I remember Hunter's mouth tasted sweet, like sugar. I'm sure he tasted strongly of tobacco as well, but what struck me was the sweetness.

At some point, they must've rolled Hunter onto a stretcher. I know at some point Ginger handed me a face mask with the bag attached and I changed from breathing into Hunter's mouth to holding the mask to his face and squeezing the bag every six counts. At some point they must've lifted him up into the truck. I remember kneeling in the bed of the truck. But I don't remember getting there. I remember the mask slipping as we drove the bumpy road down to Three Corners where the helicopter could land, and I remember dropping it on the bed of the truck and going back to mouth-to-mouth.

Mostly, I remember Donnie, and the chest compressions, unceasing, one, two, three, four, five, six. Somebody else took over briefly when we got the truck down to Three Corners, but they soon tired and Donnie came back on. I later learned that the average big, muscular firemen could perform CPR five to six minutes before tiring. Small, wiry Donnie pumped Hunter's chest forty-five minutes until the helicopter arrived.

The paramedics took over when the helicopter finally landed. I remember being pulled gently out of the way, someone saying there's a compression pulse down to his ankle. I remember thinking he *must* be okay.

The bed of the truck was suddenly crowded, and I climbed up over the cab and slid down the hood. I walked around the back of the truck in time to hear one of the paramedics say to Donnie, "He's gone. He's been gone for a while. You were just keeping his heart going."

I walked the fifty or so yards to the rocky beach, heedless of the wild rose scratching, pulling at me. I think I swore. I might have screamed at the waves. I did not cry.

Recipe for disaster

Take one slightly overweight middle-aged man with a poor diet and high blood pressure. Add a three-pack-a-day habit. Mix in 2 parts stubbornness and 3 days of holding his left arm and insisting he must just have strained it. Stir in a small island with no medical service, and dial back to a time without cell phones or portable defibrillators. Finish with a Coast Guard helicopter with other things to do. Wait. It will happen.

Hunter

Chapter 57
It's a Bird, It's a Plane—

By the time I moved to Cuttyhunk in 1982, the windmill was already a folkloric legend. Everyone had a different story about exactly why it was there, and why it wasn't being used. A PBS documentary was filmed during its construction, but even after I managed to get hold of a copy and view it, I wasn't sure exactly what had happened.

The bare facts were that an independent company headed by Alan Spaulding (whose family owned the West End of the island) had gotten funding for an experimental windmill and permission from the town to erect it on the highest point on Cuttyhunk Island.

I find the fact that he actually got the town to agree to let him erect it amazing, having sat through many a town meeting where an issue like who was given what piling in the harbor could drag on for years.

The facts of the windmill are these:

✔ It was built at no cost to the town.

✔ It worked.

✔ The power generated was, at that time, approximately half of the energy the town needed.

✔ The current was not compatible with the current the power-house generated.

✔ A circuit board needed to match up the two power sources would cost, at that time, approximately $14,000.

✔ The town could not agree on whether or not to buy such a circuit board.

Ultimately, no decision could be reached, and the windmill was never used.

The how's and why's and who decided what and who said what to whom differed with every person I spoke to. But the general consensus seems to be that there was a large enough faction on the island to swing the voters who thought since they never voted for the windmill in the first place, and were never told it would cost the town money, the town shouldn't have to pay anything to use it.

Like I said, when I got there, it was simply "the windmill," a Cuttyhunk landmark. Coming to the island on the ferry, you knew as soon as you saw the windmill exactly how much longer it would be until you were standing on the dock.

People referred to Cuttyhunk as "the island with the windmill on top." Norman, the seaplane operator, used to call the Allen House regularly before he began a flight and ask if anyone could see the windmill. If you could see the windmill from the Allen House, it was probably clear enough to fly over from the mainland.

In the early morning, that person answering the phone was almost always me. Often, especially in the spring, I had to tell him, "Norman, not only can I not see the windmill, I can't see table nine."

Table nine was about twenty feet from the phone. Fog on Cuttyhunk is both notorious and legendary.

The windmill stood and turned on windy days, more and more slowly as it rusted in the salt air. Finally, it stopped turning at all. New employees arriving on Cuttyhunk were given all sorts of windmill stories to test their gullibility. The fence surrounding it began to sag, and concerns were raised that parts of the windmill, most notably the blades, might detach in a hurricane or nor'easter and cause severe harm to life or property. This was, after all, not your little thin-bladed windmill like those in farms spread across California. This windmill had a body the size of a small plane fuselage and blades larger than your average skiff.

After much debate, a decision was made to tear the windmill down. The destruction happened one winter while I was off-island, and the shock of not seeing it upon returning to Cuttyhunk was surprisingly intense. Pulling up on the ferry, I couldn't help but feel something was wrong. The wrong island, the wrong time period. Something felt jarring and out of place.

Even though I had barely noticed the windmill for years, it had etched itself into my consciousness, and it took a long time for me to be able to look at the island without feeling a sense of loss.

They pulled the windmill down, but left it where it had fallen. The circuitry was outmoded and beyond salvage, and it was deemed not financially feasible to salvage the metal. The wreckage looked like that of a small plane, and in fact, that became the most popular story to tell new employees who hadn't ever heard of the windmill. I have no doubt many gruesome tales were told in staff housing, especially to employees just about to take their first seaplane ride.

Ginger had a box of island windmill postcards at the store, and she spent one winter drawing dragons flying over and clutching the windmill in their claws, and Godzilla or King Kong climbing the windmill. These proved quite popular and are now most likely collector's items.

The fence around the wreckage was tightened to prevent kids from climbing over it and possibly hurting themselves. The island wanted no part of a lawsuit brought by an angry parent.

Now Norman is gone, Ginger has left the island; most of the guys who built the windmill have died or moved off island. In the video they look so young, and strong, and confident. Few summer people remember the windmill at all. Only the old-timers, who were kids when it was built, and a few of their parents.

The windmill was built at the height of the seventies oil crisis. Lately, several of the "newcomers" who have built houses on the island, and become a force to be reckoned with at town meetings, have brought up the idea of building a windmill and hooking it into the powerhouse to provide cheaper electric power. Some families are even talking about building their own windmills, and selling the extra power back to the town.

What a concept.

Windmill postcard with dragon.

Chapter 58
Elvis Has Left the Island

The Cuttyhunk Post Office is one of the smallest in the country, occupying a roughly twelve-by-twelve section off the side of a private house. When I lived on Cuttyhunk, Ellen Veeder owned the house, and there had been three generations of Veeder women as postmasters.

You entered the Post Office by a side door that led to the partitioned-off room. On the public side were the window and the post office boxes. These boxes were in great demand and very difficult to get. Usually someone had to move off-island or die before a box changed hands. There was barely space for two people to stand between the window and the wall as most of the space inside the public area was taken up by piles of boxes and mailbags waiting to either come in or go out.

When the new telephone books for the New Bedford area came in each year, you could barely squeeze inside single file to get your mail.

Behind the counter it was just as crowded, with less than two feet between the window and the counters and shelves that lined the walls. A maximum of two people could be in there at any one time sorting mail, and at least one of them had to be quite thin.

Mary fit the bill. She was less than five feet tall and weighed maybe eighty-five pounds fully clothed, and she had been the official post office helper for years. Her eyesight wasn't the best near the end of her working years, but that didn't really matter most of the time, as there was always someone in there with her on mail days.

On days the boat *didn't* run, she had plenty of time to read addresses, postmark letters people brought in, weigh packages, and sell stamps and money orders. On days the boat didn't run, there was no reason to be in a hurry anyway.

Elvis came to Cuttyhunk in the form of a stamp about a month before the anniversary of his death. Stamps often arrive at post offices before their release date, and the Elvis stamp was supposed to be a big deal, with the release date scheduled to coincide exactly with the anniversary date. Collectors were waiting anxiously. Or so I found out after the fact, after all the fuss and attention.

It was near the end of January, and bills were due. We paid bills as early as possible on Cuttyhunk, especially in winter, as no one knew when the boat might be delayed because of bad weather, and creditors never seemed to take "I live on Cuttyhunk" as a valid excuse.

Several of us crowded into the post office that Monday, an unusual occurrence in itself, and that might have flustered Mary. Or it simply may have been that the Elvis stamps were larger and more colorful and therefore easier to see. Whatever the reason, she sold at least four of us at total of twenty Elvis stamps.

We didn't think anything of it; none of us read the week-old papers regularly or paid that much attention to anything but headline, important news. On Cuttyhunk, in the 1980s in winter, the outside world and its craziness didn't seem that relevant.

All that changed when someone spread the word that Cuttyhunk Island had been on the news the night before. Not the local news, but the national news! Word spread as it always does on Cuttyhunk, mysteriously, without telephones, and before lunchtime everyone on island knew that Tom Brokaw had mentioned Cuttyhunk on the nightly news. Luckily, someone had taped it.

It seemed a lady in Florida had received a letter with an Elvis stamp, postmarked well before the stamps were due to come out. An instant collectable. The four of us racked our brains trying to remember where we had sent those letters. Three of mine were bills, and I am sure their envelopes were immediately discarded on some giant paper heap. The fourth and final stamp had gone to the editor of a small magazine I'd requested a sample copy of. She later wrote me and thanked me for contributing to her child's education fund. That hurt. The least she could have done, I felt, was to split the profits of the sale with me.

Only four other postmarked envelopes were ever tracked down, increasing their value for both stamp and Elvis memorabilia collectors. But the story didn't end there. It seemed it was a serious offense to release a stamp before its due date. Otherwise, I guess, postal employees could make huge profits from rare early cancellations of commemorative stamps. The Massachusetts main post office wanted to know what happened. And the Cuttyhunk Postmaster didn't want to blame Mary, who would surely lose her job if they learned she was eighty-five and had difficulty reading small print.

The Postmaster took the rap, and, because it was Cuttyhunk, and so obviously a mistake, nothing more was said. But I couldn't help thinking: if only I had used just one of those stamps for the self-addressed stamped envelope required when sending out any one of the many poetry submissions I sent out every month. Just one . . .

Section IX.

Cooking with Food

"Christmas" at the Allen House

Chapter 59
Cuttyhunk Special Olympics

When you run a restaurant there are some tasks that have to be done over and over until you can do them in your sleep. Making our signature desserts, for example. Carrot cake, blueberry cobbler, apple crisp. If not every morning, then every other morning I would find myself at six a.m., measuring flour and sugar, my fingers stained and aching from scooping cups of frozen blueberries from a twenty-pound box, peeling and grating carrots. I didn't even need to set a timer for the oven. I'd be doing something on the far end of the kitchen and suddenly a bell would go off in my head. I began to be able to smell these desserts thirty seconds before they were done.

Some tasks you had to pay more attention to, either because a slip would be expensive and possibly painful, or because they were messy enough you needed to keep them contained in a small area. Higgins and I devised ways to make two of these tasks more bearable.

It all started when I noticed one of the dishwashers carrying a dozen coffee mugs from the machine to the racks where they were stored. He had them hung on every finger, and balanced precariously on top of each other. When I pointed out that this might not be the most practical or even economical way to transport the mugs, he solemnly informed me the dishwashers had a competition going as to who could carry the most mugs without dropping them. At twelve he was the current winner and had to stay in shape.

It was late in the season, so this made perfect sense to me. Many things that would have seemed ridiculous at the start of the season or in a normal restaurant in a normal location made sense on Cuttyhunk Island as the season wore on. The staff worked, ate, and slept together. They had few other people their age on island to hang with, so they usually partied together as well.

And they got bored together, especially those with repetitive jobs like dishwashing.

Maybe a normal owner in a normal restaurant on the mainland would have stopped what was essentially a foolish and possibly expensive game. I saw it as an opportunity.

When Higgins came in I grabbed two beef tenderloins out of the walk in and set up cutting boards on the counter.

"Let's see who's faster," I said.

"From ripping open the package to cut, weighed, and wrapped on the counter," she answered without missing a beat.

This was usually a tedious job, as tenderloin was very expensive and you didn't want to waste anything, but you also wanted to make sure each bite the customers put in their mouths was pure meat, no silver skin or fat.

The dishwashers were right. Competition turned tedium into fun. I have no idea who won that first contest, but every tenderloin trimmed and cut after that day was timed and noted on paper. Higgins and I got very fast.

Now we needed to get other employees interested. In the past when asked to do some small prep job, dishwashers moved at a painfully slow pace. The worst was peeling shrimp. We bought our shrimp frozen and thawed them slowly in tubs of cold water. The dishwashers peeled them, then the peeled shrimp would be refrigerated until a cook had time to de-vein them, which was simply cutting a thin line down the shrimp's back with a paring knife and removing what was actually the waste tube.

We couldn't have the dishwashers do this part. The shrimp came back to us cut in two, only partially de-veined, or hopelessly butchered in some way. Higgins had the brilliant idea of dividing into teams, her brother, Bill, and Higgins against Dave, the other dishwasher, and me.

The boys stood by the sink, peeling shrimp and tossing them into aprons Higgins and I stretched like bowls over our knees as we sat next to them. We de-veined each shrimp and put it on ice. The first team to finish won. In addition, we kept timed records, just in case one team had to peel and de-vein a box of shrimp without the other team available to race.

The highlight for me came when Dave and I won every time for almost a week, and Bill asked his sister to please wake him when she prepped shrimp, even though it was technically his day off.

One day a large piece of cardboard appeared on the dish room wall, listing each event and the current leader and time. After that, competitions of various types raged for the rest of the season. Prep had never been accomplished faster, and the dishwashers had never been happier.

The next year I oh-so-casually asked a new dishwasher how many coffee mugs he thought he could carry at one time. He looked at me as if I were insane.

"What, and break them all and have to clean it up?" he asked.

That was the end of the kitchen Olympics at the Allen House. But oh, what a glorious season it had been.

Chapter 60
Bits and Pieces 2
A. Caviar á la Mirror

We were rich.

Well okay, we weren't rich, but we certainly felt that way.

Nina and I had more disposable income than either had ever dreamed of. We were making more than $400 a week each, our rent was paid, we were on group health insurance, even ninety percent of our travel off and on-island was paid for, as these trips were almost always for business. We were rolling in dough.

We decided to behave like the immensely wealthy people we felt we were. This was extremely difficult to do on Cuttyhunk Island. Here, the *really* extremely wealthy people dressed down, drove beat-up vehicles if they had a vehicle at all, and in general acted as if they had no money. There was nothing to spend money on the island itself. It wasn't as if we could go out for a fancy dinner; we *were* the fancy dinner, such as it was. There was no place to shop, and no place to wear anything nice if you had been able to shop. And we certainly had no time to go off-island for fun.

Higgins found us an outlet to satisfy our need to feel affluent. One dry goods supplier had enclosed an insert in his catalog for a small company in Maine that imported Russian caviar. Amazingly, Nina and I had managed to grow up with taste for real Russian caviar living in a small town in East Tennessee. Leon made regular business trips to Russia and almost every time he came to visit my dad, he brought caviar. Not knowing anyone in the small town whom they thought would appreciate it, my parents shared it with us. It had been a rare and amazing treat, and now we were wealthy enough to indulge ourselves.

Higgins had developed a taste for Russian caviar at food shows in Boston where everything on display was set out for people to taste.

We decided to throw a caviar party. It would be mostly for the three of us, but we would let anybody on the staff who wanted to have a taste of real caviar. *And*, we would, for the first time in our lives, be able to eat as much as we wanted.

We ordered four-ounce tins of each of the three caviars, Sevruga, Osetra, and Beluga. I still remember the prices. The Sevruga was $85, the Osetra, $110 and the Beluga a whopping $135. You have to remember these were mid-80's prices. I have no idea what they would be today. I can't afford to find out.

The day the caviar arrived, we made the announcement that after dinner there would be a caviar tasting. We felt it was up to us to train our staff's palates, especially since we were pretty sure none of them would like the stuff and want a second taste. To make doubly sure of this, we reminded everyone they were eating fish eggs. Generous as we were, we still wanted most of the caviar for ourselves.

I'd had more than a bit of a wild streak in my youth, and thought it would be amusing to show how grown up I was, exchanging spending money on drugs for spending it on exotic food. So I set the three containers of caviar in crushed ice on a large mirror with a credit card next to it. I got the joke even if no one else did.

We had a blast. About half the staff elected to try the caviar, although none of them liked it. That was fine with us.

And word got around, as it usually did on Cuttyhunk Island. Nobody said anything to us, but a week later one of the Garfields came by with a large piece of foi gras. Someone had sent her an entire goose liver from France and there was no way she and her family could consume it before they went off island. She thought that perhaps we might enjoy it. Somehow she knew we had expensive and delicate palates. The word was out, and that, too, was fine with us.

B. Holiday Spirits

Those first few years the Allen House got very quiet in the fall. We were still staying open until mid-October, mostly for fisherman, and even with the many renovation and fix-up projects always under way, time got a little heavy on our hands. The staff staying after Labor Day began to feel more like family than employees, and a kind of bonding took place. Fall is a special time on the island, usually clear, with warm days and cool nights. Nina and I actually made it down to the beach for a few bonfires. Fall was when we held our private Cheryl Wheeler concerts. And we had Thanksgiving and Christmas.

I don't know who came up with the idea, probably Higgins. I imagine the conversation went something like this –

"What the hell am I going to make for staff meal tonight? I am so freaking tired of trying to come up with something."

"Why don't we order a turkey and roast it?"

"Okay, order a turkey. Hell, order a can of pumpkin while you're at it. Let's pretend it's freaking Thanksgiving."

Thus an idea was born. We announced to the staff that the day after tomorrow was Thanksgiving. They loved the idea, everyone except Higgins, who now realized that she would not only have to roast a turkey but make stuffing, mashed potatoes, sweet potatoes, and pumpkin pie.

Everyone chipped in to help, peeling and mashing potatoes, washing sweet potatoes, and cubing bread for stuffing. We invited Ginger and her boyfriend, and they brought a homemade blueberry pie. After dinner service was done, we cleaned up and reset the big table in the inside dining room, adding small tables and chairs as needed.

It was a grand feast, and put everybody in a wonderful mood. Such a wonderful mood that we decided to have Christmas the next week.

Now people *really* got into the spirit of things. I came into the inside dining room one morning to find a small pine tree leaning against the wall. That afternoon it was standing in a corner in a homemade stand, and by the next night it was completely decorated.

We got some funny looks from houseguests but the employees explained straight-faced that it was an island custom to have Christmas in October.

"Christmas Eve" brought another surprise. When Higgins and I carried out platters to the waiting group at the table, we saw that there were small wrapped packages at each place.

Mary Beth explained they'd raided the lost and found box up at the desk. This box was usually chock-full by the end of the season with things people had left in the restaurant and showers. After we closed, we usually donated the items to a shelter along with the twenty or so bottles of half-used shampoo and conditioner we'd collected from the shower stalls. Mary Beth decided she'd try and determine which items best suited individuals who would be at Christmas dinner. These items were then wrapped and distributed as she and her cohorts saw fit. One year, I received an only slightly torn pair of black silk long johns, a gift I much appreciated when the weather got colder. Another year, when I was bemoaning the lack of a girlfriend, I received a blonde, blue-eyed Barbie doll.

Pumpkin Flan

Makes 6 cups
1 cup sugar
½ cup water
½ cup pumpkin
1/3 cup sugar
1 tablespoon cornstarch
1/8 teaspoon nutmeg
1/8 teaspoon cinnamon
1/8 teaspoon ground clove
5 egg yolks
2 cups light cream

Heat sugar and water until caramelized and pour mixture evenly into six cups. Mix together pumpkin, sugar, cornstarch and spices. In separate pan, heat light cream just to simmer. Stir in pumpkin mixture and cool. Mix in egg yolks and pour into caramelized cups. Bake in a water bath @ 350 for one hour. Let cool and set.

Chapter 61
Help! (I Need Somebody)

When Higgins decided it was finally time to leave the island after six seasons, I felt bereft. Not only was I losing my kitchen manager and a great cook, I was losing a dear friend. I couldn't imagine finding anyone else with her sense of humor, someone who would sing and dance in the kitchen with me. Who else would I come to know well enough to move around the kitchen at top speed without ever coming close to getting in each other's way? But she *was* leaving, and I was going to have to look for someone else.

After four years of bad luck with ads in the *Providence Journal* and *Boston Globe*, Nina and I decided it was time to try an employment agency. After interviewing three candidates and studying their résumés, I chose Nicole. Although she had less actual kitchen experience than the other two applicants, she had a great deal of managerial experience. And more importantly, she seemed hungry. She seemed to want the job and like the idea of being on an island. I hoped desperately this was someone who would last more than one season.

Nicole did last more than one season, but not as kitchen manager. We found her more useful as a general manager. She took over scheduling as well as keeping the books, and dragged us kicking and screaming into the 20th century by coaxing us into buying a computer. She and Nina worked out marketing plans, trying to pull in more parties and possibly some off-season conferences. We had all the business we could handle in July and August, but often empty rooms in the spring and fall that we were anxious to fill. Although our business was growing yearly, our annual net income was staying flat. We hoped the additional spring and fall income would help the bottom line, as we had discovered that every time we added a new facet to the business, we had to add at least one new employee.

Acquiring those new employees was a full-time job in itself, and we were always looking. When Mary Beth sent us Pelky and Mo from her winter resort job in Vermont, we thought that might be an idea worth exploring: going after more off-season employees at ski resorts. We were fairly successful in that regard with dishwashers and desk help, but we still had giant gaps to fill every season.

Nina and I were once again repainting walls, listening to a story on the Vineyard radio news about how a large percentage of Cape and Vineyard help came from other countries. This story focused on illegal Irish immigrants. I turned to Nina and said, "Damn, that's it. We'll just go get a boatload of Irish immigrants."

I said it, but Nicole researched it. She found an employment agency that handled young people from every country in Europe who wanted to come to the United States for a summer. We thought we had found the answer to all our prayers.

The employment agency sent us a list of applications. They covered mostly Eastern European countries, although several were from France. It seemed English, Swiss, German, Spanish, Italian, and even Irish young people were not interested in spending the summer on a tiny island in the middle of nowhere. They wanted to go to resorts or theme parks, places where there were more opportunities to see America on their days off.

We chose a number of applications, and sent our request back. The number of applicants quickly winnowed down. More and more of them were opting to work in cities or resort areas, or dropped out when it was made clear to them we were not within commuting distance of Cape Cod. Finally, we came up with a desk person, a cook, a housekeeper, a waiter, and a dishwasher. The cook and housekeeper were from France, the others Eastern European.

We had chosen only employees whose English was rated good, very good, or excellent, but our scale was clearly different from the agency's, and we were unpleasantly surprised to find that **good** meant a person could speak almost no English, and understand about half of what was said to him or her. **Very good** seemed to mean the person would be ok if you spoke slowly and did not use slang. **Excellent**, thank god, actually *meant* very good as these were the employees we'd chosen to work with the public as waitstaff and front desk people.

The first disaster was the French cook. He considered himself a chef, and while his food was very pretty, his dishes took a *long* time to prepare. He was completely unsuited for the fast pace of the line in July and August. He could probably have come up to speed if he'd spoken more English, but he could barely understand us when we spoke slowly, and in the middle of a dinner service slowly was not an option. Finally, we brought in a young island woman who spoke fluent French as an interpreter. This proved to be our undoing. She quickly convinced him he was misused and should ask his sponsor to move him. Just like that, we were out a cook.

To make matters worse, the housekeeper was the only other person on the island who spoke French. When the cook left, she left with him. The employment agency was required to replace employees that did not work out, but that took time. And even before the cook and the housekeeper left, we'd had to let go the Yugoslavian dishwasher who, it turned out, spoke no English at all.

We were more than a little upset with the agency. But the two employees who remained were a couple, and they worked out very well, so we agreed to give it another try the next year. This time we would call each potential employee ourselves, and damn the expense. We were going to be the ones to determine how well they spoke English, and we were going to be the ones to tell them about the island. No more surprises.

But our second year wasn't much better. The island was just not what these Europeans thought of when they thought of America. Sadly, we returned to ads in the papers and scouring ski resorts for help.

Chocolate Velvets

The dessert <u>everyone</u> could understand

5 tablespoons light Karo syrup
6 teaspoons water
1 cup chocolate drops
4 teaspoons vanilla
1 pint heavy cream
1 can sweetened condensed milk

Bring Karo and water to boil, then remove from heat. Add chocolate drops and vanilla and mix till melted. Cool slightly. In a chilled bowl whip heavy cream and condensed milk. Beat till soft peaks form. Fold in slightly cooled chocolate mix. Place bowl in freezer for 6 hours minimum. Spoon into individual serving glasses. Keep frozen until ready to serve.

Chapter 62
Kitchen Renovation[3]

In our grand tradition of bigger *must* be better, we set out to re-model the kitchen. Again. Actually, technically we weren't to blame. Although the kitchen was small and cramped for the amount of busi-ness we were doing, we'd never thought to remodel on a grand scale until Nina's husband, Mark, told us he knew of a whole kitchen in Boston that was about to be demolished. A friend of his was doing the reconstruction, and we could have any of the equipment we wanted if we hauled it out of there. Mark offered his men and his trucks to move anything we wanted down to New Bedford. He would store it in his shop until we were ready for it.

Mark loved Nina a whole lot. It never occurred to me until we had closed the inn how much this must've cost him. He never said a word about it.

Nina and I drove up to Boston on a cool fall weekend. The building in question belonged partially to AT&T, and what we were looking at was their cafeteria. It was filled with equipment that we salivated over, but could not really justify having. In the end, we picked out several stainless steel tables and a cooling unit that had glass doors on both sides so a pantry person could put salads or dessert in from one side and the waitresses could pick up from the other. We took a small deli unit, figuring we could put it somewhere for our expanding takeout business, and two under-the-counter refrigerator units. And the hood. We took this giant hood with its own exhaust system. We had to. It was just so extremely cool.

Of course, none of this stuff would fit into the kitchen we had. Mark's business was slow at the moment, so he sent over a construc-tion crew who proceeded to tear down the (by now) useless shack, move the kitchen out ten feet in its place, and connect the salad pantry to the kitchen by way of a small strip of a building that became our office. We'd used the shack for an office since we built staff housing, but it was getting too nasty even for us. And it was hard for us to be completely separated from what was going on in the inn and kitchen. This way we could work in the office and still keep an eye on things.

The addition cost us $56,000. God knows what it would've cost us without Mark. But we budgeted for $50,000 and, oddly enough, that's what it came in at. This seemed to happen a lot when we worked with Mark.

During the remodeling, a doorway was cut from the kitchen into the gift shop so we could become the takeout queens of Cuttyhunk Island. We figured that with just one or two more employees and a slight re-training, we could put dinners out the front, a complete takeout café out the back, and still have room for catering. We were now employing almost everyone on the island over the age of fifteen for the evening shifts. We had become easily twice as big as any other employer on the island.

It had to happen. We finally exhausted ourselves. I had gotten sick several years earlier, and couldn't quite seemed to recover my earlier energy. Nina had taken a year off when Matt was born, and we decided we would keep Nicole on as general manager, and I would take a year off while she managed the kitchen.

The kitchen was busier than ever. I sat in my apartment and worried about all the things that were not going exactly the way I felt they should. I talked with Nina daily. I couldn't help myself. The Allen House was *my* baby, and I identified with it so strongly that any problem, any negative comment was a personal insult. I was a pretty sad case that summer, and not exactly rested when the season ended.

Nina and I had a long talk with Dad that winter. We both felt we had taken the Allen House as far as we could. We had conquered the island, dealt with two hurricanes, weddings from three to three hundred, crazy fishermen, and demented guests.

We had taken everything they could throw at us and begged for more. But it had been several years since we had done anything really new. We were tired of sending out brochures, of staffing, buying T-shirts and souvenirs at gift shows. We had catered yacht club parties so often we didn't need to look at the lists from the year before. We had dealt with fires, a thief, and foreign staff. We were not only tired, we were bored. It was time to sell.

Section XI.

What We Know

Front View—Allen House

Chapter 63
About Food

Here's a brief recap and history of food service on the island in no particular order.

Once upon a time there was the Allen House, which in its grand heyday used to serve lobster dinners for a hundred people who took ferries over from the mainland. That was when Lucille and Clarence Allen ran the Allen House. Before that it was the Poplars and I believe it only served houseguests and possibly their friends and relations. After Clarence died and as Lucille aged, she sold the Allen House to Mildred and Ken with the stipulation that she live in the house and be taken care of until that was no longer practicable. At some point during Lucille's decline, the Bosworth House opened. It had three rough rooms upstairs for fishermen, but a much nicer dining room than Mildred and Ken ran.

Mildred and Ken ran the Allen House as a boarding house, feeding their houseguests first and others as the food supply allowed, first-come, first-served. Saturday night was hot dogs and beans. Haute cuisine. At some point during this time, Bonnie opened a bakery in her house, selling bread and cookies and muffins and fruit squares. Bruce and Dickie sold lobsters down at the fish dock. For a dollar more a pound, and if you ordered before four p.m., Carolyn would cook the lobsters for you and have them back down at the fish dock at six. Muggsy, who ran the general store, died. His daughter took over and began selling ice cream cones, making sandwiches, and baking muffins and breakfast breads. Bonnie began to sell sandwiches and ice cream from a shack down on the fish dock. It had been her father's shack when he fished off Cuttyhunk, and after his death it somehow remained in the family, even though nobody fished anymore. They are a very old island family. Seth opened a raw bar out of his shack on the dock and opened his lobster bakes to the public occasionally.

That is a rough history up until I come into the picture, at which point my memories are a little clearer, although I must say that ninety eight percent of my attention was focused on the Allen House, so I might easily have missed something.

The triumvirate bought the Allen House from Mildred and Ken and began to turn it into an inn and fine dining restaurant. The inn part worked well; the fine dining idea toned down a bit after the first couple of years. The place still functioned as a boarding house for those staying there, but additions were made to the menu which could be purchased at additional cost, and the porch was refurbished as a dining room and opened to the public.

The Allen House began to offer the Bosworth House some competition. Dickie stopped lobstering. Seth's oyster and clam business became successful enough that he could hire kids to shuck oysters and clams for appetizer platters in the early evenings. Later he added shrimp, a shrimp and crab dip, and a floating raw bar.

The Allen House made the final changeover from boarding house to inn and restaurant. The Bosworth House closed, and after a few years was sold as a private residence to the elder Parsons. Bonnie built an addition and began serving breakfast. The Barrys put a pizza oven in their garage and began to sell take-out pizza and ribs. Bonnie added breakfast items to her shack at the dock and began staying open all day.

Several hot dog and sandwich carts made brief appearances, usually lasting one season, maybe two, before changing hands.

Seth expanded his lobster bakes on the beach business. We expanded the kitchen for the third and final time and began serving takeout pizza, wings, calzones, and sandwiches in the evenings. Bonnie stopped serving breakfast. Bruce began to sell fresh fish along with lobsters from his shack.

We sold the Allen House. Bonnie built on and began serving breakfast again. Nina opened Small Fry, a takeout island version of fast food near Three Corners next door to the Barrys. The Barrys started serving lobster dinners on picnic tables down their driveway. Nina sold Small Fry and it became Bart's Place, gradually evolving from fast food to casual dining. The Moore's house was sold and became the Cuttyhunk Fishing Club Bed and Breakfast. Bonnie took over its operation and stopped serving breakfast at her place, instead hiring a cook and opening the bed and breakfast to the public in the summer. The Barrys stopped serving anything. Seth began cooking lobster dinners in the courtyard of his new house near the docks

The general store changed hands; a new store was built that began serving pizza, sandwiches and fresh baked goods. Bart's place closed, and reopened a year later as Bart's cart, a high-end lunch and dinner cart.

The Barrys began to serve pizza and chicken again.

Chapter 64
About Frontiers

Cuttyhunk Island, the last frontier. Or so it felt when I first arrived. In many ways the island seemed not to have any connection to the state of Massachusetts at all. The dump was a prime example. When I first came on-island, Potter was the trash man and ran the dump, and I paid little attention. You put out a bag of trash, and it disappeared. I thought no more about it than I did in the city I'd come from.

Shortly after I started in the kitchen, Potter retired and the job went to Hunter. One day I was throwing away some broken glass and Steve saw me.

"Put that in a box before you throw it away," he said. "Hunter picks those bags up by hand."

It was the first time I'd realized there wasn't a dump truck on-island. Hunter not only had to put the bags into his truck by hand, he had to take them out the same way at the dump.

I began to wonder about that dump. Hunter picked up most of the island trash on a rotating basis, but as we got busier he began stopping by every day. One day, he came in the afternoon, just as I was taking a break. The ancient pickup truck was full, and on impulse, I asked if I could go along. I was a bit older than the kids who usually bummed rides with Hunter, but he took my request in stride and shoved a pile of Pepsi cans, oily rags, and candy wrappers off the seat onto the floor and grandly motioned me in. Hunter's truck, like his garage, was not for the faint of heart. I hadn't had much time off to explore, and when I did head out to the West End, I always took the left fork of the road, the one that ended in a path along the cliffs and then all the way out to the West End. It was private property, but back then walkers who didn't trash up the place were welcome to explore. I had never taken the right-hand fork.

The dump was quite a sight. In fact, I can honestly say I have never seen anything like it, before or since. And I was no stranger to town dumps and landfills, having done my share of illegal scavenging during my theater days.

But this dump was something special. *Everything* the town discarded ended up here. Bagged trash, junked appliances, old car batteries, sheetrock and old wood from building projects, worn-out clothes, old furniture; when someone on-island had no more use for something, it was Hunter's turn. Then, if Hunter couldn't figure out a way to use it, it ended up at the dump.

Periodically, Billy or Tyler would come out with the decrepit town backhoe and shove all the stuff into a huge pile. Then, on a day when the wind was blowing away from town, Hunter would set it on fire. He used old motor oil if he had it, gasoline if he didn't. Hunter was frugal with the town's money. In July and August when our season got busy, he'd use the old oil from our fryolators to ensure a good burn.

Every so often a call would come in to the front desk from the Coast Guard station over in Menemsha on Martha's Vineyard. If the employee was new he or she, usually looking a little worried, would call Nina or me to the phone. We'd pick up to hear someone say, "We've got another report that Cuttyhunk Island is on fire. You guys aren't on fire, are you?"

If I was the one who had answered, I would call out to Nina, "Hey, you aren't on fire, are you?"

And she would answer, "Nope, how about you?"

I would reply, "Nope, don't think so," and inform the Coast Guard that it appeared we were not on fire.

The desk person usually continued looking concerned until we asked them to breathe deeply.

"Smell that?" we'd ask. "That's not a wood fire. That's Hunter, burning the dump."

Once you'd smelled it, there was a particular distinction to a dump fire that set it apart from any other sort of burning smell.

After a fire, Hunter would get someone with the backhoe to rake through the pile again, and push aside any metal or other things that wouldn't burn, and when that pile got too big, they'd dig a hole and bury the lot. This had gone on for countless years before I got there, but, like many other island "differences" it ended during my tenure. The people who owned the land the dump sat on had asked for years for the trash to be handled differently, to no avail. Within five years of my arrival, the requests were worded more and more strongly until finally they threatened to close the dump entirely. Little was done by the town, however. Old appliances and cars were taken to the town dock until there was enough trash for a barge, but ninety percent of refuse continued to go to the dump. Nina and I were seriously worried by that threat to close the dump. We had no idea what we would do with the restaurant waste if the family made good on their threat. We were, except for the town docks, by far the biggest waste producers on the island. Luckily for us, when the family finally did make good on their threat, it was just after we had sold the Allen House. And predictably enough, when they did close the dump, the town was astounded. It was as if the intervening years of pleading and threats and damage assessments and environmental impact statements had never happened.

Today the Cuttyhunk trash system is a model of environmental rectitude. Everything that can be recycled is, stored in huge dumpsters that sit down at the town dock until they are taken off by barge to a state recycling facility. Trash is collected in specially marked bags whose cost is determined by size, and only trash in those bags is allowed to be collected. This trash, and trash from boats that can be dropped off at the dock for a fee, is compacted, and the compactor is also sent off-island to a waste burning and heat reclamation site.

The dump area was dug up, the ground lined with plastic, and the waste reburied and covered over. Today it looks pretty much like any scrub area on the island.

The dump was only one example of Cuttyhunk's frontier mentality when I first arrived.

All new houses built were required to have septic tanks, but all the older ones were hooked into the town sewer system. Or what was laughingly called the town sewer system, as it was a series of old pipes linking the houses that ran straight out into the ocean. This, too, became a matter of concern after the first few years I was there. The triumvirate had the front yard dug up and three huge tanks installed when they bought the place, and Dave rented the town backhoe and enlarged the septic field to make sure it would be adequate. So the Allen House was up to code. But when the EPA showed up and demanded everyone on the old system put in a septic tank, they quickly ran into problems. Many of the older houses were built almost on the water, on land that would definitely be classified as wetlands and therefore unbuildable by today's standards. But they were grandfathered into the system, or, they would have been if there'd been a real system. After several years of negotiating (do you sense a theme here?), a compromise was reached in which everyone who *could* put in a septic tank would, and what was left of the old system would be re-routed to some sort of specially designed holding tank that hopefully would destroy enough bacteria to bring the wastewater down to an acceptable level before it was discharged. Into the ocean, of course.

There was, for once, little infighting among the various groups of islanders, even though the town paid for the new system while those who could put in septic systems had to cover their own costs. Almost everyone had a family member whose house was on the line, literally or figuratively. The EPA sent someone out to test the outflow from the pipe every three months for a while, and eventually declared the system a success. Another Cuttyhunk idiosyncrasy destroyed in the name of progress.

The original ferry Alert was retired in 1987, and the Alert II took over. I firmly believe that was the beginning of the end. At least of the way of life I was just growing to know and love on Cuttyhunk. With the Alert II came the ability to carry more than twice as much freight per trip, which meant more building supplies could be brought over to build more houses. But the most important change was that the Alert II could carry a car. It had to be a small car, and the tide had to be exactly right both on the mainland and on the island to be able to get the car on and off of the ferry. But it could be done.

And done for a great deal less than it cost to bring a car or truck over on the barge.

Suddenly, almost everyone who'd gotten by for years with a golf cart, an old postal jeep, or four-wheeler had to have a car. Everyone who'd gotten around on foot had to have a golf cart. No longer could you walk down to the ferry dock to get your paper and let whichever islander owned the freight business that year bring up your groceries or your mother's suitcases. Now it became vital to have your own car and drive down to pick up whatever was coming over on the ferry. Not only did this cause major traffic jams as there was so little space available on or near the dock to park, but it took business away from someone trying to make a living carrying freight up the hill.

I certainly don't blame the Alert II for trying to make enough money to stay in business and pay for the new boat. And I don't blame the year-round islanders. A four-wheeler can get damn cold in the middle of winter. But I felt then and feel now it is entirely unnecessary for summer residents to bring on the Geos, Suzukis, small trucks, and other vehicles they seemed suddenly to deem vital for survival on the island. And short-term renters having the use of golf carts instead of walking? It just doesn't feel right to me. It doesn't feel like Cuttyhunk.

The Poplars—circa 1911.

Chapter 65
About How to Sell an Inn

Once Nina and I made the difficult and painful decision to sell the Allen House, we began looking for the best way to sell such a unique property without spending too much of our own money. We first listed with a high-end realtor who specialized in oceanfront properties, but soon realized we had a problem with this particular oceanfront property.

Anyone who could afford the Allen House had enough money so that they didn't need put in the incredible amount of time and energy required to run it properly. Those people who did want to run such a business could not afford to buy it. After our first year pushing the property that way without success, we decided to go another route.

We had advertised in *Yankee Magazine* since Leon and Enna's reign, and a large percentage of our customers came from those ads. Although *Yankee* was published in New England, we knew from experience it was mailed all over the United States to ex-Yankees and Yankee wannabes. *Yankee Magazine* was where we needed to be. But an ad the size we'd need to properly describe the Allen House, with pictures and all the information would take a full page, minimum, and be enormously expensive. Nina and I decided to try something else first.

Every issue *Yankee* published a listing of one unique property for sale. Usually it was a home, but in one issue they *had* featured a small general store somewhere in Vermont. We hoped we might be an unusual enough prospect to catch someone's eye at the magazine. The writing of the letter fell to me, although Nina's expert eye was on me at all times to make sure I didn't get carried away. We wrote what *I* felt was a most compelling letter to the editor, enclosed a brochure, a map of the island, and information about the business itself.

And waited.

Yankee Magazine chose us.

They sent a writer and photographer out in the middle of February to take pictures and get information for the article. The writer was pleasant enough, and easily satisfied.

The photographer was a different matter. He must have posed us thirty times in the freezing cold. I would muffle up between shots, raising my hood, wrapping a scarf around my face. Then he would announce he was ready, and I would have to strip down, unbutton my coat and adopt a carefree, happy smile and attitude.

The longer we spent in the wind, the more difficult this became. Finally, he decided to place us on a small bluff where he could shoot us in the foreground and most of the rest of the island behind us.

Nina and I thought this was a great idea. At this point, we would have posed upside down if it meant we were nearing the end of the photo shoot. The photographer posed us on some large rocks just past Churches Beach. It was a great shot. I know it must have been a great shot, because he took it at least ten times. I could not feel my butt when I was finally allowed to stand up and I was pretty sure that my ears had frozen and fallen off my head.

The article ran that spring, and I have to say the photos were excellent. The photographer was kind enough to send us a copy of that shot of ourselves on the bluff, and it seemed I had managed to keep from looking as uncomfortable as I felt. Nina, as always, looked great. The article generated a lot of interest and, we thought, found us our new owners. But it was not to be, at least not the way we'd imagined.

Chapter 66
The End *(really)*

That summer, the realtor called. We had an offer.

It was a third less than the price we had already come down to, which was a third less than our original price. But the market was lousy, nothing was selling, and the offer was in cash, no mortgage, and payable in full at closing. The company had put $5000 in escrow to show they were serious.

What company, we wanted to know?

The realtor didn't have much information, other than the company was called Coastal Realty, Inc., and appeared to be a group that owned several inns and restaurants on the East Coast and was looking to expand into New England. That was enough for us.

After some serious discussion about the price, Nina and I came back with a counter offer, only to be told the price offered was firm and non-negotiable, cash in hand at closing. The housing market was tanking, we were exhausted, and this was the first real offer we'd had in more than a year. We talked it over with Dad, and finally decided we couldn't bear to keep running the place, waiting for a better offer. We had already contracted with New England Culinary Institute for the current year, and had reservations booked. So we asked if they wanted the place now, or at the end of the season. We assumed they would want a viable business, with a seamless transition between owners.

We waited.

The company that had made the offer had hired a lawyer on Martha's Vineyard to deal with us. We were to deal strictly with him.

The lawyer finally responded to our questions. We could run the inn for the current season as we already had the mechanism in place, and the transfer would take place in the fall. We agreed. Since we'd done all the start-up work, we might as well take a year of profit, one we wouldn't automatically feel compelled to pour back into the business.

The lawyer said Coastal Realty wanted an inspection. He sent out a crew from the Vineyard that went over our place with a literal fine tooth comb. I expected one of them to whip out white glove any second. They were on the roofs, in the basements, under the crawlspace of the gift shop. Finally, seemingly satisfied, they left.

We waited.

They sent out a lead paint inspector. We held our collective breaths. We had been painting the inn and annex with the same lead-based marine paint Ken and Mildred had used, one side of each building each year. It was the only paint that lasted more than a year in the wind-driven salt spray that lashed the buildings every winter.

The report came back clean. No lead paint on the inside, even on the windowsills. We were amazed, since we had no idea what had been used before our tenure, but grateful.

Then the asbestos report came back. We knew we had asbestos in the basement. I'd been duct taping it back up to the hot water pipes for years. What we didn't know was that the laws had changed since we bought the inn, and we were going to have to pay to have stuff removed. Amazingly enough, there was no asbestos found in the annex, and none in the walls, a major saving grace. But the stuff in the main house basement had to go.

Once again Mark came to the rescue. He called in some favors and got a team out to the island in record time, at about half the normal cost of such a job. It still cost us $18,000 to watch five men and one woman garb up in Tyvek® suits with ventilators, hose down the entire basement, and then carefully bag every scrap of the stuff I had so cavalierly dealt with each summer. When they had finally finished, we called the lawyer and informed him the inn was now asbestos-free.

Again, we waited.

Back and forth it went, all summer. Would we replace missing roof shingles? At this, and every other request from then on, we put our collective foot down, as instructed by Dad and Mark. According to them, we had done all that was necessary for the sale, and now the buyers were just trying to nickel and dime us. They wanted the sale as much as we did, Dad said, and he insisted we stand firm.

By this point, Nina and I had gone for several months dreaming of a life beyond the Allen House, and from being upset about the low price to terrified we were going to lose the sale. When our denial of the last two requests brought no negative response, it became suddenly much easier to breathe.

We wanted to be helpful. We asked if they wanted our mailing list, and were told yes. But the answer to did they want our recipes, our employee manual, our files on previous parties, all the information we had so carefully collected and bound into notebooks for the next owners was: no. Nina and I found this all a bit odd, but decided that either Coastal Realty, Inc., was a franchise of sorts who wanted to run the place its own way, or there was an island person partnering the deal who wanted to run the place, but didn't want us to know who he or she was. The whole deal had been shrouded in secrecy from the beginning. We were curious, but not curious enough to queer the deal. We wished them well in our minds, and hung on to all the files just in case. The last thing the lawyer asked that summer was for us was to sign a five-year, non-compete clause. This we agreed to readily. Neither Nina nor I had any desire to start up another restaurant now that we'd sold this one.

Finally, just after we had closed for the season and the week before the real estate closing, the lawyer called. Every detail had been finalized, he said. Except one. In order for the sale to go through, the place had to be broom clean. That meant every bed, every table and chair, every piece of restaurant equipment had to be gone before we got our check. Nina and I were both puzzled and panicked. Why would a company want to scrap everything? Sure, the furniture was crap, but new restaurant equipment cost a fortune. Didn't they want to keep anything?

The answer was no. Broom clean, or no deal.

He gave us one week. Had we known in the middle of summer, we were sure ninety percent of the furniture could have been sold, or at least given away, to islanders. Had we more time, we could have gotten a decent price on some of the equipment, or been able to donate it to charity. Now we were stuck. We called the few listings in the phone book for used restaurant equipment suppliers, and finally found one who would bring a barge out and take everything away. The price was ridiculous, but the important thing was he said he'd take *everything*. We had no time to waste. I was due to leave for Russia the next week on a long-anticipated and carefully planned trip. I had my visa. If I didn't go when I was supposed to, the trip was off.

The Sunday before the barge was to arrive, we opened the Allen House to the islanders who were left. Anything they wanted we let them take. A friend of ours with an antique shop was coming on that same barge with a moving van, and he would take anything he thought he could restore and sell in his shop. The rest was fair game. Everyone on the island got new mattresses, dishes, some pots and pans. Bonnie took the sheet pans and the mixing bowls for the bakery. Nina took some filing cabinets and her treasured adding machine. We gave Nicole the computer, and put the stuffed striped bass in Dad's attic, along with the antique cash register. We gave everything of possible historical significance to the newly formed Cuttyhunk Historical Society.

The barge came on Tuesday and the guys stripped the place clean. On Thursday Billy took us over to Martha's Vineyard to sign the papers.

Our lawyer (again courtesy of Mark) met us at their lawyer's office in Edgartown. We hoped we might meet the new owners there, and possibly find out what was going on. But their lawyer had only a sheaf of signed papers with the name Coastal Realty. We were as much in the dark as before. While we were signing the papers, Billy went to talk to some of his Vineyard cop buddies. We had a celebratory lunch and headed back to the boat where Billy met us with the news that, while he was hanging around, a woman had come into the office and said the Reverend Porter wanted to know how things were going, to which the secretary replied we were still in there.

Nina and I were puzzled. What did Reverend Boone Porter have to do with our business?

We knew he hated living directly behind the Allen House. He'd complained for years about the noise, the smell from the kitchen, the smoke from the new boiler. He had threatened to take us to court to get us to raise the smokestack on that boiler another fifteen feet above code because he claimed when the wind blew a certain way his house smelled like smoke. We had raised the pipe at our own expense just to stop his complaints, but he still lambasted us regularly about the noise from staff housing.

I was already a month into my Russian trip when Nina discovered what was really going on, and fortunately knew nothing until I got back. If I had been told the truth, it would have ruined the rest of my trip.

Coastal Realty, Inc., was a cover name. It was a dummy corporation set up by the Porters. They never had any intention of running the Allen House. In fact, they immediately tore down staff housing and the new kitchen we had hoped might increase the value of the place. Everything we had invested in the Allen House went to the dump, where islanders promptly fished out anything usable. That was something, at least. We could sit in Bonnie's Bakery the next few summers and look at our kitchen door, our track lighting, our sinks and toilets in the bathrooms.

The Porters put a seven-foot picket fence around the entire property, cutting off several time-honored rights of way, and poured hundreds of thousands of dollars into the buildings to turn them into apartments for relatives who rarely visited.

I stayed on the island for several years before moving to Virginia. Nina is still there, with Mark, and their son, Matt, has gone off to college. Mr. Porter died almost ten years ago, and Mrs. Porter several years after him. The Porters are the only people on-island Nina and I will not say hello to.

When I returned to visit, less and less frequently, I'd stay in my father's house. It sits across the drive from a seven-foot white fence that does not quite hide what is left of the building I once identified with so completely. Now that my dad has gone, and the house is partially mine, I'm going to come more often, try to reclaim my sense of the island.

People still, all these years later, come up to me and tell me their Allen House stories, and remark how much they miss the place. I don't miss the eighteen-hour days, the difficulty staffing, those few irate customers. I don't miss having my life controlled by a business. But do I miss the Allen House?

Yeah.

I do.

About the Author

Margo Solod was born in Morristown TN and graduated from the University of Tennessee with a degree in Theater Arts. She was an itinerant lighting designer and master electrician for several years before ending up on, of all places, a small island 14 miles off the MA coast. The rest is history, or should be.

She lives now in the Shenandoah valley of VA with her partner Deborah and an ever-changing number of dogs. Jesse the dog actually made it down here and into the new cabin, and lived to be thirteen years old. Me, I'm still here. Sometimes I'm on the island. Maybe I'll see you there.

View from the top of the hill. Classic.
Every tourist has one, every brochure as well.
This is from our second brochure.
Photo courtesy of Fredi Solod.

Made in the USA
Middletown, DE
12 January 2021

31455331R00166